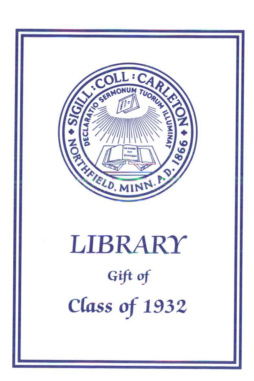

THE JEWS OF LEBANON
Between Coexistence and Conflict

To

Rona Bar
Isaac
Mindy Blackstock
Abigail Mann
Deborah Myers-Weinstein
Cheryl Rivkin

The Jews of Lebanon

Between Coexistence and Conflict

KIRSTEN E. SCHULZE

sussex
ACADEMIC
PRESS

BRIGHTON • PORTLAND

2 4 6 8 10 9 7 5 3 1

First published 2001 in Great Britain by
SUSSEX ACADEMIC PRESS
PO Box 2950
Brighton BN2 5SP

and in the United States of America by
SUSSEX ACADEMIC PRESS
5804 N.E. Hassalo St.
Portland, Oregon 97213-3644

British Library Cataloguing in Publication Data
A CIP catalogue record for this book is available from the British Library.

Library of Congress Cataloging-in-Publication Data
Schulze, Kirsten E.
The Jews of Lebanon: between coexistence and conflict / Kirsten E. Schulze.
p. cm.
Includes bibliographical references and index.
ISBN 1–902210–64–6 (alk. paper)
1. Jews—Lebanon—History. 2. Lebanon—Ethnic relations. I. Title.
DS135.L34 S38 2001
956.92'004924—dc21   00–140215

Printed by TJ International, Padstow, Cornwall
This book is printed on acid-free paper

Contents

List of Illustrations

———

Foreword by Avi Shlaim

Almost anything connected with the Arab-Israeli conflict or with the history of the Jews in the Arab countries is susceptible to intense passions and partisanship not only on the part of official spokespersons and propagandists but, only too often, on the part of scholars as well. Over the last decade or so, a group of "new" or revisionist Israeli historians have been challenging, with the help of official documents, the traditional Zionist version of the birth of the State of Israel in 1948 and of the fifty years' conflict between Israel and the Arab world. The response of the orthodox historians and the keepers of the Labour Zionist flame was not long in coming and it gave rise to a fierce and ongoing debate. This is the most emotionally-charged but also one of the most interesting debates in the entire field of modern Middle Eastern studies. Related to this debate, and scarcely less heated, is the controversy surrounding the history of the Jews who lived under Arab rule before and after the creation of the Jewish state.

Nearly all of the existing literature on the subject is written by Jewish scholars and much of it is permeated by a pro-Jewish and anti-Arab bias. This literature dwells at length on the hardship, discrimination and humiliation that the Jews are said to have endured in the Middle East throughout the ages. It also emphasizes the second-class status of the Jews, the legal restrictions imposed on them, the officially-sponsored persecution and the pogroms. The emergence of Zionism in the early part of the twentieth century is said to have triggered particularly vicious Arab responses all around Palestine. In addition, this literature stresses the intolerance of Islam towards other religions in general and towards Judaism in particular. The general picture that emerges from these accounts is not a balanced one with lights alongside the undoubted shadows but a one-sided one, focusing almost obsessively on the hatred and on the suffering visited upon the Jews by Arab society. In this respect, conventional accounts of Jewish life under Arab rule fit neatly into what the American-Jewish historian Salo Baron once called the lachrymose version of Jewish history: a history of misery and degradation, of oppression and harassment, of trials and tribulations, all culminating in the Holocaust.

Kirsten Schulze does not subscribe to the traditional version of Jewish history. She notes that the literature on the Jews in the Middle East is seriously flawed and she sets out to redress the balance. Redressing the balance does not mean going to the other extreme of painting a rosy picture; it means avoiding bias, prejudice, and political agendas, and striving to provide a fair and comprehensive account of the life of Jewish communities in the Arab world which includes the positive as well as the negative aspects.

The specific subject of Dr Schulze's book is the history of the Jews of Lebanon in the twentieth century. On this subject she is eminently well qualified to write. She is well versed in the history and politics of the Middle East and she has a command of Arabic and Hebrew. She has published extensively on the Arab-Israeli conflict, including a book on *Israel's Covert Diplomacy in Lebanon*. In this book she argues that Israel has pursued an active policy of intervention in the domestic politics of Lebanon through the alliance with the Maronites from 1920 until 1985. This challenges the conventional view that Israel only acts in self-defence against external threats and that she refrains from interfering in the internal affairs of the neighbouring Arab states.

The book before us focuses on the history of the Jews within Lebanon rather than on the country's external relations, though Israel does feature in the story to the extent that its actions impinged on the position of the Jewish community in this deeply divided country. The book has many merits. First, the research effort that went into the making of this book is really impressive: Dr Schulze has collected a vast amount of information from archives, private papers, newspapers, and other sources, and she has made a valuable contribution of her own by conducting interviews with a number of prominent Lebanese Jews. Second, she uses this rich panoply of sources to brilliantly illuminating effect. Third, her account is pretty comprehensive, ranging over the social, economic, political, cultural and religious aspects of the life of the Jews of Lebanon. Fourth, she succeeds in placing the Jewish community in the broader context of Lebanese and Middle Eastern politics. Last but not least, Dr Schulze has made a highly significant and substantive contribution to the study of minorities in the Middle East. Her most interesting conclusion is that Lebanon's treatment of its Jews was no worse, if it was no better, than its treatment of its other 22 minorities.

Avi Shlaim
St Antony's College, Oxford

Acknowledgements

_____

This book could not have been written without the contribution of a large number of people, all of whom I wish to thank. For their time, patience and support I wish to thank Nadim Shehadi, Fuad Debbas, Eugene Rogan, Joseph Mizrahi, Rabbi Elbaz, Robert O. Freedman, Gad Barzilai, Raghid el-Solh, Douglas Krikler, Tudor Parfitt, Gary Davis, Avraham Sela, Uri Lubrani, Michael Glatzer, Shimon Rubinstein, Boutrus Labaki, Theo Hanf, Tarif Khalidi, Menachem Klein, Eyal Zisser, Zahavit and Rafi Cohen-Almagor, Antoine Bassil, Fouad Abu Nader, and Joseph Abu Khalil.

The financial support for the research was provided by the British Academy, the Lucius N. Littauer Foundation, the Ben Zvi Institute, and the Nuffield Foundation. Without their contribution, publication of this book would not have been possible.

Most importantly I would like to thank those Lebanese Jews who shared their treasured memories and photographs with me: Stella Levi, Vikki Angel, Joseph Lichtman, Shula Kishek Cohen, Shlomo Leviatan, Zaki Levi, Ezra Tamir, Toufic Yedid Levy, Charles Raidibon, Moni Sfinzi, Camille Cohen Kichek, Itzhak Levanon, Jacques Neria, Nathan Sofer, Alex Sofer, Odette Ozon, Marcel Nahon, Nissim Dahan, and the Jews still living in Beirut who will remain unnamed but not forgotten.

Gratitude is extended to the Central Zionist Archives, the Israel State Archives, the Haganah Archives, the Public Record Office, the National Archives and Record Administration, the archives of the Centre for Lebanese Studies, the Ben Zvi Archives, the archives of the Alliance Israélite Universelle, and specifically to Robert and Elliot Stambouli who permitted me to see the papers of their father Jacques.

I also want to thank Elizabeth Elbaum and Daniel Todman for their assistance with the task of translating documents and transcribing tapes, and to Ian Jackson who in his spare time at the Public Record Office compiled a very helpful and timesaving list of files on Lebanon for me.

And finally, I would like to extend my deepest appreciation to Catherine Moutell and Rona Bar Isaac for their comments on the first draft; to Anthony Grahame, Editorial Director at Sussex Academic Press, for his assistance in seeing the book through the press; to my mother for proof-reading the text; and above all to Avi Shlaim for his suggestions, support and, of course, writing the foreword.

Abbreviations

AIUA	Alliance Israélite Universelle Archives
BZA	Ben Zvi Archives
CZA	Central Zionist Archives
HA	Haganah Archives
IAF	Israeli Air Force
IDF	Israel Defence Forces
ILMAC	Israeli–Lebanese Mixed Armistice Commission
JSPP	Jacques Stambouli's Private Papers
PASC	Palestine Armed Struggle Command
PFLP	Popular Front for the Liberation of Palestine
PLO	Palestine Liberation Organization
PRO	Public Record Office
NARA	National Archives and Record Administration
NLP	National Liberal Party
UAR	United Arab Republic
UN	United Nations
UNSC	United Nations Security Council

Note on Transliteration

The transliteration of Arabic and Hebrew words is based upon the system used by the *International Journal of Middle East Studies* with the exception of proper names and personal names. Proper names appear in their familiar latinized form found in Western literature on the Middle East. Personal names appear in the form used by the individuals themselves, or as they appear in archival documents.

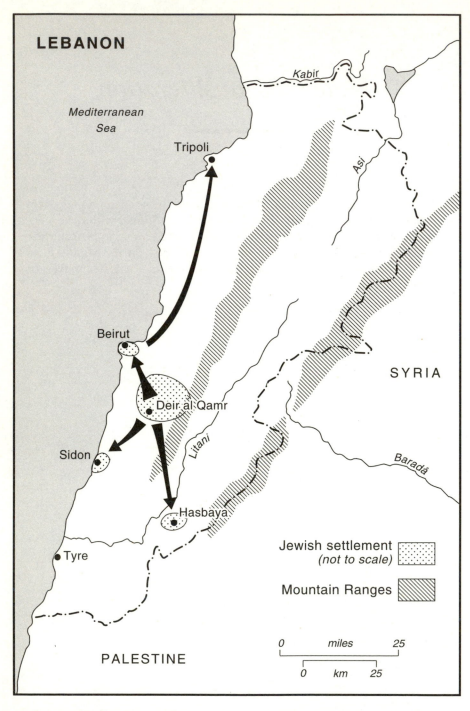

Jewish settlement and migration in nineteenth-century Lebanon

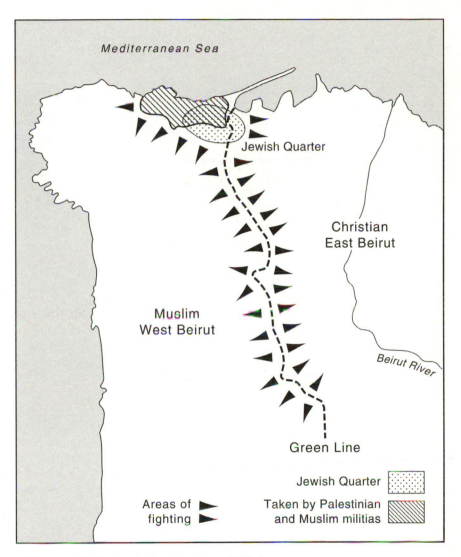

Mediterranean Sea

Jewish Quarter

Christian
East Beirut

Muslim
West Beirut

Beirut River

Green Line

Areas of
fighting

Jewish Quarter

Taken by Palestinian
and Muslim militias

The Jewish Quarter in the Civil War, 1975–6

Cèdre, mes yeux las de pleurer
Ne veulent que jouir de la beauté
Je puiserai en ton nom mille et une énergies
Car ma foi reste entière en notre paradis.

Alberto Sidi Delburgo

Introduction

The Lebanese Jewish community has occupied an obscure place in the history of Lebanon, where, as one of the smaller minorities among twenty-three ethno-religious groups, it has received little attention in studies of state and society. Much of this obscurity is due to the size of the community which at its largest never numbered more than an estimated 14,000. Another reason can be found in the nature of most scholarly work on Lebanon itself, which has been preoccupied with civil strife and the Muslim–Christian division. Lebanese Jews who were predominantly apolitical, who tried to nurture good relations with all confessional groups, who were rarely represented in the army or militias, did not fit into the analytical framework imposed on Lebanon's twentieth-century history. Yet one can clearly say that Lebanese Jews were no less Lebanese than their Christian or Muslim counterparts. They too had a vested interest in the identity of the state, and whilst not promoting a political project of their own, these Jews shared the vision of Lebanon as an independent, multi-communal, Levantine country as advocated by many of the Maronite notables as well as the Lebanese merchant and banker community. Indeed, it could be claimed that from a socio-economic perspective the Jews embodied the Levantine stereotype.

Jewish Life in the Arab Middle East

The conventional image of Jewish life in the Middle East focuses on the *dhimmi* status in society, legal restrictions, degrading treatment, and persecution. While this impression may, in fact, be supported by a number of historical accounts it is equally not borne out by others. Yet, it is this image that has captured the imagination of those interested in the subject. Consider Saul Friedman's account of Jewish life during the time of the Fatimids:

> The attempt to isolate, ridicule, and debase Jews was carried to an extreme

in the reign of Fatimid Caliph al-Hakim in Egypt (966–1021). A self-deluded fanatic who considered himself the redeemer of mankind, al-Hakim maintained that the Jews still worshipped the golden calf, and he required them to wear little images of this animal around their necks. When this humiliation failed to induce conversion to Islam, the monarch decreed they should wear cowbells around their necks. This device also failed; therefore, the caliph ordered the Jews to wear six-pound wooden blocks about their necks. Finally, on Passover in the year 1012, al-Hakim ordered the destruction of the Jewish quarter of Cairo with all its inhabitants.[1]

The *Bulletin de l'Alliance Israélite Universelle* in 1885 gave this account of Jewish life in Yemen:

> The Jews of Sanaa complain of the humiliations which they are obliged to bear: they are made to clean the sewers and they take them in gangs to do this forced labour and they force money out of them by obliging them to buy foodstuffs which have gone off. Jews are not allowed to walk on the right hand side of an Arab; they must only wear black clothes and they can only make their purchases in the market once the Arabs have made theirs. They ruin the Jews with taxes and treat them in the vilest manner.[2]

As Maurice Roumani stated in *The Case of the Jews from Arab Countries: A Neglected Issue*: "not only did Jews suffer oppression – including discrimination and pogroms which bring to mind the worst medieval Europe – their entire existence in lands under Muslim rule was based on sufferance, not rights, this despite the fact that Jews had lived in those lands long before".[3] Degradation, second-class status, restrictions, and hatred are all evident. What is missing, however, is a deeper analysis of the situation, one which gives a comprehensive picture of both positives and negatives.

In a similar manner, the *Farhud* is often singled out as the essence of Iraqi Jewish life. As the most traumatic event of modern Jewish history in Iraq the pogrom of the Jews of Baghdad on 1–2 June 1941 could not but leave a lasting impression. In Daphne Tsimhoni's description of the *Farhud* Muslim masses "for two days . . . massacred, wounded, raped, and looted, while the British forces, informed about these horrible events, abstained from intervening. . . . The casualties numbered 160 Jews murdered, hundreds wounded as well as enormous destruction of Jewish property. Nearly every Jewish home in Baghdad was affected by this pogrom."[4]

The excerpts above all give a similar impression of Jewish life in the Arab world. The themes of discrimination, oppression, and persecution are prominent. An additional factor in the twentieth century is the advent of Zionism which is often seen as triggering particularly vicious Arab responses. Generalizations such as all Jews were either forced out of Arab countries after the creation of the State of Israel, or left because the situation became so intolerable, are central to this argument. Indeed, Morroe Berger claims that 96 per cent of Arab Jews were forced to leave.[5] Statements such as Egyptian Prime Minister Fahmi al-Nuqrashi, who, upon the arrest of a number of Egyptian Jews in 1948, said that "all Jews were potential Zionists, all Zionists were communists and that the combination of those two with the situation in Palestine presented a danger to all non-communist states"[6] support this image.

Given the conflicting accounts and contradictory evidence of Jewish life under Islam, ranging from persecution to equal rights, the question remains as to what extent each of these accounts holds true and to what extent this paradigm is applicable to the Jewish experience in Lebanon.

A complex mosaic

This book tells the story of the Jews of Lebanon in the twentieth century. It provides a complex mosaic of intra- and inter-communal relations reconstructed from archives of the community, archives of the *Alliance Israélite Universelle*, the Israel State Archives, the Central Zionist Archives, and the Public Record Office, as well as private papers and a substantial amount of oral history from Lebanese Jews who have remained in Beirut as well as those who chose to leave. What becomes clear is that this account does not fit the stereotype of Jews in many other Arab countries, namely that of a fifth column or the enemy within. Rather, Lebanese Jews were a minority among many. Interestingly though, this is not how they generally have been perceived by outsiders. For instance, a feature-length article in the *Jerusalem Post Magazine* on 20 August 1982, after the Israeli invasion of Lebanon which inevitably sparked interest in the community, states that

> Palestinians occupy the former Jewish quarter today, as they have since 1948 when the Jews fled. The government confiscated all abandoned Jewish property for 'the Palestinian Arab refugees.' These Palestinians still live in houses with *mezuzah* niches on the doorposts and work in shops once owned by Jews. The former *beit midrash* is now a Palestinian carpentry shop. The synagogue stands empty, although in an apartment on the roof lives a Palestinian family.[7]

This *Jerusalem Post* article refers to the Jewish quarter of Saida, a city which had a community of 3,500 Jews. Closer inspection reveals that the Jews fled only temporarily in 1948; in fact, it was the Lebanese government which protected their property and restored it to the Jews upon their return. The community did not leave until the second civil war. Even then,

Jewish property was not confiscated by the Lebanese state. Although some of the abandoned houses were taken over by Palestinians, these Palestinian families became the closest friends of the remaining Jews. The *Jerusalem Post* article proceeds with an interview with one of the last remaining families in Saida: "Ask the Levys why they remained and you will hear a familiar litany of reasons why Jews remain anywhere in the Diaspora. We had a business to maintain. The children are in school. The grandmother is too aged and infirm to face moving. And anyway our situation isn't bad. And it's always been our home."[8] Such a patronizing attitude does not reveal a true understanding of the situation faced by Jews in Lebanon.

An even more glaring example of misconception and overgeneralization of the experience of Jews in the Middle East is contained in Saul Friedman's book *Without Future: The Plight of Syrian Jewry*, which begins with a chapter on the "Myth of Islamic Toleration," setting the tone for the rest of the book. The section on Lebanon is a particularly crafty mix of half truths. Friedman selectively using a bombing incident which killed 14 Jews in Tripoli (Lebanon) in 1945 as his point of departure, claims that Jewish students were dismissed from schools[9] in 1947/8, and that 10,000 Jews fled Lebanon after riots – 10,000 from a community which, according to the table on the next page, only comprises 5,000 members. Then he jumps to the 1980s and the kidnappings, creating the impression that the community reeled from one trauma to another. His account is seriously flawed. It completely discards the tolerance of Lebanese society, the protection the Lebanese government afforded the Jews, the equal rights of Lebanese Jewry, and the fact that they did not leave during any of the Arab-Israeli wars. Moreover, the Lebanese Jewish community increased rather than decreased after 1948 – so much so that it caused many laments in the Jewish Agency in Jerusalem which had been trying to motivate Lebanese Jews to move to Israel to no avail.

The above cited accounts on Lebanon fit neatly into the general picture created of Jewish life in the Middle East. Closer analysis, however, shows that the Lebanese Jewish community and its relations with Lebanese Muslims and Christians contradicts the prevailing view that Jews everywhere in the Middle East were second-class citizens and that after the establishment of the State of Israel in 1948 they became the target of 'anti-Semitism' and persecution. Unlike the Jewish communities in many other Middle Eastern countries, the Jewish community in Lebanon grew after 1948 and it was not until the civil war of 1975 that the community started to migrate and to emigrate. The Jews of Lebanon were just one of Lebanon's 23 minorities, with the same rights and privileges and subject to the same political tensions of minority infighting. The creation of the State of Israel in 1948 did not change this situation. The 1982 Israeli invasion of Lebanon, however, did. And the 1985 withdrawal of the Israel Defense Forces left the Jews vulnerable.

Jewish Life in Lebanon

The development of modern Lebanon in the twentieth century was accompanied by population movements within the Jewish community. In 1911 Jews from Syria, Iraq,[10] Turkey, and Greece,[11] as well as some families of Persian origin, settled in Lebanon. The number of Jews in Beirut alone increased to 5,000.[12] Conversely, in 1913, with Jewish settlements increasing in Palestine, the Jewish families from Hasbaya[13] moved to the Galilee settlement of Rosh Pina on the initiative of Baron Rothschild.[14] Only three families stayed behind.

In 1926 the French Mandate powers drew up a constitution which provided the basis for a multi-confessional democratic political system based on the French values of liberty, equality and fraternity. When Lebanon gained independence in 1943 a National Pact was concluded between the principal confessional groups based on a census conducted in 1932 and the constitution. Lebanon became a consociational democracy in which political representation was allocated on a 6:5 Christian–Muslim proportional basis. The presidency went to the Maronites, the premiership to the Sunnis, and the speaker of the house to the Shi'a and so on. The Jews along with the Latin Catholics, Syrian Jacobites, Syrian Catholics, Nestorians, and Chaldeans shared a minority seat in the parliament.

The rights of the Lebanese Jewish community had been recognized in a civil constitution in 1911. This made them one of the more progressive minorities. In comparison, Muslims and Christians at that time were recognized only on a religious basis. Recognition on a civil as well as a religious level meant effectively that the head of the Jewish community was its president rather than the chief rabbi.[15] The Jewish community president dealt with inter-communal relations, representing the community politically, socially and economically. In keeping with Jewish tradition, intra-communal relations were guided by Jewish law. Indeed, personal status laws in Lebanon were in the hands of all of the respective communities. Accordingly, the Jewish community had a Rabbinic Tribunal which dealt with marriage, divorce, and other personal status issues.

By the time of independence in 1943 the Jewish community had become concentrated in Beirut with only a few families remaining in and around Saida and Tripoli. The number of Lebanese Jews increased dramatically with the influx of thousands of refugees from Iraq and Syria in 1948 as a result of the first Arab-Israeli war. These refugees were granted the right to stay in Lebanon. They did not, however, receive Lebanese citizenship. The 1948 war did not have a disastrous effect on the Lebanese Jewish community. The Lebanese government actively protected the community from Arab nationalist and Palestinian elements in Lebanon – but even Arab frustration over the situation in Palestine rarely manifested itself in aggression against the local Jews. Lebanese Jews themselves did not consider the war to directly affect them as they saw themselves clearly as Lebanese nationals – so much so that there were Jewish soldiers in the Lebanese Army fighting in the war of 1948.

Lebanon, compared to its immediate neighbour Syria and indeed most other Arab states, had a more tolerant and liberal attitude toward its own Jews and toward Jewish refugees seeking asylum in Lebanon. Thus, in 1948 the number of Jews had increased to 5,200 and by 1951 to 9,000, 6,961 of whom were Lebanese citizens.[16] Indeed, Lebanon was the only Arab country in which the number of Jews increased after the first Arab-Israeli war.

Syrian and Iraqi Jewish refugees settled in Beirut's Wadi Abu Jamil while at the same time the established Lebanese Jewish bourgeoisie started to move out of the Jewish quarter to Qantari and to Michel Chiha Street.[17] The upper middle-class Jews living in more fashionable areas were engaged in commerce and finance. Most notably among these are the two banking families – Safra and Zilkha. The poorer Jews in Wadi Abu Jamil worked in the garment, soap, and glass industries or as peddlers.

Relations between the Jewish community and the other Lebanese minorities remained amicable. Characteristic of cross-communal interaction and friendship were celebrations of religious festivals to which Jews, Muslims and Christians invited each other. Lebanese Jews today cherish the memory of their non-Jewish neighbors bringing bread into the quarter at the end of Passover.

The tradition of sharing each other's religious festivals continued after the first Arab-Israeli war. In 1951, during the Passover celebration, the president of the Jewish community, Dr Joseph Attie, held a reception at Magen Avraham synagogue which was attended by Sami Sulh, Abdallah Yafi, Rachid Beydoun, Joseph Chader, Habib Abi Chahla, Charles Helou, Pierre Gemayel and Msgr. Ignace Moubarak, the Maronite Archbishop of Beirut.[18] The Jews were patriotic, seeing themselves as Lebanese nationals, and they also were perceived as Lebanese by the other communities.

Tacit alliances were created with Christian leaders, such as head of the Maronite *Kata'ib* party Pierre Gemayel, as both Lebanese Jews and many Maronites advocated the strengthening of Lebanon's Christian character which was seen as a guarantee of keeping Lebanon a refuge for minorities in the Middle East.[19] Indeed, Pierre Gemayel from 1948 onwards stressed on many occasions that his party considered the Jews to be fully-fledged Lebanese citizens and that Lebanon was "about all minorities living peacefully together".[20] A number of Jews were *Kata'ib* party members, and the community as a whole supported Gemayel in the elections. An interesting side note to *Kata'ib*–Jewish relations are *Kata'ib*–Israeli relations which were secretly conducted from the 1920s up to 1984.[21] The *Kata'ib* and later Lebanese Forces leadership made a conscious decision not to involve the local Jewish community in order not to endanger their status among Lebanon's minorities.[22] The Israelis after the invasion of 1982 were not so sensitive.

Friendships with prominent Lebanese politicians and good business relationships in addition to the governments' dedication to religious tolerance ensured that the Jewish community had government protection in troubled times. During the 1948, 1967 and 1973 Arab-Israeli wars the Lebanese Army posted guards to the entrance of the Jewish quarter.[23] During the civil wars of 1958 and 1975 the Maronite *Kata'ib* party and later the Lebanese Forces protected Jewish interests militarily, the Jews not having their own militia.

The liberal atmosphere in Lebanon had encouraged the growth of the community to 14,000 by the time of the onset of the first civil war in 1958. The instability created by the hostilities led to emigration from Lebanon by all communities. However, it affected the Jews quite drastically since the general instability followed by the crash of the Intrabank in 1966, and the burden of the Palestinian refugees from the 1967 war, had an adverse effect on the economy and finance sector which the Jews so heavily depended upon. Thus, by 1967 the community had decreased to 7,000, falling to less than 4,000 in 1971.[24]

The 1967 Arab-Israeli Six-Day War also left its mark on Lebanon leading to an overall decline in the security for all communities. In December 1970 a bomb exploded in the Jewish Selim Tarrab school.[25] This was such a departure from the co-existence between Lebanon's Jews and other Lebanese minorities that the Minister of the Interior, Kamal Jumblatt, publicly apologized. Yet, this bomb was a sign of what was to come in Lebanon's immediate future as the security situation in the country deteriorated, the government of Suleiman Franjieh lost its credibility, and inter-communal tension rose. Many Jews as well as many Christians and Muslims started to leave their disintegrating country. In line with their self-definition as Lebanese citizens, the Jewish families immigrated to Europe and the United States and settled among other Lebanese émigrés; only a few decided to settle in Israel. Then, in 1975, the second Lebanese civil war broke out. Wadi Abu Jamil, being very much in the center of the city found itself on the greenline between the pro-status quo mainly Christian forces and the anti-status quo coalition of Sunni, Shi'a, Druze and Palestinian forces. As a result of the war, the synagogues and the Jewish school were closed and economic activity was severely restricted.[26] Many buildings, including the main synagogue and the *Talmud Torah*, were damaged.[27] Only 450–1,000 out of the 4,000–6,000 Jews were still in Lebanon in 1978.[28] By 1980 this number had further decreased to 200–300 with only 20 remaining in Beirut.[29] Along with Christian and Muslim Beirutis, many Jews had fled to the more peaceful countryside; most, however, left Lebanon. Jewish lives were, for the first time, in serious physical danger – not from Palestinian radicalism, Arab nationalism or anti-Semitism, but from an ethnically divided society at war with itself. An estimated 200 Jews were killed in the cross-fire between warring factions in 1975–6.[30]

The on-going Lebanese civil war entered a new phase with the Israeli invasion of Lebanon in 1982. The Jewish community benefited from the Israeli presence which guaranteed their safety and opened access across the border to relatives living in Israel. Many Lebanese Jews took this opportunity and left Lebanon, a few settling in Israel and many more travelling via Israel to Europe or the United States. In 1984, with the Israeli withdrawal from Beirut, the situation of the remaining Jewish families deteriorated rapidly. Up to the Israeli invasion the relations of the Jews with Christians and Muslims had remained good despite the war.[31] However, from 1982 onward, the Jews in the minds of some Islamist militias had become associated with Israel and the darkest period of Lebanese Jewish history began. Eleven leading personalities were kidnapped and killed. Others were evacuated overnight from Wadi Abu Jamil by the *Kata'ib* and moved to the safer area of the Christian enclave where they remain until the present day.

A Literary Survey

Some references to the Lebanese Jewish community have appeared in a limited number of books on Lebanon and books on Jews in the Middle East. Through these references it is possible to obtain a fleeting impression of what Lebanese Jewish life was like in the past. In many accounts, however, these references do not extend beyond a paragraph and thus, while providing relevant information, they are only indicative of a subject which has been hitherto neglected. This book aims to situate Lebanon's Jews in Lebanese history and thus fills a gap in the existing literature while also presenting a new angle on both the history of Lebanon and the Arab-Israeli conflict. Helena Cobban in *The Making of Modern Lebanon* mentions that the Jewish community during the upheavals of the 1970s shrank from around 2,000 to near extinction.[32] Michael W. Suleiman's book on *Political Parties in Lebanon: The Challenge of a Fragmented Political Culture* comments in passing upon the Jewish element in Lebanon's business community as well as their political insignificance, while focusing on the larger minorities. Elizabeth Picard's excellent book *Lebanon: A Shattered Country* gives a very brief overview of the position of the Jewish community, ending with an accurate analysis when she says that "belonging neither to Islam nor Christianity, the Jewish community had chosen to inscribe its history in that of a modern Lebanese state, thus reflecting the country's dynamism and weakness – and particularly its vulnerability to its surroundings".[33] Probably the most comprehensive contribution on this subject is that by Luc Henri de Bar in his book *Les Communautés Confessionelles du Liban* which includes a full chapter on the Jewish community. Moreover, Bar has an interesting take on the Jews describing them as "well integrated into their environment". He raises the question whether this was purely the result of Lebanon being Christian as well as Muslim which provided the space for the Jews to contribute to the country's prosperous economy. They were never drawn to either pole, "didn't ally themselves with one or the other, against one or the other".[34]

Most other authors writing on Lebanon, however, ranging from Theodor Hanf's seminal work *Coexistence in Wartime Lebanon: Decline of a State and Rise of a Nation*, Kamal Salibi's *House of Many Mansions: A History of Lebanon Reconsidered*, William Harris' *Faces of Lebanon: Sects, Wars, and Global Extensions* to Stephen Longrigg's *Syria and Lebanon under French Mandate* neglect the Lebanese Jewish community completely. A little more information can be gathered from those books dealing with Israel's 1982 invasion of Lebanon and Israeli–Maronite relations, often making references connecting Lebanese Jews to both Israel and to the Lebanese Maronites. Laura Zittrain Eisenberg's outstanding work *My Enemy's Enemy: Lebanon in Early Zionist Imagination, 1900–1948* and Zeev Schiff's and Ehud Ya'ari's *Israel's Lebanon War* fall into this category. Yet, altogether, the information on the small Lebanese Jewish community in books on Lebanon's complex history is scant, a situation this book aims to redress.

The place of Lebanese Jewry in the greater history of Judaism and Zionism has been equally one that could be at best described as marginal. The comparative absence of persecution and anti-Semitism plays a significant role. Another reason is the community's proximity to both Palestine and Syria, which has often led to the Jews of Lebanon being mentioned but not studied in academic works on those respective communities. This has occasionally resulted in the denial of the existence of a Lebanese Jewish identity and claims that Jews living in Lebanon were actually Syrian Jews. A closer look at the historical origins of the Lebanese Jewish community, however, reveals that the Jewish presence not only dates back to biblical times, but also that Jews living in Lebanon were not just Syrian migrants. In fact, an analysis of the genealogical composition of the Lebanese Jewish community reveals Spanish, Maghrebi, Turkish, Greek, and Persian roots over many centuries as well as Syrian, Iraqi and European backgrounds over the course of the nineteenth and twentieth centuries. In keeping with other Lebanese ethnic communities the Jewish community was comprised of refugees which had left other parts of the Middle East to find safety in Lebanon's geographic position and in a more tolerant society.

Walter P. Zenner's chapter on "Jews in Late Ottoman Syria: External Relations"[35] in Shlomo Deshen's and Walter P. Zenner's edited volume *Jewish Societies in the Middle East: Community, Culture and Authority* is one example of seeing Lebanon's Jewish community within the context of a greater Syria. He makes references to both the Jews of Saida and Beirut as well as their agricultural roots in Deir al-Qamr. Unfortunately for those interested in Lebanon, there is no more than a glimpse of Lebanese Jewish life under Ottoman rule. Raphael Patai's two books *The Vanished Worlds of Jewry* and *Tents of Jacob: The Diaspora Yesterday and Today* as well as Hayyim J. Cohen's *The Jews of the Middle East 1880–1972* and J. J. Benjamin's travelogue *Acht Jahre in Asien und Afrika von 1846 bis 1855* fall into the same category. Norman Stillman's *The Jews of Arab Lands in Modern Times* and the *The Jews of Arab Lands: A History and Source Book* add to the subject of Lebanese Jewry in the form of published documents including a report on the Jewish community in Saida (1902), a complaint by the Jews of Beirut about their Chief Rabbi (1909), the Chief Rabbi's defense (1910), and Abraham Elmaleh's attempt to spread Zionism (1927) – just to name a few. They are an excellent source from which to gain an insight into the dynamics of the community, its socio-political position, as well as conveying an impression of the time. Another interesting piece of work is P. C. Sadgrove's inquiry into the "Beirut Jewish-Arab Theatre" raising the issues of culture and identity at the end of the nineteenth century. A further contribution on the wider subject has come from Joseph B. Schechtman who in his book *On Wings of Eagles: The Plight, Exodus, and Homecoming of Oriental Jewry* has a full chapter on the Jews of Lebanon in which he attempts to balance Lebanon's special status among Arab and Middle Eastern states with the status of Middle Eastern Jews in society. Accordingly he does point to the "peaceful and uneventful life" of the community, but then follows with an almost stereotypical statement for the region, saying that events in Palestine ended this idyll.[36] The rest of his account, up to 1959, does not change this picture. S. Landshut's brief overview of Lebanese Jewry in his book on *Jewish Communities in the Muslim Countries of the*

Middle East makes only references to the situation in 1948, but manages to capture the complexity of events nevertheless. An interesting, more substantial, and highly relevant contribution on the subject of the Jews of Lebanon is Abraham Elmaleh's edited volume *In Memoriam: Hommage à Joseph David Farhi* which gives an account of the life and achievements of one of the most distinguished presidents of the Lebanese Jewish community, Joseph Farhi, as well as an impression of this particular time in Lebanese history as viewed by Farhi's contemporaries, who all played prominent roles in the community.

Altogether, it can be said that information on the Lebanese Jewish community has been sketchy at best, leaving room for a much more comprehensive account which this book aims to provide. It will be essentially a political history of the community as it will focus on the position of this minority within the broader socio-political system of the state. This does not mean that economic, cultural, and religious aspects will not be touched upon, but they will play a comparatively minor part. Focal points in this study will be identity, nationalism, Zionism, inter-communal interaction, and the involvement of the Jewish community in Lebanon's civil wars as well as the Arab-Israeli wars. Related questions that will be explored are the relationship between Lebanese Jews and other Jewish communities such as those in Syria, Palestine under the British mandate and later Israel; whether the creation of the state of Israel changed life for the Jews of Lebanon; and, finally, whether the history of the Lebanese Jews throws a different light on the Arab-Israeli conflict.

1

A Voyage through History

Little is known about the Jewish experience in the area of present-day Lebanon before the twentieth century. Occasional references in travelogs and history books provide only an impressionistic glimpse of this small community. Yet this Lebanese mosaic of Jewish life, while fragmented, provides another dimension to the general experience of the Jews in the Middle East. The history of Lebanon and its Jews is one which has always had elements of distinctness and autonomy which produced a society with different inter-communal relations other than its neighbours. For the Jews of Lebanon neither the myth of a golden age of Islamic tolerance, nor the image of Christian bigotry, nor the picture of Muslim fanaticism hold true.

The pre-twentieth century experience of the Jews of Lebanon was characterized by centuries of safety, hospitality, and tranquillity. The fates of the Jewish communities were interwoven with the rises and falls of the cities in which they lived. Following the war of 1860 the Jews were swept up by the tides of modernization, inter-communal migration, and the restructuring of Lebanese society. By the turn of the century the community had developed from one that was Arabized, rural, geographically fragmented, and relatively obscure to one that had become centered around Beirut and Saida, had become urbanized, and that had adopted a distinctly francophile Levantine identity – a community which tied its future to the emerging modern multi-cultural state.

The Historical Legacy

The presence of Jews in Lebanon dates back to biblical times when the ancient cities of Tyre and Saida were known as "the crowned" and "merchant to many nations". The arrival of the first Jews in Lebanon is said to have been 1,000 BCE.[1] Under Solomon (970–930 BCE) Lebanese cedars were used for the construction of the temple in Jerusalem and influence was exerted through trade connections with King Hiram of Tyre.[2] It is also said that as a sign of his love King Solomon built a palace for the Queen Sheba in Baalbek. Further testimonials to the existence of Jewish communities date from the period of the Hasmoneans with references in the Mishnah and the Talmud to villages and settlements in the Lebanese mountains and Mount Hermon.[3] During the reign of Aristobulus (104–105 BCE) some areas around Mount Lebanon were conquered and forcibly Judaized.[4] In the chronicles of the Jewish communities, the community of Hasbaya stood out for preserving the tradition of its fore-fathers.

During the Roman period, the House of Herod ruled over parts of Lebanon. An increase in the Jewish population in that region was regis-tered after the Bar Kochva revolt in 132 CE. The Jews who had migrated to what is now Lebanon were mainly agriculturalists from Judea and the Galilee. They found refuge in the villages at the foothills of Mount Hermon. They did not consider themselves to be living in exile as the agri-cultural commandments, such as those relating to the sabbatical year, extended geographically to just south of Saida.[5]

In 502 CE it is reported that the Beirut synagogue was destroyed in an earthquake.[6] Under the reign of the *Khalif* Umar (634–644 CE) Lebanon became part of the expanding Arab Empire. As the Empire contained large Christian and Jewish populations the previously harsh policy of Islam towards the Jews (in Arabia) changed to one more tolerant in order to avoid a wide-spread exodus. Tolerance, however, did not mean an absence of restrictions. Jews were allowed to live under Muslim rule on payment of a poll-tax. Traditionally, rich Jews had to pay a specified sum each year, the well off paid half and the poor a quarter. They were also forbidden to carry arms, testify against Muslims, or marry Muslims. While a specific dress code was the norm in many places, this was not enforced in Lebanon.[7] Moreover, these restrictions did not prevent Jews in Lebanon from holding positions of authority such as medical or finan-cial advisers at the courts of the *khalifs*.[8]

The Arab author al-Baladhuri relates that the *Khalif* Mu'awiya (661–680 CE) settled Jews in Tripoli. A Jewish community also existed in Baalbek in 922.[9] Rabbi Saadia Gaon, who lived there, wrote that he had students from "Baal Gad", the biblical name for Baalbek.[10] The Palestinian academy established its seat in Tyre in 1071[11] and Itzhak Ben Zvi during one of his travels noted that the small Jewish community in Tyre dated to 1170[12] and consisted of families integrated into the local milieu. They were Arabized or *musta'aribin* – loosely translated as those who adopt Arab manners.[13] They were engaged in glassmaking and inter-national commerce.[14] The communities in Lebanon were not isolated either. The Cairo Geniza recorded a number of inter-marriages between Jews from Lebanon with those Egypt, Syria and Palestine in the eleventh century.[15] Benjamin of Tudela, in the twelfth century, claims that Jews lived in the same area as the Druze with whom they traded and engaged in crafts.[16] They were well integrated into their environment and the majority of them were Arabized.[17] In 1173 Benjamin of Tudela found 50 Jews in Beirut, while local Jewish tradition holds that the synagogue and the cemetery dated from 1300.[18] The traveller Rabbi Moshe visited Saida some 450 years ago and found 20 families of "Jews acting like Arabs" living there.[19] In the fourteenth century references to the Jews of Hasbaya were made in a manuscript describing them as the "Levites of Hasban".

A book of *responsa* by Rabbi Yom Tov Sahalon, one of the great sages of Safed, during the time of Joseph ben Efraim Caro (1488–1575), makes it clear that the Jews of southern Lebanon clearly looked toward Safed for spiritual guidance. As is evident from the *responsa*, Rabbi Sahalon was asked by the Jews of Hasbaya about the law regarding a resident who sowed his field during the sabbatical year. His response provides some interesting insights into the Hasbaya community at that time: A rabbi served in the community, known as the Sage Rabbi David; the community was led by *Sheikh* Yosef Menashe; and Hasbaya was ruled by *Emir* Ali, presumably a Druze. But it also makes it very clear that rulings handed down by the sages of Safed were legally binding for the area of Hasbaya.

> Holy congregation, may the Protector of the Eternal truth protect every sacred thing in Hasbaya. Regarding that which we have heard, that one man who lives there among you has done wrong . . . that he has sown in the sabbatical year. . . . Perhaps he thought that since (the village of Hasbaya) is not the Land of Israel it is permissible to plant there in the sabbatical . . . Maimonides wrote . . . that the sabbatical is observed in Transjordan and in Syria as commanded by the scribes, so we find that he has transgressed the words of the sages and his sin is too great to bear.
>
> . . . And the law should be that he must uproot all that he has sown, even though he did it unknowingly . . . we have thus seen it fit to decree upon him that he give it to the poor of Hasbaya like the Sage Rabbi David, who is a disseminator of Torah, a teacher, a slaughterer and a leader of prayer services, shall give him a generous portion . . . And if he turns a rebellious shoulder, we decree upon the wise and elevated *Sheikh* Yosef Menashe that he should go to *Emir* Ali . . . and tell him: the sages of Israel send you regards and tell you that so-and-so has violated the prohibition of the sabbatical year according to our faith, and if he does not act in accordance with the Torah you should take from him all the grain produced from his field.[20]

Evidence such as this illustrates aspects of Jewish life in Lebanon in the period prior to the Ottoman Empire. And even though information is scant, it bears testimony to the existence of long established Jewish communities in what is present-day Lebanon, including the cities of Tripoli and Beirut which had 1,535 Jewish residents between 1570 and

1590,[21] as well as Saida, Tyre, and the Druze areas of the Shouf and Hasbaya.

Lebanon under Ottoman Rule

The Ottomans conquered Lebanon in the sixteenth century in their drive for territorial expansion from Turkey through Syria, ending ultimately in the defeat of the Abbasid Caliphate in Cairo. The inclusion of Mount Lebanon into the Ottoman Empire had a number of important repercussions for the predominantly Druze–Maronite area. Maronites from the northern region of Mount Lebanon began to migrate to Kisrawan, among them the Khazin family, which settled in Balluna and the Gemayel family which settled in Bikfaya.[22] Both families played a leading role in the Maronite community, the former in the seventeenth and eighteenth centuries and the latter in the emergence of the modern Lebanese state. In the Druze community, after a number of local rebellions led by the chieftains of the House of Maan, the Fakhr al-Din family, followed by their Sunni relatives of the Shihab family from Wadi al-Taym, became the leading dynasty.

Both played an important role in Druze–Jewish relations. The Shihabs reigned until 1841, falling victim to the deteriorating Maronite–Druze relations and Lebanon's encounter with modernity. Until this point Maronites, Druze, and the small Jewish community lived amicably in the same area. "They had seen the ascent and fall of dynasties arising from each or any of their communities, had acted as close and accepted neighbours, had been indifferently landlord or tenant or worker on estates of every ownership; they had sustained, in community of interest, scene, language, livelihood, and familiar friendship, a scarcely troubled symbiosis."[23]

The precarious inter-communal dynamics of Mount Lebanon were adversely affected by the ten years of Egyptian occupation under Mohammed Ali, changes in Maronite society, the destruction of the old feudal leadership, and growing Ottoman jealousy of suspected foreign "interference", primarily French. The result was a social fracturing of the Mountain, which turned into a bloody civil war in 1860. The Druze massacre of an estimated 11,000 local Christians triggered the landing of French expeditionary forces in Beirut, as France had traditionally considered itself to be the protector of the Maronites.[24] It also gave birth to a new Ottoman statute, known as the *règlement*, in 1861 and instituted in 1864, which institutionalized the communitarian political system which has characterized Lebanon ever since. The Mountain was directly administered for the Ottoman Sultan by a governor aided by an elected council representing the local communities. The system stipulated that the governor be a Christian appointed by the Sublime Porte but effectively chosen by the European powers. It further stipulated that the council have twelve members, two for every principal community, dividing the council confessionally into six Muslim and six Christian representatives.[25] Thus, the result of Turco-European negotiations to resolve the strife was the establishment of an autonomous regime for Mount Lebanon, lasting until 1915.

This autonomy was strengthened by the fact that the Courts of Justice after 1879 were based on the Ottoman model, the law was Turkish, a customs barrier now separated Lebanon from Syria, taxes were collected and paid to Istanbul, and schools were the concern of the local communities. Autonomy, however, while cherished, was not the solution to Mount Lebanon's communal tensions. "Although the regime from 1864 to 1915 prevented recurrence of the horrors of 1860, and secured a half-century of tranquillity, the position was not without its defects, which time was not diminishing. It had been installed in the sole interests of a single . . . community, the Catholic and French-protected Maronites. . . . The power of the clergy among the Maronites, which during the nineteenth century had replaced that of the old feudal leaders, was unchecked and, for the community as citizens, must be counted unfortunate. A due balance of power as between the central and local governments was never established, suspicion and mutual aversion always prevailed."[26]

The Lebanese Jewish Community

The Ottoman approach towards ethno-religious minorities was embodied in the *millet* system which guaranteed community autonomy in the areas of some civil and all personal status laws, the full control over property and schools, and the right to be heard by the Sultan through their appointed leaders, as well as exemption from military service. Christian and Jewish communities became virtually states within the state.[27] This was the case particularly in Lebanon where secular and religious affairs of the community were often in the hands of the same person who consequently assumed an almost autocratic position of power.

The Ottoman reforms, according to Norman Stillman, contributed to the undoing of the Jews of Arab lands in the long run. "The large, newly emancipated and more assimilated Christian minority in the Levant came into fierce competition with the Jews. . . . In their struggle with the Jews, the Levantine Christians also helped introduce and disseminate Western anti-Semitism in the Arab world."[28] Clear evidence of this for the broader region were the blood libel accusations in the 1840s, but these were more of a Damascene phenomenon than a Lebanese one.

The first major influx of Jews to Lebanon came in 1710 when a significant number of Andalusian Jews fled from the Spanish Inquisition to the safety of the Shouf mountains.[29] The Shouf held particular appeal to these Andalusian and *Maghrebi* Jews as they were told that the mountains were inhabited by neither Christians nor Muslims. The Druze welcomed the Jews for they as a community in the Middle East had also suffered from Sunni intolerance, thus preferring *dhimmi* neighbours on the whole.[30] Under the protection of the Druze *emirs* they settled in the villages of Deir al-Qamr, Ba'qlin, Mukhtara,[31] Ayn Qaniya and Ayn Zahlata.[32] In fact, Fakhr al-Din provided the Jewish refugees with a room for prayer signalling both welcome and a notion of permanence. Deir al-Qamr is said to have numbered 80 families at the beginning of the 19th century.[33]

Deir al-Qamr had been the administrative and political center of the Manasif district since the seventeenth century. It was a small village at that time, in the heart of the mountain, when it became the capital of the Maan dynasty. During Fakhr al-Din's reign it acquired its distinct fountains, marble courts, mansions, and a *serail* of Italian inspiration. More and more buildings were constructed and Deir al-Qamr to many became a "paradise". By the nineteenth century it had become the trade center of the region with a population of 4,000, and one of 7,000–10,000 by the late 1850s. It was the most urbane town in the mountain.[34] In addition to its "old" agricultural Jewish community, it soon acquired a "new" one of merchants, money lenders, and peddlers centered around the town bazaar.

Unlike Jews in other Middle Eastern countries, the Jews in the Shouf were predominantly agriculturalists. Like their Druze neighbors they became involved in Lebanon's silk production, cultivating mulberry trees and breeding silk worms. Others were olive and wine growers.[35] Indeed, the agricultural occupations are still reflected in Lebanese Jewish names such as Diarné ("Deir" al-Qamr), Zeitouné (olives) and Khabié (vessel for olive oil).[36] The name Diarné is further connected to the Chaabans, the Danas, the Hanans, the Hasbanis, the Makhloufs, and the Srours. In addition to agriculture, some Jews engaged in commerce, the manufacture of soap, and the extraction of iron from the surrounding ore deposits.[37] As a community they were known for their courage, and legends were told about their heroism and the exploits of their brave daughters who knew how to defend their lives and their honour.[38]

The longing for Jerusalem was never far from the surface in this small community. Shortly after their arrival in the Shouf some Jews planted a small forest of cedars in the area of the village of al-Barouk, eleven kilometres from Deir al-Qamr. The Jews in this village were engaged in the cultivating of vineyards and olive groves, and the raising of goats. A family which is still linked with al-Barouk is that of the Anzaruts. Legend holds that the cedars were planted by the Jews of al-Barouk to provide the timber for rebuilding the Temple in Jerusalem. In fact, until today, there is a forest in the Shouf known as *al-arz al-yahud* – or the cedars of the Jews.

Under the reign of Bashir II (1788–1841) the Jewish community flourished. In Mukhtara the Jewish community had its own synagogue and cemetery. An estimated 15 families were there in the first half of the nineteenth century. During this period the Maronite claim to the territory in the Shouf increased and caused Maronite–Druze tensions. Added to this were regional tensions including the 1840 hostilities against Syrian Jews as a result of blood libel accusations.[39] They had been accused of killing a monk. The same year the Jews of Rhodes were blamed for the death of a ten-year-old Greek boy. In 1848 the Damascene Jews were further accused of the ritual murder of a disappeared infant.[40] Anti-Jewish feeling in the area was high and did not leave the Lebanese communities untouched.

In 1848 the disappearance of another child led to a ritual murder accusation which shattered the peaceful life of the Jewish community in the Shouf. "A Christian boy named Yusuf, son of Assad Abu Shakr from Deir al-Qamr, disappeared on the eve of Passover. A horrible blood libel was brought upon the Jews. Nine respected members of the community were arrested and the smell of a pogrom was in the air . . . In the end the boy was found dead in a field and neither the identity of the murderer nor the cause of the death were determined."[41] The hostilities spread and the Jews of Beirut were only saved from physical harm because of the intervention of the Dutch and Prussian consuls.[42] In many ways, these incidents were indicative of the tension leading to the 1860 war.

The blood libel accusation did not find sympathy with the Druze and, in that sense, it remained a single incident without lasting impact. It did, however, fall into a broader regional upheaval characterized by rising ethnic nationalism, emerging economic competition between local Jews and Greek Orthodox newcomers, and general insecurity which adversely affected a number of Jewish communities in the Levant.

The prime impact of this wave of anti-Jewish sentiments in the Levant was an increase in Jewish immigrants to Lebanon which was still more tolerant than the neighboring areas. Thus the number of Jews in Lebanon, which had already expanded through an influx of Turkish and Spanish Jews, grew further in 1848 when Jewish families from Damascus fled to Lebanon. Yet while the Jewish communities in the Shouf and Beirut had encountered some problems, the small communities in other parts of Lebanon remained virtually untouched by events. For example, a travelog description by J. J. Benjamin gives the following impression of Lebanese Jews (probably referring to Hasbaya) in January 1848:

In some villages there are Jewish families which are popular with the Druze and who like the indigenous (people), are farmers . . . They are very religious, but uneducated. Their children, namely the girls, take the herds out in line with patriarchal custom as the bible tells of Rachel. I was told a story which took place a couple of years ago, that a young girl was attacked by a Druze, who wanted to rape her. The girl warned him that violence would be met with violence. The Druze ignored her pleading and her threats and accosted her, which is when she pulled out a pistol and shot him. When this case came to trial, the girl was not only not punished, but was praised for her courage.[43]

The next major upheaval in the history of Lebanese Jewry came with the complete disintegration of Maronite–Druze relations in the Shouf, resulting in the war of 1860. Many Maronite and Druze villagers were forced to flee the area and migrated to the coastal region around Beirut. The on-going hostilities meant that the Jews who had settled in the Shouf also started migrating from 1850 onwards, especially when the Druze abandoned Deir al-Qamr. The Jews of Deir al-Qamr decided to leave with them as relations with Maronites had been strained through the blood libel accusations,[44] while the Druze protected the Jews during the war and helped them leave the mountain.[45] Thus the year 1893 signalled the end of the Jewish presence in the Shouf.

At this point the community split into three smaller groups. Between 1850 and 1860 the first group, mainly of *Maghrebi* origin settled, in the area of Saida in South Lebanon,[46] which had had a sizeable Jewish community since 1522.[47] In 1738 Rabbi Haim Yosef David Azulai encountered a flourishing Jewish community in Saida.[48]

The second group settled in the area of Hasbaya on the slopes of Mount Hermon. The third and largest group settled in Beirut, not only because of the economic opportunities the coastal city offered but also because of the already existing Jewish community. Beirut at that time was in the process of transition from a small port town to a bustling city. Located on the northern end of hills, bordered to the north and west by the Mediterranean, and to the south by the Mount Lebanon range, it naturally drew Lebanese of all communities to it. In the center of the city the streets were narrow and winding. The houses had thick stone walls, surrounding courtyards hiding them from the view of the casual passerby. They were crammed together, flat roofed terraces touching. In the heart of the city was the lively bazaar with numerous shops, booths, inns, and coffee houses.[49] It was around this area that the ancient Jewish community had made its home and to which the Jewish migrants flocked. The head of the Damascene Jewish community Rabbi Moses Farhi, during one of his journeys in the 1830s, described the Beirut Jewish community as "fifteen native families" (making it clear that they were not recent Jewish immigrants) who had "a neat little synagogue" which had its own large garden, planted with lime and citron trees.[50] Rabbi David d' Beth Hillel, who travelled the region over the period 1824–32, provides a similar description:

> Beirut is built at the foot of Mount Lebanon which is on the Mediterranean; it is a large town and has some very fine houses and *chans* for travellers, but the streets and markets are narrow after the ancient customs . . . The town abounds with every kind of trade because it is the entrance to Damascus from the sea. This place manufactures a great quantity of silk, as there are an abundance of trees for the support of the silkworm . . . There are about 15 families of native Israelite merchants speaking Arabic; they have a small synagogue and have customs similar to those of Judea.[51]

Other sources estimate the size of the community to have been 25 families in 1840,[52] and 1,000 in 1850, further increasing after 1860.[53] Later on some of the Beiruti Jews also moved north to Tripoli, which according to Rabbi David had "about 15 families of native Israelites who have a neat little synagogue in which are written in Hebrew characters the words 'the synagogue of Sinim'. Behind it is a garden of lime and citron trees."[54] In 1881/2 there were 3,541 Jews in Beirut and Tripoli,[55] rising to 5,000 alone for Beirut in 1901[56] with 1,908 pupils in the *vilayet* of Beirut.[57] In 1914 there were 4,568 in Beirut, 72 in Tripoli, 6 in Hasbaya and one in Baalbek.[58] Thus, in essence, the Jews in Lebanon were living among the Druze, Christians, Shi'a and Sunnis, reflecting not only Lebanon's multi-communal identity, but also that the Jews were widely accepted as just another of the country's 23 minorities.

The town of Saida in the 1830s was surrounded by a "little wall in which are very good streets and houses built of hewn stones, and the climate is wholesome. There are of native Israelites about 25 families, principally merchants; they have a small synagogue, they speak Arabic and have the same customs as the Israelites of Judea."[59] The community of Saida had been embellished by mainly *Maghrebi* Jews from the Shouf who brought with them rural traditions which they implanted onto the terrain around this predominantly Sunni city. This was most noticeable in the Jewish ownership of some of the citrus groves and plantations around the fertile coastal city. By 1860 the community in Saida had grown to such an extent that it called for the formal construction of a synagogue, rather than the use of prayer rooms in a community member's home.

In 1902 Saida was a city of 15,000–18,000 residents. There was no significant commerce or industry and most residents made a living off the gardens outside the city or were fishermen. Overlooking the Mediterranean Sea the small buildings were made of stones gathered from the fields. The alleys between the crammed houses were narrow and winding. The entrance to the Jewish quarter of Saida was through a low narrow gate. "Imagine a long courtyard, narrow and dark, a sort of corridor, as sinuous as can be, whose width is never more than two meters. On either side are two and three storey houses – or rather cells cut into the walls, not receiving even a little of the dim light from the side of the narrow passage that forms the street."[60] In a small square stood the main synagogue and the *Talmud Torah*. The Jews of Saida, at the turn of the century, were described as generally poor. They were predominantly peddlers with a few owning citrus groves outside the city. Most of the landowners were Muslim. Since the region itself was not particularly prosperous, peddling meant leaving the home and family after *Shabbat* and returning the following Friday before sunset.

In the nineteenth century the poll-tax for Jews was abolished.[61] And in 1911 the Ottoman government officially recognized the Jews as one of Lebanon's confessional groups and conferred upon the community the same rights other confessions had already received. This, in essence, meant that not only were the Jews generally perceived as equal by other ethno-religious communities in Lebanon, they also had the same rights and responsibilities under the law. In addition, under Ottoman law, the Jewish community had juridical autonomy in the areas of marriage, divorce, inheritance, all business law, certain aspects of housing, and ritual law. Jewish authorities were able to impose fines, ostracize, mete out corporal punishment, and even carry out capital punishment indirectly through the organs of the state.[62]

The southern Lebanese village of Hasbaya, situated on the gentle slopes of Mount Hermon, also had a sizeable Jewish community. Hasbaya featured much more prominently among Jews and non-Jews from outside Lebanon than any other community. This is partly due to the geographic proximity and thus accessibility to those visiting Palestine. There exists, however, evidence that the attention this community received was due to the ambiguity over whether they were not in fact Palestinian Jews, as some definitions of biblical Palestine included that part of South Lebanon. The latter is based on an ancient tradition regarding the boundaries of the Land of Israel including Sefanta as a border point. Sefanta is generally considered to be synonymous with al-Safna which lies to the north of Hasbaya.[63]

The book of *responsa* by Rabbi M. Galanit from 1777 discusses the case of a Hasbani Jew who was imprisoned by the Druze *emir*:

And the day came to pass when imprisoned under him were gentiles and a few Jews who the Emir decreed should be imprisoned, and among them was one Jew named Mourad Siher Al-Rodisli who with one of the gentile prisoners . . . dug a tunnel . . . and escaped with all the Emir's prisoners who had been imprisoned there. . . . After time passed, one gentile came, a Druze from Hasbaya, whom the Emir sent on a mission from Hasbaya to another place.

Based on this testimony Rabbi Galanit released a Jewess from the status of *aguna*. Among the witnesses mentioned in this episode were Nissim Bechar, Yitzhak Maatik and Rabbi Yosef Zerahia – all from established Hasbaya families.[64]

In 1835, the traveller Rabbi Yosef Schwartz visited Lebanon and related the following about the 30 Jewish families of Hasbaya: "They were very much loved by the Druze and they were strong men, men of valour and workers of the land. . . . Even their daughters tend sheep with bow and spear in their hands to fight with wild beasts and ambushers." The Jews of Hasbaya cultivated grain and vineyards, and tended to sheep and cattle. The Hermon Jews had a monopoly on producing soap from olive oil, marketing and selling in all of Lebanon. They also raised silk-worms and dyed clothes.[65]

Church of Scotland missionary John Wilson encountered the Hasbaya community during his travels in the region after hearing about them in Jerusalem. His diary entry of 15 April 1843 gives an impressionistic account of Passover:

> We arrived in Hasbaya at six thirty, and we found the lodgings which Mordechai our Jewish guide who accompanied us from India procured for us in the house of the Jew Moshe Ben Yosef Valido, more accurately, a temporary dwelling in his courtyard. We were not allowed to sleep or eat inside in case we would being in *chametz* and desecrate Passover, which the family were busy preparing for. We received all the attention we expected from these simple people. They gave us shelter, and of course, on our part we did not interfere with them in any way in their carrying out religious duties. Mordechai joined them in the reading of the Passover *Haggadah*, the Passover service which is held by the family. They maintained a festive mood during the reading or during the ceremonies which included a cup of wine, bitter herbs, *matza* and meat that was placed before them.

Wilson's account continues with a brief history of the community in the entry of the following day (16 April 1843). He states that all families were Sephardi and that there were approximately twenty households comprised of an estimated 100 people. They were all Lebanese with the exception of one Palestinian from Acco. Their ancestors had settled in Wadi al-Taym one hundred years ago and most of them traced their origins back to North Africa. Only a small number, two or three, were professional traders. The others all seemed to be involved in agriculture to some extent, as can be gathered from similar references by Schwartz,

who writing at the same time as Wilson, tells of thirty families in Hasbaya.
He describes them as "strong people, brave men, and they work the land
just like the gentiles of the mountain, and their daughters are also shep-
herdesses".[66]

Wilson's diary gives yet further insight into the small community:

> They have a small synagogue, but no *beit midrash*. They have no inclina-
> tion for study. But a few of them understand Hebrew, and about eight to
> ten read and write Arabic. They very much need the holy scriptures in
> Hebrew and we were very sorry that we could not fulfil their request. Their
> *hakim* Avraham Ben David, who is the governor, the butcher, the teacher
> and the cantor, said that he is prepared to work as a headteacher of a school,
> if they will appoint him to such a post, aside from teaching Talmud. They
> complained that the demands of the Turkish government places a great
> burden on them, and that under the rule of Ibrahim Pasha they would pay
> only 450 Grush per annum, and now they are required to pay 3,200
> Grush.[67]

This diary entry raises a number of interesting points. The community like
much of its Christian and Muslim counterparts had an illiterate majority.
It can also be assumed that the structure of the community was essentially
as tribal and patriarchal as the other Lebanese communities. This is
supported by the fact that there was one Jewish leader who much like a
village *mukhtar* represented his people on secular matters, attended to
their religious needs, educated their children, and adjudicated disputes.

The Hasbaya Jewish community attracted attention again a couple of
years later in 1859, when a rather curious letter appeared in the journal
Hamaggid. It was a letter from a father to his son in which he recounts
the abuse he received from the Druze *sheikh* of Hasbaya. Having been
asked by the *sheikh* to cure his possessed wife and unwilling and unable
to comply, the Jew Shalom was beaten, stabbed with a sword, and thrown
into a pit. After the local Jews, Christians and the regional governor as
well as some twenty Druze clerics intervened, Shalom was released. He
fled to Beirut where he was welcomed by the local Jewish community. He
ended the letter by begging his son to come to him before he died.[68]

This letter seems to be at odds with the idyllic picture of Hasbaya
painted in books, diaries and travelogs of the 1840s and 1850s. It is difficult to say retrospectively to what extent this letter characterizes a decline
in the inter-communal relations of the village ten years later. It is a
confusing, almost inconsistent document within itself, showing, on the
one hand, the brutality of the Druze *sheikh*, but, on the other hand, the
successful intervention of a substantial number of non-Jews – Christian
and Druze – to rectify the situation. Moreover, the Jew Shalom did not
flee across the close border to Palestine but instead travelled the much

longer distance to Beirut. In many ways it would be easy to dismiss this letter completely on the basis of the Druze *sheikh*'s "derangement" as a result of the grief over his ill wife, or even seeing it as a rather elaborate ploy by a father to get his two adult children to move back home and take care of him. The main argument against this is a reference in an account by the mother of a Lebanese Jew by the name of Salim Hasbani who spent most of her life in Hasbaya even though she was originally from Mukhtara. She remembers that a number of families left Hasbaya temporarily during the Druze–Maronite War of 1860. These families went to Damascus, but decided to return to Hasbaya half a year later.[69] This suggests that there were indeed upheavals in the Hasbaya community with the arrival of Jewish families from the Shouf, the departure of some Hasbaya families to Damascus, and others to Beirut and Saida. As a mixed village of Druze, Christians, Muslims and Jews the Druze–Maronite tensions had made themselves felt. Indeed, the 1860 civil war which had started in the Maronite district of Kisrawan, spread from the mountain onto the plains and to the anti-Lebanon range, including Hasbaya.[70] On the other hand, these inter-communal tensions were not characteristic of Hasbaya and should thus not be taken out of context.

The geographic proximity of the slopes of Mount Hermon and the emerging Jewish settlement in Palestine were, no doubt, the largest factor in the dissolution of the Hasbaya Jewish community. There had always been more of a spiritual link of this community with Zion which can be gathered from the tradition of burying their dead in nearby Abel al-Saki believed to be in the Land of Israel.[71] With Jewish immigrants acquiring land in the Galilee and the increasingly active Zionist movement, the Hasbaya Jews started being drawn more and more towards their co-religionists across the border. A visit of Baron Rothschild features quite prominently in the local history. Oral history holds that in 1887 Rothschild passed through the area and aroused the curiosity of the Hasbaya Jews who had never seen a "wealthy" Jew before. They climbed down from the slopes of Mount Hermon to greet him. He was surprised to see Jews living in the mountains in Lebanon and asked them who they were and how they lived. Then he asked whether they needed anything, at which point they asked for a new synagogue and school. All that was left of the old synagogue was the southern wall. Rothschild paid for a new synagogue to be built at the expense of 170 Lira and provided the community with a *hacham*.[72]

Trade links, religious ties, and economic and financial opportunity opened the way for the eventual migration of most of the families to nearby Rosh Pina in Palestine, a move that had been encouraged and financed by Baron Rothschild.[73] The migration started in 1888[74] and by 1913 only three families still remained in the Lebanese village on the slopes of Mount Hermon. Rothschild's other "contributions" to Hasbaya were of a less permanent nature. The ancient wall of the original synagogue is still standing, while the walls of Rothschild's new building collapsed long ago.

Culture, Education and Religion

Lebanese Jews after their interlude in Mount Lebanon became an urban population who were Arabic-speaking and French educated. In that sense, they lagged behind other Middle Eastern Jews who tended to have ceased to be an agricultural people during the seventh and eighth centuries, but unlike other ancient populations, returned to life as a nation of merchants and artisans.[75] They have been described as assimilated into the Arab population save in greater Westernization of mind and habit.[76] They managed their own community within the *millet* system with their own schools as well as those of the *Alliance Israélite Universelle*. In addition to the schools of the *Alliance*, missionary schools started to attract more Jewish students from the mid-nineteenth century onwards. The Church of Scotland had three schools in Beirut alone. Generally these schools were unsuccessful in their proselytizing efforts. In the case of Lebanon, most missionary schools were French and this specifically meant that classes taught on Saturdays resulted in Sabbath desecration for the children of the mainly upper middle class Lebanese Jewish families.[77]

Lebanese Jews like other Middle Eastern Jews participated in the country's culture as well as that of their own community. With Beirut emerging as an intellectual and literary center within the region in the nineteenth century, it is not surprising that Beirut's Jews were included among the playwrights. Most prominent were the lawyer and businessman Antun Yusuf Shihaybar and his brother Ilyas, a school teacher at the Jewish school in Beirut, as well as Zaki Cohen and his son Selim. The Shihaybar brothers' plays which were written and performed in Arabic and are currently in the possession of the Abulafia family in Israel include *dhabihat ishaq* (the sacrifice of Isaac), *al-marid al-wahmi* (the imaginary invalid), *mudda'i al-sharaf* (the would-be gentleman), and *intisar al-fadila* (the victory of virtue). Zaki Cohen's plays were written and performed in Hebrew – making them the first plays in Hebrew performed in Beirut in 1876 – and his son Selim's plays were in Arabic. The latter's included *intisar al-haqq* (the victory of truth), *'awd al-sa'ada* (the return of happiness), *khashf al-hijab* (the unveiling), *al-muqamir* (the gambler), *Badr wa ikhwanuha* (Badr and her brothers), and *al-musrif* (the profilgate). In addition, there were a number of unknown plays by Salim Dhaki performed in March 1882, April 1894 and April 1895.[78]

These plays provide an interesting insight into the extent of Arabization of the Beiruti Jews. With the exception of Zaki Cohen's plays, they were written and performed in Arabic. They featured characters whose Jewish identity was clear, emphasized by the use of some Hebrew words and the discussion of questions of the Jewish faith, history, and persecution.[79] They also made allusions to Arabic history, Quranic verses, classical Arabic poetry, and European literature. Thus they combined Jewish, Arabic and European elements – in many ways a classic Levantine mixture. The broader impact of these plays on Beiruti society is indicative not only of the way the Jews framed their own identity as Jewish, Arab and Levantine/Lebanese but also of their acceptance within an equally mixed-identity Muslim-Christian community. The plays were appreciated by high officials and notables from all communities. Niqula Fayyad, well-known physician, poet and writer, once said that the "most famous plays were those performed in the school of Zaki Cohen in al-Ashrafieh. I used to attend them clandestinely and envied those who had received an official invitation."[80]

The example of the emerging Jewish–Arab theatre in Beirut highlights some of the links between cultural expressions of the Jewish community and its educational establishments. Indeed, much of the Jewish theatre tradition was linked to the Jewish school which in the 1870s and 1880s presented plays at the beginning or end of the academic year.[81] Both the Shihaybar brothers, the Cohens, and Dhaki taught at the *Tiferet Yisrael* school which was, in fact, established by Rabbi Zaki Cohen in 1874. The school was unique in the sense that in addition to educating Lebanese Jewish children, it also became a private boarding school for the children of prosperous Jewish families from Damascus and Aleppo only a year after its establishment and remained so until its closure in 1904. It combined religious subjects with a very high standard of secular studies, boasting a wide range of languages including Hebrew, Arabic, Turkish, French, English, and German. Despite the entry of the *Alliance Israélite Universelle* onto the educational scene in Lebanon, *Tiferet Yisrael* was the center of both educational, literary and cultural activities of the small Jewish community, which in 1856 had numbered only 500, doubling by 1880, and tripling by 1889. With its language of instruction being Arabic it was an exception within the greater Jewish education establishments in the Middle East.

The *Alliance Israélite Universelle* established a primary school for boys in Beirut in 1869 and a primary school for girls in 1878. A co-educational primary school was also founded in Saida in 1902.[82] Unlike *Tiferet Yisrael* the schools of the *Alliance* were exclusively secular in orientation and the language of instruction was French. The *Alliance Israélite Universelle* as a movement was founded in Paris in 1860. Its aim was to work throughout the world for the emancipation and the moral progress of the Jews.[83] The underlying principles of the movement were those of liberty, equality and fraternity of the French Revolution.[84] The interest of Western Jews in the fate of their co-religionists in the Middle East was sparked by the 1840 Damascus blood libel case. So when the *Alliance* was created it pursued the fight for Jewish rights world wide under the talmudic motto "all Jews are responsible for each other".[85] Added to the classic spirit of emancipation was a liberal doses of the classic (colonial) French civilizing mission. In order to be able to extend equality and emancipation a concerted amount of regeneration of Jews living in "backward" societies was needed. Thus, what the *Alliance* as an institution embodied and sought to instil in the Lebanese Jews was a French value system, the French language, French appreciation of literature, music and culture. These ideological underpinnings were, on the one hand, linked to the integration of the Middle East into the world capitalist market and, on the other hand, based on general perceptions that Middle Eastern Jews without distinction were unenlightened, ignorant, superstitious and fanatic. In short, they were a source of deep embarrassment to their enlightened European (French) brethren.[86]

To the chagrin of the emerging Zionist movement the *Alliance* had an almost anti-Zionist stance. Moreover, its assimilationist approach angered the traditional religious establishment. Yet, it has been pointed out that to see the *Alliance* purely within the French colonial context is also incorrect. Middle Eastern Jews were not the classic "other" in the perception of French Jewry which was part of the great French civilization, but an extension of it.[87] Thus, through the *Alliance* French Jewry sought to draw Middle Eastern Jews into civilization. What is present in the relationship between French Jews and Middle Eastern Jews, lacking in other French missionaries and their colonial subjects, is a real sense of eventual equality rather than mere likeness.

The impact of the *Alliance* on the Lebanese Jewish community cannot be overestimated as it profoundly added to their identity, and, in the emerging national divide, placed them clearly in the francophile and pro-Western camp. It also meant that the French mandate was yet another period in which Lebanese Jewry flourished – at least until the Vichy regime.

Religion comprises the final element within the triangle of Lebanese Jewish social life, interacting with both culture and education in the formulation of Jewish identity in nineteenth century Ottoman Lebanon. The synagogues filled their traditional roles not only as vehicles for religion and culture but also for social integration, stratification, and control. The construction and location of synagogues in many ways documents the development of the Lebanese Jewish community.

The first modern synagogue in Beirut was located in the area of the Place de l'Étoile and al-Ahdab Street where it stood until 1922. The traditional quarters at that time placed the Greek-Orthodox community to the east around Ashrafieh and the Sunni Muslims to the west around Basta. Most of the Jews who had settled in Beirut lived in the area of Souk Sursock and Dalalin next to the Roman Catholic Church of Mar Elias. In the late nineteenth century they started moving towards Wadi Abu Jamil, along the Ottoman government buildings in the *serail* and along Bab Idriss and into the valley. As time went on Wadi Abu Jamil became the religious, social and economic centre of the community. To imagine the Jewish quarter as a ghetto would be a mistake. It was a section of Beirut which had taken on distinct communal characteristics, no more and no less than the Armenian quarter, Maronite, Greek-Orthodox, or Sunni parts of the city. Wadi Abu Jamil did not receive its first synagogue until long after the settlement of the community in that area.

Two grand "private" synagogues were built in the mountain resorts of Aley and Bhamdoun. This was a response to the traditional seasonal migration of many middle class Lebanese urbanites to the mountains during the hot and humid summer months. Middle class Jewish families in accordance with this tradition decided to build a synagogue in Aley in 1890 and in Bhamdoun in 1915. Between 1850 and 1860 a synagogue was also built in Saida.

Religious and community life in Beirut as well as that in Aley and Bhamdoun was a combination of "Levantineness" with Syrian, Iranian and Iraqi *minhagim*.[88] Much of religious tradition was transmitted orally rather than through learned texts as Lebanese Jewry was only slightly more literate than its other Middle Eastern counterparts at that time. This resulted in the notion of the "saintly" rabbi who was able to solve all problems without consulting texts right up to the twentieth century.

A prominent factor within Lebanese Jewish religious expression was popular religion or popular mysticism. Like their Muslim neighbours who pilgered to tombs of saints, the Jews also practised both "high" and "low" Judaism. One such manifestation of "low" or popular religion was the pilgrimage to the reputed tombs of the sons of Jacob, said to buried in Lebanon.[89] The tomb of Rabbi Reuven near Hasbaya had similar importance. Salim Hasbani recalled that this particular tomb was also visited by gentiles. There is an interesting tale connected with Rabbi Reuven's tomb:

Next to the tomb there are four olive trees and a piece of land. It happened 80 or 90 years ago (Salim Hasbani recalls in 1929) that the tombstone was destroyed. One of the *Emirs* ruled the land. At the same time there was a well-respected Druze whose name was Salim Bek Shams. The Druze told the Jews that the Rabbi (Reuven) came to him in a dream at night and said to him: "You should know that I am destroyed, if you don't undertake repairs I will strangle you." And he (the Druze) did not heed it (the dream). On the second night the dream recurred, and it was so on the third night. The *Bek* became alarmed and started building a mausoleum for him (the Rabbi).[90]

The mausoleum subsequently became a prominent locality of pilgrimage drawing not only Jewish worshippers, but also Christians and Druze. Near the tomb of Rabbi Reuven there was also a small cemetery in addition to the official one in Abel al-Saki.

Another example of mystical popular religion and its appeal across the communities is the assembly of the religious leaders of all communities at times of crises for joint prayers. A Lebanese Jew recalls there was a time of drought. Muslim and Christian leaders were praying for rain. They came to the local rabbi and asked him to join them in prayer and blow the *shofar*. The rabbi declared a fast for the whole community and took the children from the *Talmud Torah* to the cemetery. Before they finished the fast, the rain came pouring down. The rabbi was honoured by the Muslim and Christian leaders. And years later, after his death, they still went to the rabbi's grave.[91]

Lebanese Jews like other Middle Eastern Jewish communities had links with the Jews in Palestine. The geographic proximity meant that these religious ties which evolved around pilgrimages to Jerusalem, Safed, Hebron and Tiberias were well developed.[92] Palestinian Jewish emissaries, such as Victor Jacobson, also travelled to Beirut on a regular basis.[93]

Religion became a central issue for the Beirut community at the turn of the century as it underwent a spiritual crisis caused by the lack of a chief rabbi. This was followed by a scandal in connection with the rabbi they then had employed to fill the vacancy. The community had appealed to Chief Rabbi Nahoum in Constantinople to send an appropriate person for the position of Chief Rabbi of Lebanon, and Rabbi Danon was despatched to Lebanon to fill this post in 1908. But "the man who should have sought to unite the hearts of all (did) everything to divide them. . . . By his inconsistent character and lack of dignity, he has done everything to discredit himself in the eyes of the people and, what is worse, to discredit his office. . . . Blinded by power which he exaggeratedly thought he wielded, he threatened at every turn the newcomer and notable alike."[94] The community at that time levied its own tax on meat in order to fund its institutions. Apparently, Rabbi Danon misappropriated these funds. He also took control of the locks of the cemetery in order to personally collect tax on burials. The tax had up to that point been collected by the community committee, and the revenues had been deposited in accordance with the statues of the community in the Anglo-Palestine Bank. It was used for the burial of the poor free of charge. The patience of the community members with Rabbi Danon reached breaking point when a member of the Greenberg family died and the rabbi would not allow them to bury him before the tax had been paid. "He haggled at 2 a.m. over this issue with the dead body on the floor and the family struck by grief."[95] After this incident the notables of the community petitioned the Chief Rabbi in Constantinople to remove Rabbi Danon. The action against the rabbi was initiated by the then community president Ezra Anzarut and the committee. In his defense Rabbi Danon claimed that the opposition was down to Yaacov Semach who was a veteran *Alliance* teacher and the director of the schools. Semach, according to Danon, turned the notables against him.[96] Danon was not able to keep his post in face of the community's action. He was succeeded by Chief Rabbi Jacob Maslaton who held this post from 1910 to 1921. At the same time a shift also took place in the secular leadership of the community with Anzarut being succeeded by Joseph Farhi as the president of the Jewish community until 1924.

2

Lebanese Jews under the French Mandate: Liberty, Fraternity, and Equality

The period of the French mandate is one that left a distinct and often contradictory imprint on the minds of all Lebanese communities. The French presence was perceived as an impediment to independence by many Christian politicians. These same politicians, however, also saw French influence on the area as a welcome check on Arab nationalism in the region. In the eyes of many Lebanese Muslims the French mandatory power was blamed for the separation of Lebanon from Syria and the creation of Grand Liban. Thus the French had hindered legitimate Muslim Arab aspirations for a united Arab state. The conflict in Palestine also affected the situation in neighboring Lebanon, placing some Maronite politicians in an uneasy alliance with the *Yishuv*, Muslim nationalists in occasionally hostile opposition, and the Jews in a position which was not always as clear-cut as they might have wished. Yet at the same time Muslims, Christians, Druze, and especially the Jews remember the mandate as another golden age in Lebanon's history, a time characterized by the pursuit of culture, literature, and the art of living – a time when there was inter-communal cooperation despite differing views on the state.

Grand Liban and the Mandate

The First World War heralded the dismemberment of the Ottoman Empire. In the spring of 1920 France and Britain agreed on the exact division formula for the Arab territories of the former Ottoman Empire at the San Remo conference. The principal consideration underlying this formula as in the earlier Sykes–Picot Agreement was oil and communications.[1] France was awarded the mandate for Lebanon on 28 April 1920, giving the French the duty of framing a constitution, protecting the rights and interests of the population, as well as encouraging local autonomy.[2] The direct implication for Lebanon was the creation of the Republic of Lebanon in its "Greater Lebanon" territorial configuration.

With the arrival of colonial rule came a general abandonment of religious traditions for all urban communities and a tendency to an often superficial form of Westernization. For the Jews this meant a lapse in ritual immersion, ignorance of Hebrew, and adoption of Western dress.

> The entry of the *Alliance Israélite Universelle* educational system into the lives of the Jews in the Muslim countries turned out to be a distinctly mixed blessing. It was a good thing in the sense that it laid the foundations for the emergence and growth of a Western oriented intelligentsia. At the same time, however, the *Alliance* also paved the way for a gradual alienation from Jewish tradition and Jewish nationalism, and for the perception of Western lands – rather than the land of Israel – as objects of migration.[3]

The latter held particularly true for the Jews of Lebanon.

The departure of the Ottoman governors and the entry of French troops into Lebanon in 1919 gave rise to the long-simmering and still unresolved debate over the identity of Lebanon as a state. In 1919 there existed three key conceptions competing with each other: Arab unity, Greater Syria, and an independent Lebanon. Arab unity was supported by some Greek Orthodox notables as well as Muslim political circles. The Greater Syria option was championed by the secular intellectual establishment which considered Syria, Lebanon and Palestine as one "natural" political unit and secularism as the only answer to minority-majority integration in the region. Most Lebanese, however, supported the notion of an independent Lebanon – including Lebanon's Jews. Supporters of the third option, among them the Maronite hierarchy and the Administrative Council of pre-war Mount Lebanon, were divided with regard to the borders of this independent state. The rival territorial units were *Petit Liban*, effectively the *mutasarrifiya* (governorate) of Mount Lebanon, and *Grand Liban*, adding to Mount Lebanon the *qazas* (districts) of Baalbek, the Bekaa, Rashayya and Hasbaya. The latter was essentially the area once ruled by Fakhr al-Din and Bashir II reaching from Tripoli and the Akkar plain in the north to the Bekaa in the west, to Jebel Amel in the south. The French who had been given the mandate over Syria and Lebanon by the League of Nation were lobbied with great efficiency by the Greater Lebanon supporters, many of whom were Lebanese emigrants in Paris. The final decision in favor of *Grand Liban* was ultimately motivated by two factors: the Maronites who would have been the prime beneficiaries of a smaller state actually wanted a larger one, and within the context of mandate responsibilities *Grand Liban* was a much more economically viable unit with a stronger basis for independence. Thus, on 1 September 1920, Greater Lebanon was proclaimed by the French High Commissioner General Henri Gouraud – a picturesque, gallant, distinguished military figure and devout Catholic[4] – from the porch of the residence of the French high commissioner in Beirut.

For the Maronites the new state was the culmination of centuries of striving for liberty and independence. For the majority of the Lebanese Muslims this new state meant no longer being part of the ruling group but being a minority among many. The Jews of Lebanon embraced this independent multi-cultural Levantine state with almost as much enthusiasm as the Maronites, for their religious, social, political and economic position had not only been safeguarded but enhanced.

The political system negotiated between Lebanese politicians and French administrators was in many respects similar to the *règlement* after the 1860 war. The fundamental rights of the individual ethnic and religious communities that had evolved over the previous centuries were fiercely protected.[5] Under the mandate the confessional system was perpetuated as an acknowledgement of inalienable rights and recognition of the strongest social bonds. Yet at the same time a vocal minority pressed for its abolition, exalting national over archaic sectarian loyalties.[6] The struggle between the two, hitherto unresolved, was reflected in the 1922 Electoral Law which decreed that every representative, on the one hand, represented the whole nation rather than his specific community, but, on the other hand, the seats were distributed confessionally on a proportional basis.[7] The census conducted prior to the elections counted 3,500 Jews, 330,000 Christians, 275,000 Muslims and 43,000 Druze,[8] numbers which the historian Stephen Longrigg considered to be highly inaccurate for reasons of "concealment, misunderstanding, falsification, conjecture, and motives peculiar to the communities which in such countries always prevent accurate personal registration".[9] Longrigg highlights some of the problems with population statistics which need to be kept in mind and which also account for the variance in the numbers used here. Nevertheless, the census numbers are sufficient to provide a general estimate of the size of the Jewish community.

In 1926 *Grand Liban* was reconstituted as the Lebanese Republic, the Lebanese Constitution defining the state as unitary. Articles 9 and 10 of the Constitution were particularly important for the Jewish community as seen within the broader context of Jewish experience in the Middle East. Article 9 guaranteed the freedom of conscience, the freedom of religion, and provided the communities with the right to legislate on matters of civil status. Article 10 granted the communities the right to their own educational system, subject to state supervision. Thus the Jews of Lebanon had become one of the few, and perhaps the only one of the

Jewish communities in the Middle East which had its religious equality constitutionally protected. This made it very clear that they were regarded as one minority among many, rather than second-class citizens or even the enemy within.

The Lebanese Constitution provoked fierce Syrian and unionist opposition as it effectively enshrined the territorial integrity of the Lebanese state as unalterable. The French, however, saw to it that the effectiveness of the Muslim boycott of the state over this issue was eroded. They impressed upon the Maronite leadership the vital necessity of giving the Muslim community enough stake in the country to encourage them to help maintain the state.[10] Once the Constitution had been adopted, an assembly created, and a state bureaucracy established, a change of attitude among several Muslim leaders began to emerge.[11] The idea of an independent Lebanon became reality as the Lebanese Muslim population, despite its initial resistance, started to participate in the new system. They took part in the 1932 census, and in the same year, a Muslim stood for the presidency for the first time,[12] and from 1934 onwards a Sunni Muslim has always held the premiership. This move towards full participation was enhanced by the fact that the creation of a united Arab state in the region had been deferred until the withdrawal of the mandatory powers. Yet, while inclusive state-building took place during the mandate, inclusive nation-building remained elusive. Or, as the eminent Lebanese historian Kamal Salibi asked: "Are administrative bureaucracies, flags and national anthems sufficient to make a true *nation-state* out of a given territory and the people who inhabit it?"[13]

The vague notion of a truly multi-cultural Lebanon in which all communities were afforded parity of esteem was forced to compete with much more concise forms of nationalism such as the "Lebanonism" or political Maronitism espoused by the *Kata'ib* party, the Greater Syrianism pursued by the *Parti Populaire Syrien* (PPS), or the militant Arab nationalism of the *Najjadeh*. Even though these parties were unable to attract broad support during the time of the French mandate, they contributed to the failure to create an overarching Lebanese national identity, leaving community, religion, region, and family as the primordial identity.

During this period, Lebanese Jews unlike Jews in other Arab countries were not particularly active in the budding communist movements. While Jews had been in leading positions in the Palestinian, Iraqi and Egyptian communist parties, they did not play an important role in the Lebanese communist movement.[14] It has been claimed that this conspicuous absence may be attributed to the fact that Lebanese Jews, though fairly well-off economically, have not felt themselves to be an integral part of the population and, consequently, have not developed a social conscience in regard to the ills of Lebanese society.[15] While the economic aspect should not be underestimated, the lack of interest in the Lebanese communist movement lies elsewhere. It lies in the lack of discrimination and oppression. The attraction of communist parties in other countries to Jews was that communism strove for equality regardless of religion or ethnicity. It thus served as an equalizing mechanism. In Lebanon the Jews were equal and they were, like most of their Christian and Muslim neighbors, capitalists through and through, hence the absence of Jews in Lebanon's small communist movement.

Politics in Lebanon remained essentially tribal with the Jews having tied their future to a multi-cultural independent state. Society's progress, in comparison, was one of leaps and bounds. By the end of the mandate Lebanon had, at least to outside appearances, become a shining example of a liberal democracy and of general social advancement.[16]

Merchants and Financiers

By 1914 Beirut had an estimated 200,000 inhabitants compared to only 6,000 at the beginning of the nineteenth century. It had developed from a port town to a major capital city with a cosmopolitan atmosphere. References to the size of the Jewish community during the French mandate vary widely: Pierre Rondot establishes the number of Jews in Mount Lebanon in 1913 at 86, expanding to 3,588 in 1932.[17] The *Encyclopedia Judaica* estimates the Jewish population of Beirut alone to have reached 5,000 by 1929.[18] The French government in 1923 counted 3,303 Jews in Greater Lebanon, and the 1932 census registered 3,588 Jews. By the late 1930s the community is said to have numbered 6,000, the vast majority of whom were living in Beirut. Albert Hourani even places their number as high as 9,981.[19]

With the growth of the city came significant infrastructural development which benefited all communities alike: drinking water, gas street-lighting, trams, postal and telegraphic services, schools, hospitals, as well as printing and publishing houses. The port city became the center for manufacturing and trading companies which, unlike those in other Middle Eastern cities, were owned by Lebanese and not foreigners.[20] These Lebanese entrepreneurs were predominantly Greek Orthodox and Greek Catholic Christians, but the Jews of Lebanon also played a significant role.

In the nineteenth century, Beirut had been one of the most important ports on the eastern Mediterranean. During this time the majority of Jews were engaged in commerce, and according to travelers' reports they were prosperous, with only a small number of poor.[21] As the city developed, they took part in Lebanon's domestic and foreign trade, banking, and tourism. There are no exact details on the occupations of Lebanon's Jewry at that time, but insights gained from travelogs provide a substantive basis for the assumption that most of them were merchants or clerks and a few artisans.[22]

Lebanon's economy during the mandate underwent a number of fluctuations with the stresses and strains relating to the end of the First World War, the Ottoman debt, the settlement of Armenian refugees between 1919 and 1923, the currency reform, the great depression, and the Second World War. The daily living conditions for much of the rural population remained relatively unchanged. Life in the city, however, underwent drastic changes. In a new atmosphere of modernity new progress and enterprise were stretching the boundaries of the imaginable. One of the key changes was a shift in prosperity from the old elites to a new rising trading class of Maronites, other Catholics, Jews, and Muslim minorities who flourished through their relations with the French and their freedom from Sunni dominion.[23]

The year 1935 saw three strikes which were a reflection of the economic and political situation. The long depression had frayed political nerves and had drained financial resources. General disaffection resulted in the two week strike of the butchers in Zahle, which was a violent response to the meat-transport tax. It led to the occupation of government offices and a heavy police response including shooting and arrests. Only a few months later, in March–April, Beirut's taxi drivers went on strike. Beirut's lawyers then went on strike leading to the closure of the courts.[24]

During the period of French rule, Beirut's intermediary service role between the East and the West was reinforced. The influence of French capital in the local economy, the dominance of French political and military power in the Levant, and the challenge of British Palestine resulted in policies and investment that emphasized the expansion of ports, roads, railways, and the infrastructure, mostly centered around the capital.[25] The Jews strengthened their role in commerce within this context, although they were not among the wealthiest merchants.[26] With the exception of Joseph Farhi who was a member of the Chamber of Commerce of Beirut, a member of the Merchants Association, and a member of the *Commission des Mercuriales* of the Economic Council,[27] they played no significant role in the powerful merchants associations despite the fact that approximately 90 per cent of Lebanese Jews were engaged in commerce.[28] As one Lebanese Jew recalls, most of them were businessmen, two or three were big bankers such as the Safras, Zilkhas, and some would include the Safadiehs. Many were commercial importers, and there were some small bankers and money lenders such as the Nahmads and Arazis. They were well-respected and trusted.[29] They maintained extensive business relationships with both Muslims and Christians, and the community as a whole was prosperous, possessing sufficient resources to look after its religious and educational needs.

The overall success of economic activities for all of Lebanon's communities was the result of their reach far beyond the state's borders. Lebanon's Jews and non-Jews had trade relations with both Syria and Palestine. Indeed Lebanon was one of two principal foreign markets for the sale of Palestinian products manufactured by Jewish factories.[30]

The Jewish businesses included Anzarut and Sons owned by Ezra Anzarut and his son Jacques but managed by Joseph Farhi until 1934. Farhi then proceeded to open his own *maison de commerce* Joseph David Farhi & Co Ltd.[31] Another prominent business was Joseph Dichy Bey's *maison commerciale* which represented among others Gestetner, Boots, Agence Maritime, and Smith-Corona. In addition, there was a small number of Jewish journalists in Lebanon, for example, Eliyahu Salim Mann, editor of *Al-'Alam al-Isra'ili* established in 1921, and Toufiq Mizrahi who published an economic magazine in French called *Le Commerce du Levant*. Among the few poets and writers worthy of note was Esther Azhari-Moyal.[32]

Inter-communal Relations and Community Life

Inter-communal relations, which had been traditionally characterized by religion and family received the added dimension of social distinctions with Lebanon's move to modernity. While there generally were no great differences in the living standards of farmers and workers, the growing entrepreneurial segment within the Lebanese population gave way to a Christian and Jewish petty bourgeoisie which adopted European clothes and a flagrantly Western life-style, and a Sunni Muslim bourgeoisie with similar, though more discreet, behavior.[33]

The overall relationship between the communities was amicable, characterized by mutual respect and deep personal friendships. This does not, however, mean that there were no disturbing incidents, but that these were comparatively few, and were individual actions rather than community attitudes. For example, the Maronite community as a whole had a very good relationship with its Jewish neighbors. But this did not prevent the rather unfortunate attempt by Maronite priest Antun Yamin in 1926 to try to blackmail well-off Jews.[34] Failing to attain the desired money, he imported Arabic translations of the *Protocol of the Elders of Zion* and tried to sell them. In this he was equally unsuccessful. Nevertheless, the Jewish community president appealed to the French High Commissioner Henri de Jouvenel to ban this publication under Mandate article 26.[35] De Jouvenel declared the affair ridiculous, stating that it could not possibly have any effect on the morale of the population which, it was pointed out, was unwilling to even purchase the book. Thus the attitudes of the communities stood in stark contract to the actions of this particular priest.

Religious festivals served as one of the main focal points of inter-community interaction beyond the mundane every-day world of business and commerce. The open display of religious affiliation and celebration of holidays characterized Lebanon's multi-cultural society. With the Jews of Lebanon it was not just a mere case of tolerating their religious differences but a case of all communities participating in each other's lavish and high-spirited celebrations. The Jewish quarter was covered with flowers on holidays and at the end of Passover non-Jewish neighbors would bring bread. It became a tradition to hold annual receptions at the synagogue for Passover which furthered the amicable relations between the Jewish community and the authorities as well as other communities.[36]

For instance, in 1932, during the Passover celebrations, the Jewish community president Selim Harari held a reception to which he invited French mandate authorities and Lebanese government representatives, addressing them as follows: "We address the government of the Republic of Lebanon with feelings of profound gratitude . . . for safeguarding our rights and interests as a religious minority; we are loyal and sincere citizens."[37]

Passover 1936 provides another example. After the religious service at Magen Avraham, the Jewish community received Lebanon's notables. Representing the High Commissioner was Mr Gennardi, the Inspector-General of the Waqf, and representing the president was the Emir Jamil Chehab, the Director of Finances. Also present were General Huntziger and Counter-Admiral Rivet. Community president Joseph Farhi's address commenced with the exodus from Egypt but quickly moved into eulogizing Lebanon. "We Jews in our secular tradition love this beautiful country and our attachment is as sincere and as solid as the liberal Constitution of Lebanon and the cavalier character which its inhabitants accord us in law and in deed, equality with other citizens, guaranteeing our liberty, and assuring impartial justice."[38]

He proceeded to state that the Jews, while not politically active, served their country by enhancing its prosperity. M. Gennardi, in his speech, after spending some time on the subject of the persecution of Jews in other countries and the Jewish emancipation in recent history, proceeded to stress the ancient ties that had existed between King Solomon and Phoenician King Hiram. He finished by extending sincere greetings of the French nation in the "spirit of fraternal union".[39] The Emir Jamil Chehab speaking on behalf of the Lebanese government, stated that Lebanon had never and would never make distinctions between any of its children. "Your action never caused the government concern and I am delighted to extend to all of the community congratulations from the entire Lebanese government."[40] In addition to the French and Lebanese government representatives, a great number of religious personalities from all communities as well as representatives from most foreign consulates attended the celebration. The elaborate celebrations evident on the occasion of Passover 1936 were not an anomaly, but the norm. Religious holidays were shared with other communities and on most occasions they were lavish and grand, displaying the prosperity and well-being of the community as well as a Levantine generosity as a whole.

Similarly, on the occasion of the visit by the Maronite Patriarch Antoine Arida to the Jewish community in 1937, Jewish community president Joseph Farhi portrayed Lebanese Jewish patriotism stating that,

> For us Jews our attachment to this country is not of recent date. It has existed for thousands of years. Already Moses solicited God's favor to see the promised land -the enchanting Lebanon. Later our biblical poets celebrated the marvelous sites, the majestic cedars which Solomon preferred for building the Eternal Temple. Time has not diminished our attachment to the land which we inhabit, has nothing but fortified our feelings of loyalty and devotion to Lebanon, which in our days, following the example of its glorious ally France, is maintaining rights and a regime of liberty and justice for all its citizens without distinction of race or confession.[41]

On this occasion, the Jewish community held a particularly grandiose reception for His Beatitude. Wadi Abu Jamil had been decorated with Lebanese and French flags, palm branches, festoons, hangings, and carpets covering the walls and main facades. The entrance to the synagogue was decked with a magnificent triumphal arch. The children, the scouts, and the *Maccabi* youth lined the street leading to Magen Avraham.[42] The Patriarch and Archbishop Mubarak who accompanied him were received by Joseph Farhi, Chief Rabbi Maslaton, and the director of the *Alliance*. The Patriarch thanked the community, expressing his best wishes to Lebanon's Jews, "because we feel how precious and sincere their love is for us".[43]

Passover 1943 provided another occasion for Lebanon's Jews to express their loyalty to the emerging independent Lebanon. Community president Joseph Dichy Bey paid tribute to the liberation of Lebanon from the Vichy regime, the presence of British and French forces, as well as to the fate of his co-religionists in Europe.

> Like all Lebanese, we welcome with joy the return to constitutional life. We have already entered the constructive phase of independence and we have the courage to pursue our efforts by all means possible to consolidate and elevate this edifice equally dear to all patriots.

The call for national unity has been voiced by the president of the Lebanese Republic and the eminent heads of all religious communities has profoundly echoed in our hearts.

We recognize that to assure the prosperity and duration of our cherished country, all spiritual families which compose it need unity and solidarity. We adhere with enthusiasm to the Pact and attaining the aspirations of Lebanon.

We salute equally the presence of the distinguished representatives of the French authorities, civilian and military, of Great Britain, and of the United States. Their successful fight at this hour will see the defeat of those who want to dominate the world and reduce to slavery humanity in its entirety. The Jews have been the first victims of this war. Over four million of our brothers have been massacred – this is the tribute we have paid for our attachment to the principles of liberty.[44]

The relations between the communities went beyond official functions. Stella Levi, the daughter of Joseph Farhi who was president of the Beirut community 1910–24, 1928–30, and again from 1935–8, remembers her father going to Bkerke, the seat of the Maronite Patriarch, on a regular basis for afternoons of theological discussions with the patriarch.[45]

Joseph David Farhi exemplified the community spirit. He was born in Damascus on 27 January 1878, and was educated at the *Alliance* school in Damascus followed by the *L'Ecole Normale Israélite Orientale* in Paris, from which he graduated in 1897 with his *brevet supérieur*. From 1900 to 1901 he taught at the *Alliance* school in Sousse, Tunisia. He then proceeded to become a textile merchant by profession. He was a born leader, a symbol to the community of love of Judaism, religious traditions and civic devotion. Lebanon, the country of his choice, influenced his identity beyond doubt. In 1908 he established his business in Beirut, married the daughter of Nissim Adés – Rose – in 1910, and had four daughters: Marcelle, Suzanne, Eva and Stella. From his base in Lebanon he continued to travel to Manchester as well as other parts of the world until 1934.

From his decision to settle in Beirut onwards Farhi became active in the community. His name became linked to the establishment of community organizations, fair decision-making, commitment and energy to give the community an enviable place in society. He reformed many of the antiquated communal institutions, being as committed to Zionism and his Jewish identity as he was to his chosen Lebanese identity. He not only participated in the foundation of *B'nai Brith* in 1911 but also in *Arazei HaLevanon* (Lebanon's Cedars). His motto was to be a good Jew and a good citizen.[46]

The Jewish community, like Farhi, did not only convey its own Lebanese patriotism, but they also were perceived as Lebanese by the other communities. Maronite Patriarch Arida as well as Maronite *Kata'ib* party leader Pierre Gemayel repeatedly voiced their views that the Jews were a Lebanese minority just like any other. This is only one indicator of the close relationship between the Jews and the Maronites, which, in many ways, was more intimate than Jewish-Muslim relations. Another indicator is the Jewish community's regular contributions to Maronite church charities.[47]

The connections with the *Kata'ib* party were of utmost importance. Established in 1936, this predominantly Maronite party was the only party that counted Lebanese Jews among its members. The *Kata'ib* had been founded as a paramilitary-style youth organization inspired by European fascism and dedicated to the preservation of a Christian and independent Lebanon. The ideology or belief system is generally known as Lebanonism or Lebanese nationalism. It presents an essentially secular inter-confessional interpretation of Lebanese nationhood, although with clear Maronite roots.[48] At the heart of the party was its youth movement, which provided for some organizational links between the Maronite scouts and the Jewish scouts. There is a clear overlap of interests and even ideology between Maronite *Kata'ib* supporters and Lebanon's Jews, which accounts for an almost natural relationship between the two. Pierre Gemayel's 1937 statement that the *Kata'ib* "does not constitute a political party. It is neither for nor against anyone – it is for Lebanon"[49] very much reflects Jewish attitudes. Thus, it is not surprising that the Jews of Lebanon found their closest friends among the *Kata'ib*, friends, who in addition to the state police, assumed the role of the defender of the Jewish quarter whenever pro-Palestinian demonstrations threatened to turn against local Jews.[50]

After the end of the First World War the Jewish community underwent a number of organizational reforms led by Farhi. It was a drive towards democratization and egalitarianism within the growing community evident in the revision of the general statutes, new regulations, and the establishment of a number of commissions. Until these reforms the community had essentially been directed by one or two notables who were respected by all.[51] Farhi was the driving force behind the creation of an elected community council with an elected president. This council was comprised of approximately 15 officers supported by 150–200 community activists. The office of the community president itself was held by Farhi from 1923 to 1925, followed by Joseph Dichy Bey from 1925 to 1927.

The Community Council of Beirut assumed the function of a central body within Lebanon, recognized by the Jews of Saida and Tripoli as well as by the Lebanese authorities.[52] From 1920 to 1930 the *B'nai Brith* served as one of the main fora for discussing community concerns with regular meetings.[53] The meeting rooms also functioned as a synagogue known as the "*B'nai Brith* Temple" before the construction of Magen Avraham in 1926. In 1929 *B'nai Brith* was expanded with a women's chapter *Banoth Brith* and a youth chapter in 1938.

The reforms introduced a spirit of democracy through periodical elections, assuring that there was an influx of new ideas and new representatives. It became the social foundation for the community. Another one of Farhi's projects was the creation of the Construction Fund. The fund served the purpose of improving the synagogue in Bhamdoun, the expansion of the *Talmud Torah* School, acquiring more buildings, establishing a youth center, and a library.[54]

Farhi was an exemplary community leader in all ways: active on the Community Council, in *B'nai Brith* to which he had been elected president in 1915, a member of the Scholarly Committee of the *Talmud Torah*, the *Alliance* Schools, the Chamber of Commerce, and active in the Beirut municipality.[55] In 1933 he received the *Medaille d'Officier d'Académie* for his expansion of French culture in the Orient.[56]

He was not, however, the only personality in the community to leave a lasting mark. Joseph Dichy Bey also ranked among its great leaders. Dichy Bey was born in Beirut in 1882. He married in 1907 and was blessed with seven children: Louise, Vicky, Bella, Eva, Victor, Odette and Dolly. He became active in commerce and finance which provided him with the opportunity to work for the Egyptian state for a number of years. In recognition of his service to the state, the Egyptian King Fuad granted him the title *Bey*. In 1920 Dichy Bey returned to Beirut, founded his *maison commerciale*, and embarked upon 30 years of devoted service to the Jewish community. He was admired for his relentless energy and his generosity. He became a member of the Community Council from the day he returned, and was elected president in 1925 for the first time. He applied many of the experiences he had gathered in the administration of the Egyptian state to running community affairs. He was active in *B'nai Brith* and had good relations with the *Yishuv*, visiting Tel Aviv on a number of occasions.[57] He more than proved his leadership when, during the second world war, he assumed the responsibility for the security of the Jewish community, working continuously for the release of those community members who did not hold Lebanese citizenship and were imprisoned in special camps by the Vichy authorities.

Religion

In 1921 the community was faced with choosing a new spiritual leader to replace Chief Rabbi Jacob Maslaton. At a general assembly meeting on

20 November the unanimous choice was Rabbi Solomon Tagger. Tagger held the position of the Chief Rabbi for only two years. He was relieved of his post as his public behavior was deemed to create obstacles for and prejudice towards the Jewish community through his polemics. On 23 February 1923, Joseph Farhi was re-elected community president and was faced with the issue of Chief Rabbi Tagger. He set up an arbitration commission to examine the options. In the end, the community unanimously decided to end Rabbi Tagger's service.[58] In 1924 Shabtai Bahbout was nominated Chief Rabbi, taking office in April.

In 1926 Wadi Abu Jamil's grand synagogue Magen Avraham was constructed. It was funded by Moise Abraham Sassoon of Calcutta in memory of his father,[59] on land donated by Raphael Levy Stambouli. The building was designed by the architect Bindo Manham, the construction overseen by Ezra Benjamin and Joseph Balayla, and the project promoted by Isaac Mann. As a community effort the new synagogue was inaugurated on 25 August 1926 and its grandiose architecture and structure has characterized the former Jewish quarter until today. The *Ecole Talmud Torah* Selim Tarrab was located within the premises of Magen Avraham. Both the school and the synagogue provided the community as a whole with an impressive neighborhood as well as functioning as a vehicle for the community leadership to counter the increasing de-Judaization and religious indifference.[60]

In addition to the main synagogue there were an estimated ten smaller synagogues including the Spanish synagogue, the Kahal Reuven synagogue and the Eddy synagogue. This was a reflection of a vibrant religious life, on the one hand, and of the divisions within the community, mainly according to their origins, on the other hand. The community was predominantly Sephardi. There were, however, a small number of Ashkenazis who had settled in Beirut between the two world wars. They established their own synagogues which were basically designated rooms in a community member's house as opposed to the grand architecture of Magen Avraham.

The community was traditional in its religious observance. The Sabbath was sacred for most, as were the high holidays, which were celebrated in grand style within the community. Yet like many other Jewish communities the elders were concerned about the more relaxed attitudes of the youth. To counter these trends in 1938 a special committee to redress the spiritual situation was set up to examine the causes for their behavior.[61]

As in other aspects of community life, Farhi also played a key role in religious observance and practices. After the construction of Magen Avraham, he introduced a choir to chant traditional melodies, as well as organizing for religious instruction and a lecture series. An impression of the community's spiritual life can be gained from Abraham Elmaleh, who came from Palestine on a lecture tour to Beirut in December 1927. He arrived shortly before *Shabbat* and was welcomed by the community. It was *Hanukkah* and in a letter to the Sephardi Federation, which had arranged his visit, he gave a lively account of his experiences. He was to give some lectures to the community on Zionism, Palestine and Sephardi Jewry which had been advertised in the Beiruti Arab press as well as the Arab language Jewish newspaper *Al-'Alam al-Isra'ili*. In his letter he writes:

> On *Shabbat* morning I was invited to the service in the Great Synagogue and was honored with opening the ark and being called up third, of course, to the reading of the Torah. This splendid and beautiful synagogue which can hold approximately 1,000 men was filled to capacity with worshippers who had come to hear my lecture. After the prayers, which had lasted until ten o'clock, an enormous crowd began to stream in from the rest of the synagogue to hear the lecture. The women's gallery which also holds more than a thousand places, was filled with women and young ladies... I began my speech in Arabic after having expressed my great regret at being unable to speak in my people's language since most of the audience did not understand Hebrew.[62]

Further on in his letter he continues his account with the *Hanukkah* festivities, when he was invited back to the Great Synagogue for evening prayers and the ceremony of lighting the *Hanukkah* menorah. The number of men and women who came was around 2,000. Members of the *Maccabi* Organization and the orchestra came in their blue and white attire. He described the highlight of his mission as being his speech in French at the Club of the *Union Universelle de la Jeunesse Juive*.[63]

The reception held in his honor at the start of his visit and the gala evening at which Joseph Dichy Bey thanked Elmaleh on behalf of the community were characteristic of the Beirut community's generosity. Equally characteristic was its religious conservatism and observance. Despite the fact that many parents sent their children to Christian schools instead of the *Alliance*, and despite friendly cross-communal social contacts, conversions to Christianity were rare. Conversions to Islam remained even more obscure.[64]

Education

Hebrew schools and kindergartens had opened in Beirut and Saida in 1919 and 1920. They were initially staffed by Palestinian teachers. In 1926 Michael Tarrab, a native of Damascus who had made his fortune in

Cuba, along with his brother Raphael founded the *Ecole Talmud Torah Selim Tarrab*. In 1932 the number of students was 250 and in 1935 it had increased to 290.[65] The main subjects were Hebrew and the Bible, general subjects being introduced later. Compared with the other schools available, those of the *Alliance* or the *Mission Laïque*, the education at the *Talmud Torah* was substandard. For this reason, the majority of its pupils were from less fortunate families. Just as wealthier Jews had started to move out of Wadi Abu Jamil, they also started sending their children to French schools.

When Joseph Farhi became president of the Jewish community again in 1927, he started directing his attention towards education and budgetary reforms. He established a Jewish *lycée* and a community library in order to elevate the niveau of Jewish culture. He was an esteemed member of the patronage committee of the *Lycée Français de la Mission Laïque*. The educational reforms undertaken during this time were three-fold: they encouraged the use of Arabic as the language of instruction, they increased the teaching of Hebrew and Jewish history, and they were aimed at raising the general niveau of instruction.[66] Cooperation between the schools was also increased. A Scholarly Committee was set up to liaise with the Central Committee, the *Alliance*, and the *Talmud Torah*.

Education was mostly provided by the *Alliance Israélite Universelle*, which in 1908 was under the directorship of Mr Semah and Dr Kaisermann.[67] In 1935 the Beirut school had 673 pupils.[68] In 1936 it came under the directorship of Emile Penso. In the mid-1940s the *Alliance* opened a co-education school in Beirut.[69] Many of the teachers were supplied by the *Ecole Normale* in Paris. Hebrew language was taught freely in schools, but most Jewish students chose a French education and studied Arabic or English rather than Hebrew. Indeed, there was such little interest that the girls school did not teach Hebrew at all.[70] The preference for a French cultural orientation was especially visible among the wealthier Jews who had moved into the fashionable districts outside of Wadi Abu Jamil and sent their children to French missionary schools. This led to a certain amount of socializing and a small number of inter-marriages mainly between Jews and Christians, and also between Jews and Sunni Muslims.[71] French education was also preferred at the university level. Only few Lebanese Jewish students, as opposed to Palestinian Jewish students, attended the American University of Beirut, which had been established as the Syrian Protestant College in 1866, opting instead for the Université St. Joseph founded in 1875.

Education in Lebanon, like that in other countries throughout the mandate period, was limited by the dire economic situation and the need to have as many family members as possible in the work force. Lebanon's Jews were no different than any other Lebanese community in that sense.

While a few merchants had profited from the war, the Vichy regime, and the British-French liberation, the majority of the population was hard pressed.

Lebanese Jewry in the 1920s, 1930s and 1940s did not number among the literary greats and Lebanon's Jews, as a whole, did not become part of the educated elite. Education in many ways always took a secondary place to business. A brief glance at the *brevet* examinations provides a good indicator of this: in 1929, 1930, 1931, and 1932, three girls passed the *brevet* each year. In 1939 there were ten and in 1945 there were eight. Boys were not prepared for the *brevet* at all. Only those attending non-Jewish schools sat for the exams: in 1939 there were five, and in 1945 there were four. Up to the 1940s there was no Jewish secondary school in Beirut.[72]

Beyond the formal education provided by Jewish and non-Jewish schools, children and teenagers also benefited from the existence of a youth center, vacation camps, a library, and artistic and technical education programs.[73] There was no lack of youth organizations either. For example, the Jewish community, like some of the Christian communities had its own scout troop, which was broadly integrated into the French scouting association. To the chagrin of the Zionist representatives this scout club was far removed from any religious-nationalist sentiments, using Arabic and French as its languages and the emblems of the moon and stars.

Thus one of the aims of the rival youth organization, the *Maccabi*, became the integration of the Jewish scouts into the framework of its youth program, essentially removing it from the French international youth movements.

The numerous youth groups included *L'Amicale*, which was founded in 1908, the Hatikva Club established after the First World War, the *Maccabi*, the *Eclaireurs Israélites de Beyrouth* established in 1930, the *Union Universelle de la Jeunesse Juive* founded in 1932, and L'A.Z.A., a section of the *B'nai Brith* youth founded in 1938.[74] Cultural activities were promoted by the community's Central Committee for the Youth, which, in 1936 launched the journal *Jewish Voice* and the *Forum* in 1941. The youth also played a not unimportant role in the communal elections in 1933, 1935 and 1943 through their Party of the Youth and the Communal Action Group.[75]

And finally, there were dance clubs in keeping with the Lebanese youth of other communities. These were generally frowned upon by community elders and parents. They were seen as the focal point for those sections of the youth deemed poor and corrupted "whose only desire and interest is in dancing and instant gratification. . . . as far from the Hebrew culture or language as the East is from the West".[76] In short, life for Jewish youngsters was no different from that of the rest of Lebanon's youth with a variety of educational, social and athletic activities to pursue.

The Lebanese Zionist Project and Contacts with the *Yishuv*

The relationship between Lebanon's Jews, Zionism, the *Yishuv*, and World Jewry has always been an intriguing one. It is characterized, on the one hand, by ardent Lebanese nationalism, apathy towards the Zionist project of the *Yishuv* by the majority, but, on the other hand by fervent Zionism by a few leaders such as Joseph Farhi, good contacts with Palestinian Jews, regular visits between Beirut and Jerusalem, and some support for the concept of a Jewish state in Palestine. Accounts by the *Alliance* speak of active Zionism while accounts of the Jewish Agency at the same time lament the lack of national sentiment. The French authorities tried to discourage any Zionist expression which they viewed as a tool of their British rival. These dynamics were further complicated by the fact that actions within the framework of world Jewry were generally France-oriented, rather than Palestinocentric, separating Jewish activism from Zionism.

One example of international Jewish activity was the Beirut chapter of the *Union Universelle de la Jeunesse Juive* (UUJJ) and *B'nai Brith* protest against the imposition of a *numerus clausus* (entrance restriction) on Jewish students in Hungary, Rumania and Poland in January 1927. Farhi described the laws as barbaric and proposed aiding students from those countries to travel to the land of Israel for their studies. At a UUJJ conference in Paris, Jewish community president Joseph Farhi, vice-president Selim Harari and American University of Beirut professor Amos Landaanin sent a telegram to the League of Nations stating that "in the name of the Jewish community of Beirut, we are protesting against the *numerus clausus* existing in Hungary, Poland and Rumania. We appeal to the spirit of justice and equality of the League of Nations, to solicit its intervention to annul these unjust, inhuman restrictions."[77]

Apart from this international involvement, the community did not have a history of active participation in European Zionist events such as the early congresses or the Zionist Executive. This did not, however, mean that they were disinterested or unaware. In 1907, for instance, the director of the *Alliance* school for boys considered Zionism to have already established itself.[78] At the end of the First World War, there were accounts of active Zionism within the small Ashkenazi community and "distance" within the Sephardi community.[79] In 1925 the director of the *Alliance* Mr Danon claimed that "Zionists dominated the Beirut Jewish community and tried to give all activities and organizations a nationalist character."[80]

Yet other descriptions of the community portray Zionism as merely a cultural force. What becomes clear is that there were a few very active Zionists, within a mainly non-Zionist community, who were able to get support for some of their activities.

Zionist activity in Lebanon evolved around a number of personalities such as Joseph Farhi and Moshe Kamhine, the leader of the *Maccabi*. Institutionally, it was focused around the *Maccabi* sports organization, which was established in 1928. Kamhine had been born in Beirut in 1912 to a family who was from the Shouf. He devoted his studies to the Talmud and the Torah and other religious texts. He taught Hebrew at the *Alliance Israélite Universelle* as well as the *Talmud Torah*, and learned with and prepared students for their *bar mitzvah*. Interestingly his teaching reached far beyond the community, including foreign schools and also the Lebanese army.[81] His youth and energy made him the perfect leader for Beirut's Jewish youngsters. The *Maccabi* boasted a membership of more than 500 and as an organization had excellent relations with Pierre Gemayel's *Kata'ib* party youth wing. Kamhine was active in community commissions, the synagogue, and youth work. He is remembered for his organization of youth activities after *Shabbat*, functioning also as the community's *shohet*, and was the father of four: Shlomo, Chaim, Malka and Itzhak.[82]

An example of Zionist activity and its problems is provided by a young Lebanese Jew by the name of Joseph Azar in October 1930 who took it upon himself to advance the Zionist cause, "a spirit which was unfortunately lacking in the elders of that community". Together with Joseph Toledano, Tewfiq Mizrahi, Leonard Bukhashevsky, Avraham Shur and Jacob Franco he led the budding Zionist movement within the Lebanese Jewish community.[83] Their decision to become Zionist activists had been triggered by the 1929 riots in Palestine and, in their search for compatriots, they turned to the *Yishuv*. Azar, in a report for the Jewish Agency, gives a revealing account of the attitude of the Beirut community towards Zionism before and after 1929:

> Before the disturbances of August 1929 the Jews . . . of Lebanon manifested much sympathy for the Zionist cause and worked actively for the sake of Palestine. They had established associations which collected money for the (sic) *Keren Kayemeth* and the (sic) *Keren Hayesod*. They feared not to manifest their Zionist feelings and many of them were even proud of this. But after the disturbances conditions changed. They started to fear from (sic) anything having any connection with Zionism and ceased to hold meetings and collect money. The Jewish Communal Council of Beirut had even deemed it necessary (a point on which I do not agree with them) to proclaim that we have no connection with the Jews of Palestine. The Council endeavored to prevent anything having a Jewish national aspect because they

feared that this might wound the feelings of the Muslims. It is beyond doubt that the attitude of the Communal Council must be looked upon with great sorrow because it denotes cowardice and lack of moral courage.[84]

Both the Jewish Agency's assessment and self-assessments by other Lebanese Jews contradict the picture Azar paints of flourishing Zionism before 1929. Financial support and meetings for projects in Palestine were less a manifestation of Zionism than support for fellow Jews who were in need. It was a sign of the religious sentiments and not ideological activism. Farhi had already earlier noted local Jewish apathy towards Zionism,[85] so Azar's frustration with the lack of popular support for his Zionist ideal was not the first recognition of this situation. His charging the Jews of Lebanon with lack of moral courage came from a position of youth where everything was clearly black or white.

In their frustration Azar and his friends turned to F. H. Kisch of the Jewish Agency for advice. Kisch suggested that he direct his efforts in two directions: "Firstly to widen within the Jewish community in Syria and Lebanon the circle of adherents to the ideal of the Jewish National Home, and secondly to do everything possible to promote harmony between Jews and Arabs."[86] Kisch had raised a number of concrete possibilities for advancing the Zionist project, the first of which was the establishment of an important Arabic newspaper to be published under Jewish control in Beirut.[87] The second proposal was for a Zionist office but this would only be possible with the support of the local community. Kisch in his letter agreed with Azar on the lack of enthusiasm of the Beirut community, stressing his hope that "local leaders of your community may be won over for the support of this idea."[88]

This does not, however, mean that the Beirut community was completely inactive. Lebanese Jews raised money to combat the hostility in the local press. They also provided visiting Jewish Agency members with information on the situation in Lebanon and neighboring Syria. While accepting this information the Jewish Agency did not, as a rule, use local Jews as spies or operatives.[89] The underlying assumption was that Zionist activity by Lebanese Jews would raise charges of treason and seriously jeopardize the physical and material well-being of the community.[90] Moreover, the Agency had such good contacts in Lebanon's political circles with the likes of Maronite politician Emile Eddé, Maronite patriarch Antoine Arida, and the members of the *Kata'ib* that reliance on Lebanon's Jews was unnecessary.[91]

Zionist activity increased when ties were broken between the schools and the center in Paris, resulting in a major source of opposition to Zionism no longer being influential. More important, however, was that on a practical level the community had to turn to other Jewish organizations for support. The community in Beirut was willing to accept a Hebrew teacher from the land of Israel and cover part of his salary. Dr Rosenfeld from the World Hebrew Covenant in an assessment of the new situation believed that the *Maccabi* could become a possible instrument for increasing Zionist activities, but warned against concentrating all the activity within this framework.[92]

Youth activities underwent a brief crisis in 1941. From March to October Beirut had no youth counselor who was supported by the Jewish Agency. An emissary of *Hashomer HaTzair* was active in the local *Ben Zion* organisation, and a *Betar* student led the *Maccabi*. The older group of students within the *Maccabi* had been in close contact with the emissary from the Jewish Agency political department, but when the latter left, all activity by this group stopped. Apparently the mentioned *Betar* student encouraged the singing of Zionist songs in the Jewish quarter in the evening. This, according the a Jewish Agency official, increased with the "threat level" as demonstrations of "heroism" are highly acceptable in the Arab communities in which "our youth have been educated".[93] With the arrival of the long awaited counselor Salomon, noticeable changes took place in the *Maccabi*, primarily among the lower and middle classes. The library began operating properly and reading classes were set up. This was seen as a first step towards breaking through the superficiality which permeated the Beiruti youth, who were seen as incapable of drawing the national spirit from the sources as they were unaccustomed to reading.[94] The game room, which is equipped with Hebrew educational games funded by the budget of the *Histadrut*'s youth center, became the forum for talks, lectures, and slide shows on *Eretz Israel*. Salomon also founded the *Maccabi* choir.

Despite the community's often only half-hearted support for mainstream Zionism, *Betar*'s revisionist Zionism found some sympathy. Palestinian students who were some of the most ardent *Betar* supporters had found refuge in Beirut after having been "expelled" from Palestine for terror activities. The sympathy they found was of deep concern to the Jewish Agency, which decided that it would be best to counter it by sending to Beirut "a young articulate man, fluent in French, to fight against the influence of terrorists among the studying youth".[95]

The Jewish Agency continued to lament the lack of Zionist fervor among Lebanon's youth. Having failed to draw *Ben Zion* into a closer relationship with *Hashomer HaTzair* or similarly the Scouts into closer relations with the *Maccabi*, the youth was still seen as the cornerstone of the Zionist emissary. The youth of *B'nai Brith* seemed slightly more receptive. They were provided with Zionist literature in French.

A review by *Maccabi* chairman for Syria and Lebanon, Yosef Sneh, in November 1941 on youth activities in Lebanon and Beirut, gives further insight into the complex identity of the Jews of Lebanon and also of Lebanon as political environment in an increasingly anti-Zionist Middle East. The assessment of the socio-economic situation in Syria and Lebanon was one that reflects the wartime influence and decline of living standards experienced by many countries in the region, characterized by the "daily worries and harsh battle for existence". Young Lebanese Jews were limited to peddling, trade and some were engaged in clerical work.

> It is a common occurrence that a youngster leaves his studies and is sent by his parents – or goes of his own goodwill – to sell his abilities in the streets to earn a few pennies. This youth will never return to the schoolbench. The languages spoken by the youth are Arabic and French. Hebrew is familiar to only 35 per cent of the youth, who gained their knowledge of the language in the evening courses run by the *Maccabi*, without support from any institution in Syria or Palestine. The level of education among the youth is very low. Manners are crude, behavior and attitude to matters and people are poor, apathy towards everything is the rule among the youth, and idleness is widespread. On the other hand, the youth are active in entertainment and short-term enjoyment, and no questions disturb their relaxation. They are quietly and peacefully busy with everything that is not connected with them and their future, and is far from the values of their people.[96]

The lack of "values of their people" referred to by Sneh paints a rather damning portrait of Jewish culture and Zionism among Lebanese Jewish youngsters. This statement, however, should be treated with caution. While Sneh seems to be treating Jewish heritage and Zionism as one, his views are contradicted by those who claim that, while there indeed was a general lack of Zionist sentiments, there was nevertheless a vibrant Jewish life, one that was distinctly Lebanese.

Zionist activity remained rooted in and focused around the *Maccabi* organization which was officially recognized by the Lebanese authorities. The *Maccabi* was active in Beirut and Saida and became the framework for teaching the Hebrew language and Jewish history, pursuing general cultural activities, sports activities, scouting, education, agricultural training, and overall Zionist activities for the world movement. The agricultural element reveals some of the Palestinocentrism of the *Maccabi* organization. The agricultural issue had already been pursued at an earlier time in private conversations between Lebanese president Eddé and Eliahu Elath of the Jewish Agency in which the latter stated that "we (the *Yishuv*) see a special value in the Jewish community in Lebanon. Though national-Zionist settlement is limited within the framework of Palestine itself, we still require every Jew wherever he is to change from any other profession to agriculture."[97] Within the urban Beiruti context, however, little enthusiasm for agriculture was engendered, limiting the efforts to vegetable and flower gardens. Emissaries sent from Palestine in 1938 under the command of Davidka Nameri who went to arrange for Jewish emigration and indoctrination of the youth,[98] did not have an easy task. They established *HeHalutz HaTzair* as a pioneer youth organization.[99] The focus was on Lebanon's youth as the older generation had become "reconciled to their lot, and it was next to impossible to wean them from the attitudes and habits of generations".[100]

The attitude of Lebanese Jewry towards Zionism and the land of Israel was equally illuminating. Most Lebanese Jews were in complete agreement with the Arabs that Zionism and its endeavors in the Land of Israel were the cause of all troubles.[101] This is seen, to some extent, as being the result of assimilation rather than Zionist ideology being somehow anathema to Lebanese Jewry. This assimilation being essentially linguistic in origin brought with it other forms of assimilation. The chairman of the *Maccabi* Organization, however, did not consider the situation too bleak, seeing the lack of interest of Lebanon's Jewry as an opportunity and a challenge for Zionism. Interestingly, the "reeducation" of the Jews was not considered an end in itself, but a means to influence other communities in Lebanon. "Once opinions change in our communities it will help change the ways of thought among the neighbors. The ground will then be prepared and we can easily explain that only good can come from the development of the Jewish community in the Land of Israel – even for the Arabs."[102]

In his attempt to encourage Zionism, Sneh asked the World Hebrew Covenant to open a branch in Beirut. Many of the local residents, including those who ran the community and its education gave their support, despite earlier criticism of Zionist activities. A course for youth leaders was also scheduled.[103] The Jewish Agency Department for Youth Affairs allocated 17 Palestinian Pounds to cover the expenses in organizing such a course.[104]

An interesting development in the context of the Zionist political project was the emerging relationship between Palestinian Zionists and some elements in the Lebanese Maronite community. The Maronite clergy under the leadership of Beirut's Archbishop Ignace Mubarak and Patriarch Antoine Arida and politicians such as Emile Eddé, and members of the urban intelligentsia such as poet Charles Corm, regarded the Zionist endeavors in Palestine with affection and friendship.[105] This manifested itself in ideas ranging from forming an alliance against Islam, to plans for a political or even military union, to resurrecting the "ancient Phoenician–Canaanite relationship" as advocated by an organization called the Young Phoenicians.

The underlying belief for these ideas was that a non-Arab population of Palestine on Lebanon's southern frontier "would enable them to cooperate with that people to averting the danger arising from the Arab's efforts to create an Arab federation including Lebanon".[106] This pro-Zionist element in the Maronite community became the third component of a Jewish-Maronite–Zionist triangle, which played an important role in the Arab-Israeli dynamics further on.

The Palestine Question

Lebanon's Jews were not particularly involved or interested in politics. In that sense they occupied an almost privileged position of remaining untouched by some of the bitter Muslim-Christian disputes in the emerging Lebanese state. They were not, however, able to stay as aloof as they may have wished, as the increasingly tense political situation across the border in Palestine spilled over into Lebanon on a number of occasions. During the period of the French mandate there were two events which had direct bearing on the well-being of the Lebanese Jewish community. The first was the Western Wall incident, which led to disturbances in August 1929, costing the lives of 133 Jews and 116 Arabs in Palestine.[107] The second event was the Arab revolt from 1936 to 1939, the consequent expulsion of the Mufti of Jerusalem from Palestine, and his decision to settle in Lebanon from where he continued to agitate against the Zionists and the British.

Before 1929 most Lebanese whether Muslim, Christian or Jewish, showed little interest in events in Palestine. The Muslims were preoccupied with the Lebanese-Syrian question and many Christians were pursuing the establishment of a Christian state. Apart from a few articles published in remote intervals by the Beirut papers, the Zionist and Palestinian issue was a secondary one which was dealt with like other world problems.[108] Moreover, Lebanese Jew Joseph Azar asserted that the reason why anti-Zionist propaganda did not meet with much success was that Lebanon's population was mostly composed of merchants who kept aloof from politics and who put their material interests above everything.[109] The only reason the population took an interest in the 1929 riots was because some Muslim nationalists tried to incite disturbances.[110] These attempts, however, failed. Azar concluded from this that the opposition of the Lebanese population to the Zionist movement was of no importance.

Nevertheless, Lebanese newspapers Azar pointed out potentially posed a danger. He particularly referred to the anti-Zionist attitude of *Al-Ahrar* whose editors were "Greek Orthodox and Freemasons."[111] During the August 1929 disturbances it was the most hostile publication, exploiting the Palestine situation to increase its circulation. Yet Azar also stated that even this paper was not that dangerous and "may be gained to our cause". His assessment of *L'Orient* was more positive:

> It is worth noting that *L'Orient* and the enlightened people who support it constitute a group with whom an understanding and an agreement favorable to the Zionist movement in Palestine are possible. They are in general a strong and progressive element ready to arrive at an understanding with any people that might assist them in averting the danger of an amalgamation with the Arab race.[112]

This view very much coincided with the *Yishuv*'s opinion of that newspaper as "the organ of the enlightened Maronites who stand for a separation from whatever is Arab and Muslim and strive for the creation of a modern Christian state. *L'Orient* has adopted a praiseworthy attitude towards the Jews."[113] This left *al-Nida* with its anti-Zionist attitude as the most problematic newspaper. Azar described its editors as "fanatical nationalists who strive for the Arab Federation".

Azar's assessment of the main newspapers shows some of the underlying currents in Lebanese society and the relations between Lebanon's Jews and the other ethno-religious communities. The relative hostility of the Greek-Orthodox is no more surprising than the comparable amicability of the Maronites. The Greek Orthodox saw their future within a broader Arab context and thus were unlikely to support Zionism in any case. They were also the main economic competitor of Lebanon's Jews. The Maronites saw their future as being separate from the Arab world and sought contacts with other non-Arab and non-Muslim minorities to support their own position. Not only did they have friendly relations with Lebanon's Jews but they also had friendly relations with the *Yishuv*.[114] The anti-Zionist attitude of an Arab nationalist paper is almost self-explanatory in the political context of the 1929 disturbances. Many Muslims and many Arab nationalists viewed the Zionist project in Palestine with suspicion. That does not, however, mean that their attitude toward the local Jewish community was the same. Yet some Lebanese Jews like Selim Harari felt it necessary to take part in Muslim meetings during the riots of 1929 and to declare that there was no connection between the Jews of Beirut and the Zionists in Palestine.[115]

In 1936, during the French-Arab negotiations in Paris for the termination of the mandate status, the director of the *Alliance* in Beirut, Emile Penso, together with other community leaders drafted a joint-position paper on behalf of his own community and the Jews of Syria.[116] The paper stressed the protection of minority rights which needed to be included in the treaty arrangements. The specific demands were as follows:

1.   The same civil and political rights as those recognized for the other

elements of the population without regard to birth, nationality, language, or race, whether they be Syrians or foreigners living in these territories.

2. The protection of life, liberty, and also the free exercise of their religion both in public and private.

3. The equal right to any of the other citizens to create, operate, and control charitable, religious, or social institutions, schools, or other educational establishments.

4. An equitable share in the distribution of subventions allocated by the State or the local administrations for educational, religious, or charitable purposes.

5. The free use of the Hebrew language whether in private life, religious matters, the press, or publications of any sort.

6. The freedom of having to undertake any act incompatible with the sanctity of the Sabbath.

7. The maintenance of ritual slaughtering.

8. Finally, no measure of discrimination to be taken with regard to us.

It should be noted that all these rights already were accorded to the Lebanese Jews and that their motivation for this position paper was the fear that the declining situation in Palestine would affect their own. This fear was reflected in a letter Penso sent to the *Alliance* in Paris, stating that the Jews looked to the future with dread. "As long as the French flag was waving over our heads, we felt perfectly safe. The French Army was protecting us."[117] It must also be said that Penso was writing on behalf of both the Syrian and Lebanese communities and that much of the anxiety expressed originated from Syrian and not Lebanese Jewry. In Syria the use of Hebrew had already been severely restricted for more than a decade. Hebrew newspapers and publications had been banned and the use of Hebrew as the language of instruction in Jewish schools had been forbidden since 1923.[118] Yet some incidents in May 1936 in Saida had also provided a glimpse of what might come for Lebanon's Jews as well. With the beginning of the Arab Revolt in Palestine demonstrations with anti-Jewish slogans were staged. Houses and shops of Jews and the *Alliance* school were stoned and windows broken. The boycott of Jewish shops also began. Christian hotel owners in the vicinity of Saida were threatened not to accommodate any more Palestinian Jewish tourists.[119]

Until the Arab Revolt the emerging conflict in Palestine was viewed as an essentially local problem between the *Yishuv*, Palestinians, and the British. Lebanon's Jews, like the majority of Jews living in Arab countries, were not particularly sympathetic to the efforts of the Zionists.[120] Lebanon's Muslims and Christians had also remained aloof. The Arab

Revolt changed this situation. The effect of the Palestine question on Lebanese politics becomes clear when looking at the 1937 parliamentary reform which was essentially a domestic issue. The population as a whole had increased and, in accordance with this growth parliamentary seats were increased from 25 to 60. This raised the hope and, indeed, the possibility of the Jews receiving their own seat in parliament,[121] the number of Jews in Lebanon being approximately 6,000. Joseph Farhi decided to lobby the Lebanese president on that issue, only to receive a rather interesting and cryptic response. Eddé had received him in the presence of the Minister of Interior Habib Abi Chahla. Farhi pointed out to both that the Jewish community needed a representative and Eddé jokingly said that the Jews were already very well represented in Lebanon. "I am (said to be) a Jew and the minister here present is a Jew and premier Ahdab is also a Jew." He was referring to the clearly pro-Zionist attitude of the ministers in question. Farhi stated that he was thankful to the government for their pro-Jewish feelings but "all the same the Jews deem it essential for their prestige and interests to be represented in the coming parliament".[122] Eddé told Farhi that he was sympathetic in principle, but that he had to wait and see. Farhi then proceeded to plead his case with the French High Commissioner Count Damien de Martel. De Martel according to Farhi did not seem keen and did not ask a single question.

The desire for a seat of their own is illustrated by an open letter to the Prime Minister Khayr al-Din al-Ahdab on 22 April 1937 in which Jacques Lezemi, one of the leaders of the community, pointed out that "if our community does not noisily demand its rights, it does not mean that it is resigned. . . . Our minority group is represented in the administration by three employees only."[123] This was a situation which needed to be redressed, preferably through a parliamentary seat. The Beirut Jewish leadership wanted this seat to be one of the ones appointed by the president, thus de-politicizing the seat in many ways. They appealed through Itzhak Ben Zvi to the *Quai d'Orsay*, believing that if the French made the appropriate hints, Eddé would willingly accept such a proposal. The head of the Jewish community Joseph Farhi was suggested as a possible candidate as he was intelligent, trustworthy and devoted to Zionism, and according to Ben Zvi a man who "could be very effective both for Lebanese Jews and for our affairs in the Land of Israel".[124]

While Farhi made the rounds and found sympathy among the Lebanese but not the French, the situation on the ground underwent some dramatic changes. Political squabbling had broken out between the government and the opposition. The French High Commissioner was forced to intervene to make peace between the two on the basis of an agreed repartition of the seats in the new parliament. The new number of seats was increased to 63, divided into 42 elected and 21 nominated seats, whereby the opposition was accorded 26 members and the government 38. The battle over the seats had thus effectively ended before elections could be contested. Only one seat for minorities was created and the nominee was Dr Ayoub Tabet.[125]

Interesting within the government–opposition discourse were the accusations and counter-accusations of certain deputies being labeled "friends of the Jews".[126] These references were specifically made to those members of parliament who had sold some of their land in the Galilee to the Jewish Agency and, thus, this was less a case of anti-Semitism than a case of anti-Zionism or just expediently using the Palestine question in a political campaign to embarrass opponents. Farhi's assessment of the situation was that it was not impossible that the government hesitated to nominate a Jew because it did not want to be accused of collaboration with the Zionists.[127]

While this episode did not result in a Jewish member of parliament, it is nevertheless an illuminating one from the perspective of inter-community relations. The fact that the head of the Lebanese Jewish community was able to plead his case and gain sympathy sheds light on the position the community occupied in Lebanese society. It was a community that was well respected and accepted. It was a community which could request more political participation for their own prestige – a very Lebanese community, playing a very Lebanese game.

In 1938 inter-community relations were strained. In October of the previous year the Mufti of Jerusalem, Hajj Amin al-Hussayni, had fled Jerusalem disguised as a beggar and settled in Jounieh, northeast of Beirut. He soon started to incite the Muslim population, instigating demonstrations against Jews. Coming at the height of the Arab Revolt, the lack of a clear government response created a situation which made it possible for "certain agitators to be permitted to place bombs in the Jewish quarters of Saida and Beirut".[128]

Beiruti wholesaler Issac Diwan had expanded his business and opened up a currency exchange in Saida. He recalled the attempted bomb in Saida on 14 July 1938, as he had been the one to discover it. He had been inspecting some property when a small cord caught his eye. The cord was attached to two sticks of dynamite. It had been lit but gone out because of the dampness. Diwan notified the police immediately. The police investigated the scene, taking down Diwan's statement and suspecting a certain Ahmad al-Harari, a former gardener of his.[129]

On the evening of the same day, an unusual noise aroused panic in Wadi Abu Jamil. An unidentified person threw a bomb into the entrance of the Jewish quarter. All the windows of the nearby buildings were shattered, but no one was hurt. The police were on the scene at once and restored calm. In the wake of these two incidents permanent patrols were set up, but the Jewish community in both Saida and Beirut remained nervous.[130]

Lebanese politicians were concerned with the turn of events and the negative effect on their Jewish constituents. Premier Ahdab in a letter to Chaim Weizmann and Moshe Shertok blamed the inherent weakness of the Lebanese government for the Mufti's behavior as well the geographic proximity of Palestine.[131] But the awareness of the Lebanese authorities of the Hajj's agitating and their police patrols to protect the Jewish quarters, were unable to keep the lid on Hajj Amin al-Hussayni's activities and his appeal to the Arab nationalists in their own society. On 26 July 1939 two more bombs were thrown in Wadi Abu Jamil. Only light damage was recorded. A letter by *Alliance* Director Penso to the French High Commissioner Gabriel Puaux sums up the uneasy feelings of the community but also their belief that the Lebanese state was not to blame:

> You also know that Mr Jamal al-Hussayni, a member of the Arab Supreme Committee of Palestine and nephew of the Mufti of Jerusalem, Hajj Amin al-Hussayni, declared a few months ago at the Arab Congress in Cairo that if Arabs in Palestine do not succeed in obtaining from the English authorities the realization of their national claims, they will attack the Jews residing in the Arab countries. It appears that they are putting these threats into execution. . . . Two bombs thrown in the space of two days, in the Jewish Quarter and our school buildings, have sown panic among our co-religionists.[132]

When France and Britain declared war on Germany on 3 September 1939, the Mufti was asked to announce his support for the allies. Failing to do so, he was placed under house arrest. Disguised as a heavily veiled woman, the Mufti then escaped to Baghdad on 13 October.[133] With his departure life for Lebanon's Jews returned to normal. This respite, however, was brief and soon Lebanon, like the rest of Middle East, became caught up in the tides of the Second World War, the Jewish refugee situation, the German occupation of France, the rise of the collaborator Vichy government and the extension of its control over the French mandated territories.

The effects of the Palestine situation on neighboring Lebanon and particularly the Lebanese Jews should not be overestimated. There were occasions when Palestine intruded, but they were few and far between and generally did not affect the majority of the population. The Jews still occupied the privileged position in Lebanon of being numerically so much smaller and politically disinterested that they were outside the intra-Christian, intra-Muslim, and Muslim-Christian political feuding. Thus they were able to remain on friendly terms with all communities as is evident in relations with Maronite Patriarch Arida, Maronite Lebanese president Eddé, Sunni premier Ahdab, and Shi'a Member of Parliament Ibrahim Bey Haidar.[134]

World War II and the Vichy Regime

The rise to power of Adolf Hitler in Germany triggered a stream of German Jews leaving the country. Many of them made their way to Palestine. Some only traveled through Lebanon, while others decided to remain in Beirut. As early as 1933 the Beirut community established a local branch of the International League of Anti-Semitism, tolerated by the French authorities so long as it was not seen as provoking the German diplomatic community in the city.[135] In 1935, in response to the increasing stream of Jewish refugees, Lebanon's Jewish leaders petitioned the High Commissioner to permit German Jewish immigration to Lebanon.

The issue of Jewish immigration was not only of extreme importance for Lebanon's Jews and the neighboring *Yishuv*, but also peaked the interest of certain segments in the Lebanese population, reaching far beyond the boundaries of the Jewish community. Patriarch Arida during the rise of the Nazis to power in Germany condemned the treatment of German Jews in 1933[136] publishing a pastoral letter in *L'Orient*[137] as well as making a statement in the Egyptian journal *L'Aurore*.[138] Lebanese representatives of all communities expressed favorable opinions regarding Jewish immigration to Lebanon.[139] Jewish community president Selim Harari recalled numerous conversations with Lebanese notables including Abdallah Biham, a prominent Beirut Muslim. Harari himself, however, did not wish to see Jewish refugees settle in Lebanon, for fear that they would "disturb the position of the local Jews".[140] Eliahu Epstein, the Jewish Agency representative in Beirut at that time, even went as far as suggesting that if an official delegation called on Harari with a request to encourage Jewish immigration, "he would probably frighten the delegation away and persuade it to abandon its request".[141] Harari obviously did not find the same favor with *Yishuv* delegates as Farhi or Dichy Bey had before him. Rather than being of the proud tradition of being both Lebanese and Jewish, Harari was categorized more in line with the image of the ghetto Jew so detested by Palestinian Zionists. So, in the absence of Harari's initiative, a certain Stephan Weis sent a letter to Ponsot asking him to assist the Jews of Germany to settle in French mandated territory. Ponsot turned to Lebanese president Charles Debas and to Patriarch Arida who both replied that they had no objection whatsoever to Jewish immigration to Lebanon, as long as they did not become an economic burden.[142]

The Lebanese openness toward Jewish immigration was based on their good relations with their own Jewish community and Lebanon's history as a safe haven. They also believed that a growth in the mainly merchant community would bring with it a growth in wealth at a time when the country was in an economic depression. An additional reason for Maronite leaders was that Jewish immigration would strengthen their own position *vis-à-vis* other communities.[143] A united Jewish–Maronite economic front would counter-balance the Greek Orthodox while Lebanese Jewish political support of the Maronites and other Christians would counter the Muslims. Above all, Lebanon's offer, no matter how self-serving, needs to be seen within the context of most other states closing their borders to those very same refugees.

The outbreak of the Second World War in 1939 removed much of the attention from Lebanon's Jews and thus improved their situation. The absence of Hajj Amin al-Hussayni, who fled Beirut for Baghdad, ended the demonstrations. It also absolved the French government from the stalemated treaty negotiations for Lebanese and Syrian independence. The economic situation remained depressed and, while the French immersed themselves in military preparations, decrees, expropriations, recruitment, and reinforcement, the Lebanese continued to play a game of often ruthless sectarian politics.[144] The declaration of the state of emergency by the French High Commissioner effectively resulted in the suspension of the Lebanese constitution and rule by presidential decree with the countersignature of High Commissioner Puaux.

On 21 June 1940 Marshal Petain signed an armistice with Germany and France passed under German control. The fate of the mandated territories was directly threatened. Puaux had to accept the effective withdrawal of the French Army and authority in the Levant. The Free French movement under the leadership of General Charles de Gaulle called for resistance to Germany and Vichy France. Nevertheless, Lebanon fell under Vichy authority only shortly after the establishment of the Petain regime. Puaux only survived the armistice by a mere five months.[145] A delegation of Lebanese Jewish community leaders headed by Joseph Farhi immediately petitioned Puaux not to apply the Vichy legislation concerning the Jews.[146] As Puaux was not an enthusiastic supporter of the regime the lack of implementation of anti-Jewish laws did not pose a problem. His attitude of minimal obedience, however, cost him his position. He was ordered to relinquish his office on 24 November 1940. The High Commissioner's post fell to General Henri Dentz, a loyal Vichy follower.

The influx of German agents from September 1940 onwards had direct bearing upon the situation of Lebanon's Jews. Anti-Zionism reached its zenith with German proclamations. Dentz, however, was too preoccupied with the deteriorating economic situation to press for the full implementation of anti-Jewish laws. Thus particular problems arose only for the illegal immigration of European Jewish refugees to Palestine via Lebanon. While Lebanese Jews continued their life unencumbered as the Lebanese authorities adamantly refused to implement these discriminatory practices against their own citizens, transiting non-Lebanese Jews were imprisoned in special camps. Nissim Dahan recalls this darker period in Lebanese history as follows:

> Vichy worked with the Gestapo in Lebanon. They gathered all Italian, Greek, Iranian, Polish and Russian Jews in a camp in the mountains. . . . When the war started we had lots of air raids by the English from Egypt and we fled to the mountains. I stayed in Bikfaya. . . . Most Christian Lebanese had also gone into the mountains and created their own entity, such as Joseph Bey Karam and Mubarak who formed their own army and staged raids against the High Commissioner. . . . The *Kata'ib* protected the Jews during Vichy. Nothing really happened. There was one suicide because someone did not want to go to the camp. But nothing happened at the camp. They were treated well. It was not a concentration camp.[147]

Joseph Dichy Bey lobbied for their release during this time, and after the Allied forces liberated Lebanon, became very active in furthering their transit across the border to Palestine.[148] United in hostility to the Vichy authorities, Lebanon's population, both Christian and Muslim, showed considerable resentment against the anti-Jewish measures of the Vichy regime. The Mufti of Beirut and the Maronite Patriarch submitted a memorandum of protest to the French authorities against the discharge of Jewish government and state officials.[149] Vichy prohibition against demonstrations led the already smoldering popular discontent exacerbated by food shortages, rising prices, hoarding, black marketeering, deteriorated transport and distribution facilities, rising unemployment, and a depreciated currency, to erupt into outright hostility. Lebanese men started leaving to enlist in the Free French Army, including a number of Lebanese Jews, several of whom were promoted and decorated.[150]

In June 1941 British and Free French troops occupied the mandated territory of Lebanon, ending the influence of the Vichy regime. In the months preceding the liberation, many families had left Wadi Abu Jamil and had found refuge in the mountains.[151] Life returned to normal after Anglo-Gaullist troops took over. De Gaulle's representative General Catroux proclaimed the independence of Lebanon on 8 June 1941.[152] All anti-Jewish restrictions were lifted and Lebanese President Alfred Naccache, during a visit to Magen Avraham in December 1941, pledged that the Jews would be given a full share in the responsibilities of government.[153] Farhi, in return, eloquently reiterated Jewish loyalty to Lebanon.[154] Non-Lebanese Jews, which had been interned by the Vichy administration, were released. The Anglo-French forces provided the impetus for a new boost to Lebanon's neglected industry and the economy started to recover rapidly. This was also reflected within the Jewish community. New projects were pursued and business flourished. *B'nai Brith* embarked on a grand scheme which envisaged the intensive development of existing community structures, the establishment of a fund to build a hospital, the enlargement of a new synagogue at Aley, and the construction of a synagogue at Bhamdoun.[155] Other community projects included the establishment of an *Atelier de Couture* with provisions for apprenticeships, a nursery school for children, and a professional placement office.

Political life in Lebanon took a little longer to readjust, with the old debates over Lebanon's identity re-emerging between politicians as well as between Lebanese and French representatives. *De facto* Lebanese independence, as a result, was delayed until 8 November 1943, when the newly elected Lebanese government under president Bishara al-Khoury and prime minister Riad Sulh repealed the mandate articles through constitutional amendment.

3

Lebanese and Israeli Independence: Questions of Identity

The transition of the Levant from colonial control to independence initiated a phase of instability as a result of competing nation-building projects and the elusive quest for identity. While the Jews of Lebanon remained relatively uninvolved in the Christian-Muslim struggles, the establishment of the State of Israel south of the border made a completely aloof position untenable. As a result, Lebanon's Jews were tossed from one crisis to another and often became pawns in the domestic power games of Muslim and Christian rivals as well as the regional dynamics of the Arab-Israeli conflict. Nevertheless, the community continued to flourish and, indeed, reached its numerical and even economic zenith during this period.

Lebanese Independence and the National Pact

The prevarications of the leaders of the Free French and the intrigues of the British mission led by General Edward L. Spears meant that Lebanese independence had effectively been put on hold, despite Charles de Gaulle's promise of independence in 1941.[1] Part of the problem was de Gaulle himself. For all his genuine greatness, he was the least likely of French leaders to conduct the evidently difficult and ill-balanced task of Franco-British collaboration in Lebanon. Indeed, as events proved, he damaged Franco-British and Franco-Arab relations by his exclusive and anachronistic conception of French "rights".[2]

The course of events in the latter half of 1943 was among the unhappiest of the whole mandatory period. It threw into full evidence the curious unreality of surviving French conceptions of the Levant situation,[3] while Christians, Muslims and Jews jointly pushed for independence. On 7 October 1943, the Lebanese prime minister outlined the political program which came to be known as the "Charter of Independence". But France refused to hand over any of the powers granted through the mandate until Syro-Lebanese relations with it were clearly and specifically defined.[4] At this point the Lebanese government decided to unilaterally amend the constitution, thereby ending the mandate. The French colonial response to these unilateral changes was the arrest of most Lebanese ministers on 11 November 1943. This was followed by a decree announcing the nullification of the constitutional amendments, the suspension of the Constitution itself, and the appointment of Emile Eddé as chief of state. A general strike spread throughout Beirut, followed by angry demonstrations and riots. Portraits of de Gaulle were torn down and the British Legation was besieged by visitors. Eddé, however, proved unable and unwilling to establish a government. At the same time the two ministers who had escaped arrest proclaimed a sovereign government from a mountain village with full support of the Maronite Patriarch[5] and in defiance of the French.

The riots pursuant to the French miscalculations gave way to a wave of anti-Jewish articles in the local press. While they were hostile to the Jews, it was clearly a case of semantics since they were actually talking about the Jews in Palestine. As a letter from Beirut explained, the purpose of the articles was to distract from the domestic situation. *L'Orient* published three such articles in the last week of November. The paper had expressed a pro-French view throughout the crisis and after its offices were stormed, with windows and furniture smashed, the anti-Jewish articles were seen as an attempt to regain the public. Further, it had become known that the prominent politicians Riad as-Sulh, Henri Pharaon and Michel Chiha had bought land in the south where the new railroad had been contracted and that, of course, as a result the value of this land had risen dramatically. Any distraction from this blatant profiteering was thus welcome.[6]

Incapable of dealing with the situation, French General Catroux was forced to reinstate all of the imprisoned ministers on 20 November. Only a few days later, on 23 November, the new national flag of Lebanon replaced the Tricolour.

With Lebanese independence, the political system which was to govern until the 1975 civil war, came into being in the form of the 1943 National Pact. The Pact was an arrangement which resulted from the post-1920 rapprochement between the Maronite and the Sunni political elites, a quintessential example of political pragmatism.[7] In essence, it comprised a compromise formula on the identity of the country and on power-sharing between the religious communities. The Christians renounced the protection of Western powers while the Muslims renounced union with Syria or other Arab states. It was decided that Lebanon would be neither

Eastern nor Western but independent. All communities would be included in the exercise of power – in the civil service and the cabinet.[8] The Jews belonged to the six communities not represented in the National Pact along with the Latin Catholics, Syrian Jacobites, Syrian Catholics, Nestorians, and Chaldeans. Of these six the Jews were still the largest community.[9] The main defect of the agreement was that it represented a compromise among elites whose goal was to secure the benefits they could get from their position of power.[10] As such it did not represent the nation. Further, it allowed broad scope for interpretation, leading over time to disputes over interpretation and questioning of the Pact itself.

The Jewish Community and the Political Situation, 1943–1948

By 1943, the Jewish community had become concentrated in Beirut, with only a small community remaining in Saida and some families in Tripoli.[11] The 1944 census registered 6,261.[12] This number increased dramatically with the influx of Syrian and Iraqi Jews seeking refuge in Lebanon towards the end of the British mandate in Palestine.

Tensions over Lebanon's independence were followed by tensions resulting from the increasingly violent conflict over Palestine. The assassination of Lord Moyne in November 1944 by two Jewish Palestinian youths triggered a violent Muslim reaction in Beirut. The Mufti of Lebanon called for a boycott of Jewish activity in Lebanon. Prime Minister Riad as-Sulh, however, pleaded with the population not to lose their heads.[13] The political situation remained tense throughout the following year and in November 1945, the community faced anti-Jewish riots in Tripoli, in which 12[14] or 14 Jews[15] were killed. The community council in Beirut subsequently went to lengths to dissociate itself from Zionism, but was fighting an uphill battle with the continuing focus being on the situation in Palestine. The Jewish youth organizations *Maccabi* and *B'nei Zion* were accused of smuggling Jews into Palestine and engaging in Zionist activities. The *Maccabi* sports club was forced to sever connections with its head office in London.[16]

In 1946 Lebanon's national aspirations were finally realised with the complete withdrawal of all foreign forces. The Lebanese population and its political representatives were more than a little uneasy in face of their neighbour's Zionist ambitions.[17] Early in January decrees were issued to implement the Arab League's decision to boycott Zionist goods. In March three members of the Anglo-American Commission of Inquiry on Palestine visited Beirut at the Lebanese government's insistence. But when the Commission's report was published general strikes and some "repatriation" of local Jews were carried out. Jewish communities in Syria and Lebanon were vocal in their anti-Zionism[18] – to no avail. Two bombs exploded in two Beirut commercial establishments. Longrigg in his history of Lebanon under the mandate claimed that the shop was wrongly believed to have been Jewish and consequently bombed. Bombs also exploded at the British Consulate-General and the US Legation.[19] This seems to clearly point to a connection with the Anglo-American Commission. Yet Zionist documents on that period reveal that, in fact, it was not that clear cut. Some of the disturbances were the result of the Palestine problem, but others, such as the bombs found in the store of a Jew in Beirut, were of a completely different nature. The latter specifically were connected with a dispute between Jewish store owners.[20]

The complexity of the domestic and regional dynamics is further highlighted by the still open border between Palestine and Lebanon. This led to incidents such as David Ben-Gurion's use of Beirut airport when he had problems obtaining permission to travel from the British mandate authorities. Thus it happened that in 1946, a Jewish travel agent in Beirut chartered a Middle East Airlines plane – a DC3 Dakota – for Ben-Gurion, Moshe Sharett, and Golda Meir to travel to a Zionist conference in Switzerland.[21]

Further tensions arose in April 1947 when President Bishara al-Khoury dissolved parliament to prepare the country for the May elections. On 25 May 1947, from the early morning onwards Beirut was occupied by troops, gendarmes and police. Tanks, armoured cars and infantry units took up positions on the principal squares, streets, and outside polling booths. It was reported that special groups of supporters of the government list admitted only those who had announced their agreement to vote for the government candidates. Lebanon's press protested vehemently.[22] Despite the restrictions, 22,000 voted in Beirut as compared to 10,000 in 1943.[23]

On 8 June a new government was formed consisting of among others Sunni Prime Minister Riad as-Sulh, Greek-Orthodox Vice President Gabriel Murr, Maronite Interior Minister Camille Chamoun, Sunni Finance Minister Mohamed Abdel Rizk, Maronite Foreign Minister Hamid Franjieh, Druze Defense Minister Emir Majid Arslan, and Shi'a Agriculture Minister Ahmed Husseini.[24]

Two Women Remember: A Privileged Life in Lebanon

The memories of those who lived through a certain period of history often differ from the chronological lists of facts drafted by historians. Being memories they are, of course, shaped by later events in peoples' lives, are interpreted and reinterpreted as they are told and retold. Yet, to brush them aside as nostalgias and sentimentalities, is to disregard the more human aspects that make the past come alive. The history of Lebanon's Jews during the mandate through the eyes of Stella Levy, one of the daughters of Joseph Farhi, and Vicky Angel, who left Lebanon in 1945 and 1947 respectively, reveals a different dimension.

Stella Levy recalls that she and her three sisters led a sheltered and privileged life, which in many ways was overshadowed by their father's prominence. Her father embodied morality and Zionism in the community, and was the "father confessor" to whom everyone came. Having had a profound interest in linguistics in addition to politics, Stella Levy remembers her father's research on the similarities of Arabic and Hebrew as well as the long line of literary and political personalities who came to house regularly, including the poet and writer Bialik, the Ben Zvis, Eliahu Epstein, other delegates of the Jewish Agency and *Vaad Leumi*, and Jewish soldiers in the British Army.

The relations between her father and non-Jewish personalities were excellent. He was a personal friend of the Maronite Patriarch Arida whom he visited regularly in order to have theological discussions. She remembers that he had very good relations with the government. He organized visits by Lebanese ministers to the community on Rosh Hashana and Passover. One prominent memory is that when income tax was introduced in Palestine, her father taught the system to Lebanese government officials.

The Farhi daughters did not generally mix socially with non-Jews.

> We had some friends who were not Jewish. We were at school together but never went out with boys of other communities. If a Jewish girl was dating a Christian or a Muslim she got a bad reputation. There were a few mixed marriages, but the families tended to disinherit those who married out.[25]

Yet the Farhi girls were not "imprisoned" within a small Lebanese Jewish world. For example, they did not attend the *Alliance* school like most other Jewish children, because their father did not particularly like the director. Instead, the girls attended the Collège Protestant. "We were always the first pupils in class. My father was on best terms with the principal of the school because they discussed literature, so we never had exams on Saturdays – because the Farhi girls did not write on *Shabat*."[26] They had no formal religious education but regular private Hebrew lessons. Their father also insisted that they learned proper literary Arabic.

Stella Levy went on to university. She got an MA from the American University of Beirut, which she described as "a nest of anti-Semitism". In fact, this is the only anti-Semitism Stella Levy remembers. Her family did not encounter any problems with the Vichy authorities. During the French mandate life in Beirut was cosmopolitan and did not have an oriental atmosphere. It was agreeable, modern and European. This did not change during the Second World War. Prices went up a bit but the community did not miss anything.

The Jewish community as a whole was traditional, not orthodox. The Farhi family did not eat food that was not kosher, nor did they travel on *Shabat*. Others were less strict. On Passover they invited Palestinian soldiers to join them for the *Seder*; on *Shabat* eve they had Palestinian students at the house.

Vikki Angel's memories of the holidays have remained special. The whole family came together, including all aunts, uncles and cousins. *Purim* was celebrated with a masquerade ball, one for children and one for adults. *Hanukka* was not so important, children having only a half day off school. For Passover they got three weeks off because the school had to be cleaned. The High Holidays were celebrated in the beautiful synagogues at Aley or Bhamdoun. The Bhamdoun synagogue was particularly elaborate with chandeliers brought from Italy. The Jewish quarter and the main synagogue were lavishly decorated for holidays. For weddings it was traditional to send flowers instead of gifts, which in essence meant that the wedding party was drowning in flowers.

The community was well organized. It was administered by the *Conseil Communale*, which was elected democratically. It oversaw the life of the community, education, and health for which there were no state institutions. Charity was also an important part of the community through the *Bikur Cholim*, financial aid, the *Hevra Kadisha*, women's organizations, and the provision of breakfast for needy children.[27] Everyone paid a community tax. Those who refused to pay would not receive a Jewish burial or their children could not get married.

Stella Levy recalled that, "on the whole, the Jews took part in every sector of life".

> There was a police officer and an army officer, but most did not work for the government. They were essentially craftsmen, tradesmen and businessmen. One of my cousins was a very famous doctor. . . . Married women did not work if they did not have to. Unmarried girls did. Two of my sisters worked: one was a school teacher and the other worked in the family-owned pharmacy.[28]

Most young women, if they worked, were employed as teachers. A few went to university. Others were secretaries or nurses.

There were three sub-communities in Beirut: the Lebanese Jews, the Ashkenazis, and a small community of Spanish Jews who spoke Ladino.

They all had their own synagogues with services according to different traditions.

There was a small Zionist movement and Zionist emissaries came from Palestine to indoctrinate the youth.[29] Vikki Angel recalls that under the influence of this movement her sister ran away to Palestine to a kibbutz. But life in the kibbutz in 1944–5 was harsh and her sister had been spoilt and hated it. Her parents had real problems bringing her back to Lebanon without the appropriate papers.

Very few Lebanese Jews immigrated to Palestine.

> What we heard about Israel in Lebanon did not encourage people. Life was difficult. There were no servants. You had to work with the *Histadrut*. In Lebanon it was much easier. The geographic position made life easy: Three months in the mountains – you got three months vacation – here (Israel) people get two weeks. Women and children had an easy time. We all went to summer resorts like Aley where there were hotels, cafés, orchestras, dances and casinos.[30]

She, herself, was not a Zionist, and the only reason she moved to Jerusalem was because she met her husband on a trip to Palestine.

> When I left Beirut I didn't know there was going to be a Jewish state and that the borders would be closed. I didn't take anything with me apart from the wedding gifts. I thought I could go back on weekends to visit. In the beginning I wanted to go back to Lebanon. Then my mother came to live with us in 1966. She always regretted leaving. All Jews that left Lebanon remember Lebanon with love.[31]

Narratives and memories such as the stories of these two women are not scientific discourses. Yet they should not be dismissed as merely "nostalgia". What these two very similar accounts reflect are some of the dynamics of social life, every day worries, tensions, and beliefs – in this case those of young women in Beirut's Jewish community. Stella Levy's statements make very clear that unlike the men in her society who did define themselves in political terms, she was above all a Farhi. Family ties were close and by far the most important identifier for women at that time. Vikki Angel's statements similarly evolve around the high holidays, education, and socializing with little reference to the political situation.

The Establishment of the State of Israel

The conflict in Palestine was reaching a point of no return in 1947. It had become clear that Britain could no longer maintain control over the territory mandated to it and was searching for an honourable way to retreat.

The Jews of Lebanon started taking preventive measures, anticipating trouble. Jewish boys enrolled in the *Kata'ib* sporting clubs and scouts, where they received firearms training[32] deemed useful for defending the quarter if needed. And the *Kata'ib* sold weapons to the Jews for exactly this purpose.

When the United Nations adopted the partition resolution in November 1947, Beirut's Jewish community celebrated on the premises of Magen Avraham. An estimated 2,000 attended the festivities. In their Zionist fervor a number of younger Jews travelled south and crossed the border to join the *Haganah* for the impending war.[33] As expected, the UN partition resolution set in motion the first Arab-Israeli war and Lebanese Arab nationalists vented their frustration. A few Jews fearing Muslim action sought refuge among the Maronites. But all Jewish shops remained open, a clear indication that the majority did not feel seriously threatened.[34] On 4, 5 and 6 December 1947 bombs exploded on the outskirts of Wadi Abu Jamil at the communist party headquarters and near the US Legation. Very little damage was caused and there was no loss of life.[35] There were strikes and demonstrations.[36] In support of the Palestine cause, the Arab states had also decided to collect a special "Palestine tax".[37] The Lebanese Chamber of Deputies approved an allocation of LL1,000,000 for the defense of Palestine. Beirut municipality contributed one month's salary. Recruiting centres and the Permanent Palestine Office opened in Beirut. The press took a clear anti-American position and vindictive articles against the USSR were published. But despite this posturing, Lebanon's war effort is generally considered to have been minimal and even the financial contributions, regardless of the initial pledge, only reached a disappointing LL127,000 in Beirut and LL29,000 in Tripoli.[38]

On the night of 7/8 January 1948 an arms cache was discovered in the Jewish quarter and a number of arrests were made. Rumours that the Jews concerned were Zionist agents caused considerable excitement, and in spite of the precautions taken by the Lebanese authorities, a Jewish merchant was stabbed by three unidentified assailants.[39] Explosions occurred on successive nights in the Jewish quarter – one at the *Alliance* school in Rue Georges Picot. When it was established that the incident had been a mere case of arms pilferage,[40] the situation returned to normal.

On 9 January Palestinian Jewish students at the AUB were ordered to leave. Anti-Jewish feeling was running high at the university, and the university authorities were of the opinion that the departure of these students was in their own best interest. Some confusion seems to surround the issue of the expulsion of non-Lebanese Jewish students. Landshut, for example, claims that all foreign Jews, including the students at the American University and the French college, were ordered to leave the country in January 1948.[41] At the same time, archival evidence suggests that Lebanon's French universities announced that Jewish students irrespective of nationality were allowed to stay.[42] These orders affected an estimated 20 Palestinian Jewish students.

On 16 April Lebanon came to stand-still when a general strike was called in protest to the Deir Yassin massacre. Some damage to Jewish property in Beirut resulted.[43] On 14 May the Lebanese government declared a state of emergency. On 24 May a Shi'a mob attacked the Jews of the village of Teybl. The police fired at the mob, killing four.[44] A number of Muslim volunteers as well as a few Christians headed to the borders to aid the Palestine cause. Nissim Dahan, who was a Jewish *Kata'ib* member at that time, recalled the internal Maronite debate ending in Pierre Gemayel telling those "hotheads" who wanted to fight to "go and fight, but when you get to the frontier you will flee". His prediction was not far from the truth. Of the estimated 150 trucks taking volunteers to the border only three, according to Dahan, arrived.[45] While the exact numbers can be debated, the lack of Lebanese military involvement in the Palestine war speaks for itself.

On 26 July, Prime Minister Riad as-Sulh resigned. A new Cabinet was formed consisting of Gabriel Murr as deputy prime minister and interior minister, Hamid Franjieh as foreign minister and education minister, Hussein Aoueini as finance minister, Philippe Tacla as economy minister, Emir Majid Arslan as defense minister and agriculture minister, and Elias Khoury as health minister. Lebanon was reeling from internal instability and the repercussions of the Palestine war. A day later an explosion occurred in the Jewish quarter of Beirut in which eleven were wounded. No satisfactory explanation for the cause was given and no arrests were made in direct connection with it. Under the emergency legislation, however, 23 communists were arrested in Tripoli and three Phalangists were charged with possession of explosives.[46]

When military operations started in May, about 200 political suspects were arrested. According to a Reuters message sent from Beirut at that time they only included a few Jews.[47] Anti-Jewish demonstrations also broke out. On 15 May, in the early morning hours, a mob armed with bricks, incendiary devices, and whips proceeded towards the Jewish quarter. But when they reached the entrance they were stopped by *Kata'ib* militia guards, who together with the Lebanese gendarmerie prevented them from entering and dispersed the crowd. The *Kata'ib* party also strongly attacked the "hotheads" who went around pestering the Jewish residents of Lebanon, reminding them that Zionists and Jews were not synonymous.[48]

The community in Saida was probably the hardest hit. *Al-Ittihad al-Lubnani* reported that in December 1947 the Jews of Saida visited the Permanent Office for Palestine in order to complain about the attacks to which they had been subjected. They condemned the partition of Palestine and declared their willingness to contribute money for Palestine. In return, the Office assured the Lebanese Jews that no future malevolence was intended against them.[49] According to *al-Diyar* the Jews of Saida decided to donate LL25,000, but then changed their mind when their spokesman Ishak Divan objected.[50] Similarly, *al-Hayat* reported that several Zionists in Beirut persuaded Beirut businessmen not to contribute either.[51] In January the business community was called upon again. The collector of funds for Palestine met with some opposition from Rahime Derviche. The next day a bomb was thrown into Derviche's brother Saleh's apartment.[52]

It seems that some money was extorted in the end. The Jewish community's contribution towards the Arab Palestine fund is estimated at LL500,000,[53] thrice the amount of non-Jewish Lebanon. It also seems that "ordinary" citizens tried to benefit from the situation as well. One such incident occurred when the Zilkha Bank sent someone around with a credit note to collect a debt. The creditor tore up the note and said: "You've already got all of Palestine."[54]

In 1948, not knowing what the future held and faced with an influx of Palestinian refugees from Israel as well as Lebanese soldiers passing through on their way to the border, the majority of the Saida community fled, or according to some accounts was expelled,[55] to the countryside for the duration of the war. Their property was "confiscated for Palestinian Arab refugees" by some nationalists, but the government ordered the police to protect the Jews and enable them to return to their homes.[56] Some, nevertheless, went to Beirut where they then settled.

The country was on the verge of disintegrating. The Palestine question had brought to the surface the sectarian divisions to such an extent that the incidents against Lebanon's Jews almost paled into insignificance by comparison. On 30 May an incident occurred which provides an excellent example of the underlying tensions in the country and a context into which to place the anti-Jewish violence.

> A Christian was sitting on a full bus ready to depart to Beirut. A Muslim of alleged importance got onto the bus and insisted that his journey was more urgent. He persuaded the bus conductor to eject the Christian by force and give the Muslim the now vacant seat. The bus left for Beirut. But the Christian, having rounded up some 20 friends proceeded to the bus garage and wrecked it. The incident would have ended here had not someone else from the village concerned caused the church bells to be rung, thus summoning all the villagers, who were unusually tough, armed with sticks, stones and firearms, to the centre of the village from which they proposed to march to Tripoli. Intervention by telephone by Hamid Bey Franjieh, the minister of foreign affairs, who is a Christian notable of North Lebanon and the *mohafez* of Tripoli prevented the villagers from carrying out their

threat. Meanwhile Abdul Hamil Karameh was visiting the *kaimakam* of Tripoli with other Muslim notables and, on hearing of the incident, is reported to have remarked that Tripoli was a Muslim town and that he did not see why Christians from the surrounding countryside should be allowed to make trouble here.[57]

The passions and violence aroused by a mere full bus shows the volatility of the entire immediate post-independence period.

In the greater scheme of Lebanese confessional politics the adoption by Muslim politicians of a "Palestine first position" led to some elements within the Christian community considering an alliance with the newly established Israeli state,[58] strengthening the Lebanese Jewish-Christian bond.

In March 1949 the Israeli–Lebanese armistice agreement was signed and the politics and inter-communal relations in Lebanon returned to normal. A sign that "violent politics" had clearly ended came when on 21 July 1949 the Lebanese government announced the dissolution of all para-military organisations. The *Kata'ib* office was closed, the arms were confiscated and 13 members arrested. The Parti Populaire Syrien fared even worse with 12 members sentenced to death and 53 imprisoned.[59]

The situation for the Jews had not changed overnight, but events had been set in motion which would irreversibly affect the future of the community. As Toufic Yedid Levy recalls:

From 1948 onwards Lebanon changed character through the growing number of Palestinians which completely overturned our position. Our people, you know, were traders looking for peace and quiet. They were looking to get a return for their money . . . We weren't numerous amongst two or three million Lebanese, only 7,000. And those 7,000 weren't all Lebanese . . . the Palestinians started coming here and our situation deteriorated. Members of the community started to sell their property and left. Eventually the Palestinians started to make trouble for us. We had help from the government, from the Christians, from the *Kata'ib* – but the majority (in Lebanon) became Muslim.[60]

The implications of this impressionist memory are clear: The Lebanese state barely coped with absorbing the Palestinian refugees from the 1948 war. The confessional system was being subjected to a Sunni Muslim Palestinian "onslaught", which was perceived as an increasing threat with every additional refugee wave. It was a threat to the political status-quo and Maronite hegemony – but ultimately it was the smaller minorities who suffered first – Lebanon's Jews.

The internment camps from the Vichy period were revived in 1948. As Nathan and Alexander Sofer remember, between ten and fifteen Jews who were representative of the establishment were arrested and interned in an old army barrack in Baalbek. They were held for eight months without any restrictions on family visits. "It was not a prison. It was a precaution, not a retaliation."[61] Their Palestinian co-religionists who were residing in Lebanon at the time of the conflict were not so lucky. The Lebanese government interned many of them in a camp in Baalbek for the duration of the war.[62] Some Lebanese Jews were also detained, along with communists and members of the opposition. They were held in two rooms in a building, which had previously housed the army. The conditions of detention, according to the Israeli foreign ministry as well as Jews who were detained, were not harsh. The detainees brought their own beds and sheets, they were permitted to bring in food from the outside and receive newspapers. Relatives visited twice a week. None were tortured or beaten, the sanitary conditions were all right, and morale was high. The only drawback was that the Lebanese government made the detainees bear the expenses. It was noted, for example, that a man was taken from Baalbek to Beirut for interrogation and had to pay the travel costs of the policeman who accompanied him.[63] A list contained in the Israeli files provides a glimpse of some of detainees. The Lebanese Jews included the merchant Rudolph Kugel, the musician Adolph Sabarnatki, the engineer and director of the Singer sewing machine company Rubin, the merchant Jajathi, the owner of a hat shop Spiegel, and the commissioner Shaki. All were later released with the exception of a certain Cohen who was convicted of arms trading and transferred to one of the prisons. Jews of other nationalities, but resident in Beirut, who had been detained included the English attorney Zarfati, the Palestinian director of the *Alliance* Rana al-Malih, the Greek senior clerk at Shell corporation Aliya, the Palestinian engineer Yosef Margolies, the Palestinian driver Balanga, the French owner of an automobile service station Liteau Bahbout, and the French owner of a butcher's shop Habib Levi.[64] The detention camp in Baalbek is said to have detained 35 Jews from Beirut, 30 Lebanese communists, and 25 Palestinian Arabs between June and September 1948.[65]

A further indication of the state of war, was the Lebanese "raid" of the British consulate in Aley to obtain all visa applications for Palestine. Applicants were generally categorized as Zionists, but most were also not Lebanese. Nathan Sofer's personal experience exemplifies the tension caused by the war in Palestine further:

> The office where I worked was called PEL (Palestine-Egypt-Lebanon) Tours. The Lebanese authorities came and took our receipts, went through all our documents, but just found regular things for a travel agency. They suggested that for a fee they would return the documents and I said they could keep them. The business belonged to a Palestinian Jew, so it was

sequested. This then made the head of the Egyptian office whose name was Khaled come to Beirut and attempt to take over the office. But he couldn't because this was a Lebanese office and he didn't have the authority. Nevertheless, he started to fire all the Jews. He wanted to fire me but he couldn't because I was the manager. But Jacques Balayla was fired, Rubin Khalil, Joseph Barakat and the others. So Khaled said to me: "You may be the manager but you will do what I tell you to." He demanded that I give the office to his brother who was a travel agent in Lebanon, and I opposed it. As he couldn't fire me he wrote a letter to the security saying that I was a big Zionist and that I was involved in the gangs smuggling Jews to Palestine. So they called me to the special police for interrogation. He had sent an anonymous letter. I asked them: "What do you have against me?" They said: "We have a letter." So I asked: "Who sent the letter? Can I see the letter?" They wouldn't show me the letter, but they took me to another department headed by a Christian, who was a friend of mine. The chief of police was a Druze. The Christian told the Druze that I was a very important person and asked me what the story was. I told him the story and he went to the Druze to see the file. He showed me the letter and asked if I recognized the handwriting. We didn't have an Arabic typewriter in our office, so Khaled used to handwrite his letters. So I said, "I'm going to give you a file with copies of letters he wrote, so you can compare." I brought him the file and it was obvious. So he went to the Druze and told him that Khaled tried to fire me. The Christian officer was Haji Touma. He had known me since I was a child and during the period when we used to transfer all the immigrants from the Syrian border to Eretz Israel, the train used to stop in Beirut and he would come there and give us transit visas. We bribed him. We gave him 10 Lebanese pounds per person. So one day he said: "I'm fed up coming every time at midnight. Can't you arrange for the convoy at an earlier time?" I said: "I have a better idea. You give me the stamps and the visas and I'll give you the money." And he did. I would stamp the passports. He had confidence in me. I never cheated – I was too young to know that you could cheat.[66]

Jewish Refugees and Unavoidable Changes

The perception that the war of 1948 did not have disastrous repercussions for Lebanon's Jews prevails until today. The Lebanese Army posted guards at the entrance of Wadi Abu Jamil.[67] In addition, the *Kata'ib* also sent its militia to guard the Jewish quarter.[68] Lebanese Jews themselves did not consider the war would directly affect them as they saw themselves clearly as Lebanese nationals – so much so, that there had been Jewish soldiers in the Lebanese Army fighting the war of 1948. Others had joined the *Kata'ib* militia including Nissim Dahan and a number of his friends. They saw themselves as Lebanese nationalists, got involved with the party, and served the country in every possible way. "Lebanon was a secular state, not an Arab country. Everyone was Lebanese and served God the way they wanted."[69]

Lebanon, compared to its immediate neighbour Syria, and indeed most other Arab states, retained its tolerant and liberal attitude toward its own Jews and toward Jewish refugees seeking asylum in Lebanon. Consequently, in 1948, the number of Jews increased to 5,200 and by 1951 to 9,000 – 6,961 of whom were Lebanese citizens.[70] Thus Lebanon was the only Arab country in which the number of Jews increased after the first Arab-Israeli War.

Lebanese Jews welcomed the creation of the State of Israel and had a deep commitment to the idea of a Jewish state. But unlike Jews in other Middle Eastern states they were neither expelled from their country nor voluntarily left to live in Israel. Jewish sympathies for Israel were never strong enough to overcome a very Levantine attitude towards life.

One prevalent attitude of Lebanese Jews which alludes to this is that only those Jews who were unable to make it in the "real world of business" immigrated to Israel. And finally, Lebanese Zionist commitment can be summed up by a willingness to contribute financially and support the Jewish state from afar, but an unwillingness to live with it on a daily basis. In 1952 community president Attie accurately summed up the position of Lebanese Jewry, stating that while they were sympathetic towards Israel their first loyalty was to Lebanon.

At the same time, however, the events of 1948 brought some unavoidable changes. For instance, the Jewish newspaper *Al-'Alam al-Isra'ili* changed its name to *as-Salaam*.[71] Jewish holidays were taken off the government's list of holidays. Government assistance to Jewish educational and charitable organisations was cut. It became difficult for Jewish citizens to obtain passports and exit permits without paying more than the usual bribery rates, as well as obtaining government contracts. They also had to cope with more obstacles than other Lebanese in receiving general services from government bureaus.[72] The *Maccabi* was declared illegal, the *Maccabi* House had all its property confiscated, and the president Dr Abraham Hellman, was jailed for three weeks.[73] This did not, however, mean an end to Jewish youth activity. Rather, the youth movements, as Nissim Dahan recalls, were incorporated with those of the *Kata'ib*.[74]

There were also a number of Jewish officers in the Lebanese Army who chose to resign, including the most high ranking Jewish officer Commandant Rubin.[75] Yet others, such as Dr Sananis and Sargent Salik, didn't.[76] The crucial point is that Lebanon's Jews were not pushed out of government service positions. Elia Bassal, for example, progressed in his police career to the level of *commissaire*, leaving the *gendarmerie* only when he retired at the age of 65.[77] He took pride in his work throughout his whole career, wearing his white uniform and medals to the synagogue regularly. "He enjoyed it and the community enjoyed it, too."[78] The Jewish stenographer at the Chamber of Deputies retained his post.[79] The Beirut municipality, the Agriculture Ministry and the Army employed Jewish engineers[80] such as Mr Zeitoune, the chief engineer of the municipality of Lebanon.[81] Beyond government service Jews continued in their traditional occupations in import–export, as merchants, and bankers in addition to a small number of artists, journalists and singers.

Symbolic of the changes and the perception that these changes were rather unimportant is an incident in 1949. It is the death of a Jew named Tessler who is remembered as the only casualty. It is said that Tessler was from Safed and when the Palestinian refugees from Safed came to Beirut, he ran into the former Muslim mayor and made fun of him. The mayor did not do anything at that point. But he had a friend in the security services and they paid a visit to Tessler, confiscating his belongings and interrogating him. Tessler, of course, had nothing to reveal. The Jewish community was told that he had been arrested. They asked the government to try him in court or let him go. He was released, but the interrogators returned again and again. In the end he threw himself from the balcony.

Incidents as these often gave the impression to outsiders that the situation of Lebanon's Jews equalled that of Syrian or Iraqi Jewry. The offence this caused within Lebanese Jewry can be gathered from attempts to correct this misperception. When asked about this situation during one of his visits to Paris, Joseph Attie answered that "not only were the Jews pursuing their normal occupations, they were also integrating Jews from Syria".[82] A year later, in February 1950, the editor and publisher of the Jewish magazine *Le Commerce du Levant*, T. Mizrahi, wrote a letter to the *New York Times*:

> I must admit, as a Jew living in Lebanon, that Lebanese Jews, even in the most critical hour of the Palestinian crisis have never suffered from any particular treatment, either from the authorities or the people. At no time have the Lebanese Jews been deprived of their rights as citizens, or their liberties. They went about their business enjoying the same rights as their compatriots.
>
> The Jewish officials of the Administration have always maintained their posts, and the same kind of treatment was experienced by the Jews fleeing from the neighbouring Arab states.
>
> The Lebanese Jews consider their sympathetic ties to Palestine as purely religious, while all other ties – those of nationality, culture, language, and customs bind them to their own mother country, whose faithful citizens they wish to remain.[83]

A month later, on 17 March 1950 Mizrahi, published another article, repeating his claim. In the Hebrew newspaper *HaDor*, he stated that during the 1948 war

> not a hair fell from the head of a Lebanese Jew. The authorities did not change their attitude towards Jews. The rights of Jews were not harmed. They could continue with their businesses and their work just like everyone else in Lebanon. Not one Jewish clerk was removed from office, as happened in neighbouring Arab states.[84]

He wrote that the reason for this lay in the fact that the ties of Lebanon's Jews with the Land of Israel were of a purely religious nature. They were faithful Lebanese citizens and intended to stay such.

Focusing solely on the violence or on the protection accorded the Jews obviously has vast political implications. The events related here are not black and white, not all violence or trouble-free existence. Rather, they reflect the broader domestic tensions in Lebanon and the regional conflagration. In the end it should be remembered, that as soon as the fighting was over, the Lebanese government was the first to restore normal conditions for the Jewish population. The ban on travelling, which had been in effect during the war, was lifted, and a number of senior Jewish officials who had been dismissed were reinstated, some even promoted. Nine Jews who had fled to Lebanon from Iraq, where they had been sentenced to death in absentia, were also permitted to immigrate to Israel.[85] This, in many ways, says more about the Lebanese state than any of the bombs placed in the Jewish quarter.

On a broader regional level these unavoidable changes included the emergence of a Jewish refugee problem which significantly impacted upon Lebanon. As a result of the turmoil in Palestine from 1945 onwards and the first Arab-Israeli war 1947–9, a number of Jewish refugees from Syria and Iraq came to Lebanon, many of whom were smuggled into Palestine. In December 1945, 81 Jews from Halab, 23 from Beirut, 4 from Saida and 3 from Damascus immigrated to Israel.[86] In February 1946 a group of Jews, who were disseminating Zionist propaganda as well as smuggling co-religionists across the border, were caught. They included Zaki Hukdar and Zion Mamia from Halab, and Yaacov Pinkasi and Musa Totah from Beirut.[87] In May 1946 the Lebanese discovered another group smuggling Jewish immigrants into Palestine.[88] Nine Jews were captured on one night and four the next.

In 1946 a total of 6,000 Jews fled from Syria to Lebanon because of the deteriorating security situation and settled among the Jews of Beirut.[89] A year later, in 1947, the Syrian town of Halab suffered a pogrom. Most of the town's Jews fled to Beirut, almost doubling the size of the community. They enhanced the already excellent position of the

Jews in the financial sector with their specialised knowledge of stocks. But more important was their contribution as goldsmiths and diamond dealers. The Syrian government increased restrictions on its Jews with the result that between December 1947 and May 1948 all Jewish employees remaining in government service were fired.[90] A curfew was imposed on the community in Damascus.[91] All property of the Baghdad-Damascus Transport Company owned by the Iraqi Jew Chaim Netanel was confiscated, and his Jewish clerks were arrested on charges of "collaboration with the enemy". A detention camp for "suspicious" Jews was set up east of Damascus, and the community was under constant harassment by the press and by the population. Syrian ministers fulminated against partition and stepped up pressure on their Jewish population. Dozens of houses of worship were attacked and the government launched a fiercely anti-Semitic campaign, froze Jewish bank accounts, and confiscated the property of Jews who fled the country.[92] In December 1947 rumours were spread that the Jews were responsible for the cholera epidemic.[93]

Between 1943 and the mid-1950s Syrian Jewry shrunk from 30,000 to 5,000.[94] The number of Lebanese Jews increased dramatically with the influx of thousands of refugees from Iraq and Syria as a result of the first Arab-Israeli war. By 1949 their number in Beirut had reached 4,000.[95] These refugees were granted the right to stay in Lebanon. They did not, however, receive Lebanese citizenship and many had no desire to stay. While the refugees settled in Wadi Abu Jamil the established Lebanese Jewish bourgeoisie moved out of the quarter to Qantari and to Michel Chiha Street.[96] A new order began to emerge of a lower class comprised primarily of refugees, an upper middle class of now well-established Lebanese Jews, and, of course, the traditional Lebanese Jewish notables presiding over all. Those Jews living in the more fashionable areas were engaged in commerce, while the poorer ones in Wadi Abu Jamil worked in the garment, soap, and glass industries or as peddlers.

With the growth of the community, geographic expansion beyond Wadi Abu Jamil was unavoidable. The better-off Lebanese Jews moved to Rues Georges Picot, Petro Paoli, Chateaubriand, Agrippa, Rezkallah, Clemenceau, Bliss, May Ziade, Kantari, Rue de France, and Rue de L'Armee.[97] The biggest impact of the refugees on Beirut was on the community's education system. The number of pupils at the *Alliance* increased from 923 in 1946 to 968 in 1947 reaching 1,043 in 1948. From December 1947 new enrollments occurred on a daily basis and, according to the director Elmaleh, the school was forced to suspend admissions from February 1948 onwards.[98]

Legal emigration and illegal immigration featured highly in the refugee community. For those engaged in smuggling the refugees, smuggling other "goods" also became a lucrative sideline. In October 1948 *Le Soir* reported an incident of Lebanese passports being forged to enable Syrian Jews to flee abroad with their money. The forger was named as Salah al-Din Shatila, whose father served as an office director in the passport department. The conspirators were reported to be the Lebanese Jews David Haski, Jacques Hanan and Shimon Falwaski. The deception was discovered by the head of the secret police Emir Farid Chehab as he was about to sign the passports. The names of the implicated passport holders were: Edmond Safadieh, Yosef Safadieh, Musa Eliyahu Baida, Victoria Baida, Eliyahu Baida, Fortuna Baida, Raful Haza, Yom-Tov Shemaya, Fayez Shemaya, Mouiz Shemaya, Latifa Shemaya, Lucy Haloni, David Menashe, Frieda Totah Hazan, Maurice Anzarut, and Toufic Menashon.[99]

In May 1949 the Israeli–Lebanese Mixed Armistice Commission (ILMAC) agreed that a limited number of Jewish families residing in Lebanon would be permitted to cross into Israel.[100] In December it was recorded that 1,000 such refugees had already illegally crossed over the frontier to join their families in Israel. On 29 December it was announced in the press that the *sûreté générale* had "pounced" upon an underground network for the transport of Jews to Israel in motor launches and that over 200 Syrian and Lebanese Jews had been arrested.[101]

In 1950 the Lebanese government authorised the transit of Iraqi Jewish refugees from Lebanon to Israel via the Rosh Hanikra checkpoint. The government permitted Syrian and Iraqi Jews who had found sanctuary in Beirut to cross the frontier to Israel.[102] And, on 22 February the first group of 55 Lebanese Jews officially also crossed the border.[103] Most Syrian Jews as a norm did not remain in Lebanon, but emigrated over the following ten years to places such as New York or Israel. For example, in early March the first party consisting of 170 Syrian Jews left for Israel.[104] Another group was the Lawsai family of eight which received permission to cross the border at Rosh Hanikra on 25 March 1952 as the result of a meeting between IDF Colonel Yehoshua Harkabie, Lebanese Colonel Salem, UN General Riley, and two other Israeli officers.[105] Lebanon's unease about contacts with Israel in connection with Jewish immigration eased with the agreement of Egypt, Iraq and Jordan to also permit immigration.[106]

The opening of the Israeli–Lebanese Mixed Armistice Commission channel did not put a stop to the lucrative illegal route. On 10 July Beirut radio announced the capture of 25 Jews trying to flee Lebanon in several rowboats. A sideline to transferring Jewish refugees across the border was the smuggling also of arms and food. This business had become so lucrative that in February 1949 the "import" of meat to Israel led to a scarcity of supply in Lebanon.[107] A US report on the situation of cross-border activities in Lebanon in 1953, considered sympathy for Israel as one of the motives for smuggling goods across the border.[108]

The encounter of the Lebanese Jewish old-timers and the Syrian or Iraqi refugees was characterized by positive and negative incidents, but foremost by very personal experiences. One such story is that of Raphael Sutton who reached *bar mitzvah* age during the Syrian-French struggle in 1945. His *bar mitzvah* was hastily celebrated in the Halab synagogue and on the same day Rafi was sent by his family by bus to Beirut. He was met by relatives who, upon hearing his plight, insisted that the *bar mitzvah* be celebrated properly. So the next Saturday Rafi had a grand celebration at the synagogue in Bhamdoun, attended by the Chief Rabbi himself.[109] Rafi returned to Syria once the situation had calmed down, only to return to Lebanon in March 1948 when the Syrian Army wanted to draft him. He spent six months in Beirut before illegally emigrating to Israel with 170 other immigrants. His family followed a year later. In 1982, as a colonel in the Israel Defence Forces, he returned to that synagogue in Bhamdoun to relive one of the most cherished moments of his life.

Syrian Refugees

The accounts of Lebanese Jews of the influx of Syrian Jews rarely mentions inter-community tensions. These accounts, however, do not square with the recollections of some of these refugees. The experiences of Ezra Tamir from Halab serves two purposes: first, to highlight some of the inter-communal tensions, and secondly, to give an outsider's perspective of Beirut Jewish life.

Ezra Tamir was born in Halab and fled with his family from Syria to Lebanon in 1949. He came from a family of Oriental Zionists and it is thus not surprising that the family, after leaving Lebanon in 1967, settled in Israel.

For Syrian refugees life in Lebanon was a dangerous situation as they did not have Lebanese citizenship and consequently the Lebanese government could always deport them back to Syria. The Tamir family moved into an apartment in the Rue de France. Ezra Tamir remembers that Syrian refugees flooded into Lebanon under the most distressing circumstances.

> My cousins had been chased by dogs and soldiers shot at them when they were crossing the border. They arrived wounded in Wadi Abu Jamil. We put the Syrian refugees up in the synagogue or in various houses. They stayed for a couple of months until false papers had been prepared for them. Two or three Lebanese Jews specialized in this – having the right friends. My cousins left for the United States.

Students learned in Jewish schools until the age of 16. The primary school was the *Talmud Torah* in Wadi Abu Jamil and there was another one for religious Jews – the *Jeunesse Juive Religieuse*. There were six students to a class at the *Talmud Torah*. The secondary school was the *Alliance* which was coeducational. "I was very religious when I came to Lebanon, and they put me into a mixed class. I went to the professor and told him I did not want to be in a mixed class with all those beautiful girls."[110]

Some Christians also attended the *Alliance* school, but left whenever Hebrew classes were given. The *Alliance* taught four languages at that time: Arabic, Hebrew, English and French. The language of instruction was French, the educational system was French and the certificate exams were taken at the French embassy. The history of France and the geography of France were taught, not Lebanon's history or geography. As a Syrian refugee, Ezra Tamir could not take the *brevet* after secondary school. After the secondary school there were essentially three options: Christian schools, business, or abroad.

The community as a whole consisted of religious and secular people. It was a very liberal community. Jews would travel by car on *Shabat*. Some opened stores on Saturdays and closed on Sundays. "My family was religious and our lifestyle was with family and friends at the synagogue. There were about 10 synagogues, but none were Ashkenazi even though the rabbi was Ashkenazi."

In June at the end of the school year 70 percent of the Jews left for Aley and Bhamdoun. The richer ones went to Bhamdoun and the less rich to Aley. They came back only after *Sukkot*. "It was a fascinating way of life. The father went to work from 8 a.m. until 2 p.m. in Beirut and then returned to the mountain, where he bathed, slept, got up, went to the synagogue and then to the coffee house. The youth went out to see friends at clubs."

The ethnic configuration of Wadi Abu Jamil started to change in the 1950s. The affluent Jews moved out of the quarter and Kurds started to move in. "They hated the Jews. They lived in run-down houses and envied us. There were often fights between gangs. But to be beaten by a Kurd was the worst that could happen to you."[111]

Tensions also existed between the Lebanese oldtimers and the Syrian newcomers. Ezra Tamir attributed these tensions specifically to the Halabi Jews who were extremely miserly, while the Damascenes were much like the Beirutis. The Halabis made an issue of money and always stressed this in business deals which was perceived as uncouth. They also spoke with a different Arabic accent which made them the object of occasional ridicule within Jewish circles.

One of the differences between the Lebanese and the Syrian communities was that the Lebanese went to Saida once a year on pilgrimage "to some saint's tomb". The Syrians did not. Another difference was that Syrian children tended to go to the *Jeunesse Juive Religieuse* and learned with Rabbi Avraham Abadi for two to three hours every day. In that sense, they were more religious. The girls, however, did not have any religious education. "There were some Jewish girls who dated Christians – Muslims only very rarely. The community condemned this. When I was 16 or 17 I was part of a group of young Jews who ran after the girls and spied on them. We threatened them sometimes saying that if they didn't stop seeing Christians we'd publish this in the club. Most of them then stopped."

The women in the community stayed mainly at home and did not work. "They had children, went shopping, and played cards. They met their friends at a table playing cards and continued this wherever they went – to South America, the United States." Syrian Jews married amongst themselves. There were no prohibitions against marrying a Lebanese Jew, but Syrian parents thought a Syrian match to be better.

Most Syrian Jews emigrated from Lebanon in 1958, seeing the civil strife as a sign to move on. Ezra Tamir's family stayed until 1967. They left two weeks before the Six-Day War and made their way to Israel through Istanbul.

4

The First Civil War: Conflict of Identities

The question of national allegiance and loyalty was not concluded with independence, national sovereignty, and self-determination. Rather, it had opened Pandora's box. For Lebanon's Muslims and Christians it meant continued struggle over the nature of government and the identity of the state, which ultimately resulted in the first civil war in 1958. For Lebanon's Jews this meant continued challenges to their loyalty as Lebanese citizens, particularly when inter-communal suspicions and tensions were high.

Dual Loyalties

The creation of the State of Israel, the Arab boycott, and the outcome of the first Arab-Israeli war as a situation of "no-war, no-peace" affected Lebanon in no uncertain terms. Lebanon's war effort had been pitiful, almost 100,000 Palestinian refugees had spilled across the border, and the economy came to bear the brunt of regional upheavals. Within the delicately balanced confessional system the Palestine question became a test of loyalties. Some Maronite politicians were accused of complicity with Israel, while some Sunni politicians pushed for the integration of the refugees, which would, of course, tip the confessional balance in their favour. With the Palestine question becoming the litmus test for loyalty, Lebanon's Jews also were subjected to repeated public scrutiny. The question of dual loyalty arose from genuine security concerns as well as being economically or personally motivated. Yet while there were a number of disturbing incidents, these did not have popular or official support. As a result Jewish community life continued unencumbered and even flourished.

In 1951, Nazem Kadri, parliamentary deputy for the Bekaa, raised the issue of compensating Palestinian refugees with Lebanese Jewish money.

His demand provoked a series of articles and editorials in defence of Lebanese Jewry. Kesrouan Labaki, for example, in an article in *Le Soir* stressed that "persecution of a Jew because he was a Jew would go against the very principle of Lebanon's existence". Lebanon existed because it had resisted all assaults on its liberties, because it was a place of tolerance for all victims of religious persecution and political oppression. The Jews were Lebanese citizens and had the right to be treated justly and humanely. Indeed, "the Jews of Lebanon are no less Lebanese than Mr Nazem Kadri, Mr Zouhair Osseiran and all the demagogues who applauded".

> We know numerous Jews in Lebanon. Of some we speak highly – we honour their friendship. We know they are Lebanese, that they love this country the way we love this country, that they take part in our pains and joys, our ambitions and national ordeals.
>
> We do not have the right to treat those Jews as Zionist agents. They have under all circumstances given proof of their attachment to Lebanon and their participation in the Lebanese community.
>
> It is possible that among the Jews of Lebanon there are Zionist agents. The authorities will pursue those, arrest them, try them, condemn them according to merit. But these authorities are the same ones who will also find all those Israeli spies who are not Jewish. . . . If Mr Nazem Kadri and Mr Zouhair Osseiran took the pains to go through the archives of the police and tribunals they will find that the great majority of Israeli agents since 1947 were not Jewish.[1]

Interestingly, Lebanese Jews did not actually see the articles appearing in *An-Nahar*, *Al-Hadaf* and *Ash-Shark* calling for the confiscation of Jewish property to compensate Palestinian refugees as being directed against them. Rather, they saw it as anti-Israeli propaganda, which could easily be countered by annually paying off the involved newspapers with 20,000–25,000 Lebanese Livres.[2]

In 1952, Lebanese Deputy Emile Boustani started a campaign against Lebanese Jews which was motivated by conflicting business interests.[3] In the words of American Minister Harold B. Minor at the American Legation in Beirut, Boustani was "expansive and self-centred. It is probable that his vehemence in campaigning against the Lebanese Jews is motivated by his egotism and his business activities."[4] His campaign undoubtedly raised the profile of the Jewish community, which had been keeping very much to the political margins. Boustani, a Christian, did not find much sympathy among his parliamentary colleagues who perceived him as encouraging reckless tendencies among the small anti-Jewish element in the country at the expense of Lebanon's national interests. His tactics, while deplored, were not without economic foundation. As a result of his campaign his own profile was raised and his popularity in neighbouring Arab states rose, directly benefiting his business.[5] Part of this campaign was a call to expel two Jewish officers from the Lebanese Army. The officers in question were medical officer Capt. Nissim Sananes and one of the artillery supply officers. The Minister of Defence, Emir Majid Arslan, pointed out "that these officers had been serving in the army for several years, and stated that the commanding general was competent to judge these men's loyalty". Fellow Lebanese Army officers said that they considered "Jewishness" to be a religion and not a nationality and these two officers in question were Lebanese nationals.[6] Boustani's parliamentary motion to discharge the two officers was decisively beaten when a vote was taken.[7] With this vote Lebanese delegates had expressed their opinion that Lebanese Jews did not have dual loyalties. Indeed after the vote Defence Minister and Druze chieftain Arslan sneered to reporters "we do not have to take lessons in patriotism from the manager (Boustani) of the C.A.T. Company."

Community President Joseph Attie did not see Boustani's campaign as a cause for serious concern. He had full confidence in the continuing support of Lebanese president Bishara al-Khoury and the broader Christian community.

The Jewish Community and the Political Situation, 1949–1957

Relations between the Jewish community and the other Lebanese communities remained amicable, still characterized by shared religious festivities and a fervent display of Lebanese nationalism by Lebanese Jews after 1948. As Lebanese citizens, and contrary to the situation in many other Arab states, public office and the army were open to the Jews[8] even after the establishment of the State of Israel.

Economically the community flourished in the 1950s. The textile industry, which had already begun serious development, progressed rapidly. The impulse to industrialization in general had been notably strengthened by the wartime experience.[9] Some changes, however, needed to be made because, with the creation of the State of Israel, Lebanon had lost its Palestinian market, presenting a major drawback.

During 1949 Lebanon was busy consolidating its own economic position and combating union movements.[10] In the early 1950s, it was estimated that Beirut conducted about LL 1 billion of foreign-exchange operations per year, and, by 1951,[11] over 30 per cent of all private international gold trade went through Beirut.[12] The movement towards the consolidation of the "merchant republic" and the extension of power of Lebanon's mercantile-financial bourgeoisie continued under Camille

Chamoun's administration which attempted to weaken the political influence of the old quasi-feudal landowning elite and to strengthen the base of the international service economy.[13] In both Syria and Lebanon much of the real power still lay with "independents" usually representing a landed or monied interest and at heart non-political.[14]

In 1949, Bishara al-Khoury, through a special suspension of the constitutional provisions, was reelected president of the republic. His second term began without too many problems, but challenges to his leadership slowly started to emerge.

In 1951, during the Passover celebration the president of the community, Dr Joseph Attie, held a reception at Magen Avraham which was attended by Sami Sulh, Abdallah Yafi, Rachid Beydoun, Joseph Chader, Habib Abi Chahla, Charles Helou, Pierre Gemayel, and Mgr. Ignace Moubarak.[15] US *chargé d'affairs*, John H. Bruins, described the Passover celebration on 27 April as a classic example of Lebanon's traditional observance of religious freedom. An estimated 3,000 attended the celebration and the day passed uneventfully despite continuing Arab resentment at Israel and tension over Syrian-Israeli border incidents.[16]

Tacit alliances were created between Jewish leaders and leaders of Christian parties, such as Pierre Gemayel, who, from 1948 onwards, stressed on many occasions that his party considered Jews to be fully-fledged Lebanese citizens and that Lebanon was "all about minorities living peacefully together."[17] In 1951, the *Kata'ib* had its first member elected to parliament and then had half a dozen representatives in each successive legislature.[18] In 1952, the *Kata'ib* expanded its support base allowing any Lebanese man or woman over twenty-one to become an active member. This opened the path of active participation not only for non-Maronites but also for women.[19] A number of Jews became fully fledged *Kata'ib* party members moving up from their previous associate status. The Jews were generally courted in the elections as they voted as a block. The person to benefit most was the *Kata'ib* candidate Joseph Chader whose popularity with the community remained unsurpassed, especially given the fact that the official minority representative in no way showed interest in the community.

Friendships with prominent Lebanese politicians continued to flourish. Maronite leader Pierre Gemayel started to bring his sons Bashir and Amin along,[20] signaling the closeness of the two communities. Sunni leader Sami Sulh also ranked among the Jews' favourites. Good business relationships, in addition to the governments' dedication to religious tolerance, ensured that the Jewish community had government protection in troubled times.

On 11 February 1952, Sami Sulh formed a new Cabinet. His programme promised to reinforce the Army, amend the electoral law, grant woman suffrage rights, safeguard the rights of the workers and

support the new economic agreements with Syria.[21] The Jewish community at this time was represented in parliament by Marquis Musa de
Freige, a Roman Catholic. De Freige, though, did little to represent the
community's interest, or indeed the other five minorities he was elected
to represent. The community's political security had always been outside
the realms of the minority deputy. President Attie maintained good
relations with Lebanese president Bishara al-Khoury.

On 23 September 1952, Camille Chamoun was elected president.
Khoury's second term had been cut short by a "coup". Toufic Yedid Levy
remembers the turmoil surrounding Chamoun quite vividly because of his
own involvement.

> During the 1952 elections he (Chamoun) called me. I was in charge of the
> Jewish electoral district and we wanted to have someone in parliament. We
> generally voted for Joseph Chader and we helped the *Kata'ib* to get their
> people in. Joseph Chader would not have become an MP if it hadn't been
> for the Jewish support. Chamoun knew that. He called me to his residence
> and wanted us to vote for his man. I said: "Sorry, we can't. Your govern
> ment never helped us when we had trouble from the Palestinians. The only
> ones who helped us were the *Kata'ib*.[22]

In the autumn of 1953 a number of bankruptcies were declared in Beirut.
This shook the world of finance for some time.[23] Apart from this,
Chamoun's presidency and indeed life in Lebanon, proceeded smoothly
until broader regional events forced themselves onto the agenda. With the
political change in Egypt, the rise to power of Gamal Abdel Nasser since
1952, the spread of pan-Arabism and the Suez Crisis, the "national question" again gained attention.

The Suez Crisis did not affect the situation of the 6,692 Jews in
Lebanon,[24] but it did set in motion the political tensions which resulted in
Lebanon's first civil war. President Camille Chamoun, in line with his
strong pro-western orientation, was the only Arab leader not to break
diplomatic relations with Britain and France after their joint-attack with
Israel on Egypt. This made him vulnerable to challenge by Muslim
Lebanese seeking to include Lebanon in this greater Arab movement.

Community Life, 1943–1958

The elation over the end of the struggle for Lebanese independence was
tampered only by the news emerging from Europe in 1944 and 1945. The
steady stream of Jewish refugees had already provided the Beiruti community with a glimpse of the persecution of European Jewry. And even
though Lebanon was geographically distant that did not mean the

community remained unscathed. One of the tragic cases, which did not emerge until much later, was that of Elie Dana. Born in Beirut on 17 May 1883, Dana was living in Nice, France in 1943. He was arrested, sent to Drancy assembly camp on 27 October 1943, and, on 20 November 1943, deported to Auschwitz. He had disappeared in the turmoil of the war and was not heard of again. The Red Cross eventually found his name on the Auschwitz transport list, but as no proof of his death existed, was unable to issue a death certificate.[25]

In 1944 the education commission of the community, after an in-depth study of the situation, decided to initiate a number of projects. The LL300,000 in their possession went towards the construction of another floor on top of the Selim Tarrab school which was to become a youth room and a library. A level above that was to be made into apartments for the use of the school. The construction of a new synagogue in Bhamdoun was also on the agenda. Further, a workshop for sewing and embroidery was to be set up for young women. The synagogue in Aley was due for refurbishment. A sports ground, a center for hygiene, a convalescent home in the mountains, youth holiday camps, and scholarships for high education based on merit were also part of the ambitions of the commission.[26]

The year of 1945 was an eventful year for the Jewish community, a year of upheaval and tragedy, both internally and politically. On 8 May 1945 the community was faced with the death of one of its key leaders: Joseph David Farhi. The whole community descended into mourning for the 67-year-old who passed away in the early morning hours. Community life came to a complete standstill. His funeral at the grand synagogue was attended by numerous political and religious personalities from all communities. Chief Rabbi Bahbout and community president Dichy Bey gave voice to the grief of the community[27] and a memorial fund was established in his name.

Life in Lebanon was good and the economy was booming. The majority of Lebanese Jews were wealthy enough to afford a comfortable life-style, which included spending the summer months in the mountains away from the heat and humidity of the city. In fact, an estimated 4,000 Jews migrated to Bhamdoun each summer, renting summer lodgings from local residents. Despite the fact that the Bhamdoun synagogue was only used during the holidays, no money or effort was spared when it was built in 1945. Three crystal chandeliers lighted the vestibule and 12 more the sanctuary.

The community as a whole was still not Zionist enough for its co-religionists in the *Yishuv* who on occasion had a rather Machiavellian perspective on this issue. For example, Chaim Weizmann, in May 1943, called for special attention to be paid to the Zionist activity in Lebanon, "both due to the need to instill the Zionist idea within the community and due to the important role that . . . the Beirut community could play in relations between the Christians in Lebanon and the Jewish Yishuv".[28] According to Weizmann there existed excitement among the Maronites for the Zionist project. Beiruti Jews who had ties of trade and friendship with many of the heads of the Christian communities, could be of great help "provided they knew which line to take".[29] Weizmann proceeded to suggest inviting some of the Beirut Jewish leaders – at their own expense – to discuss this issue. The leaders he specifically had in mind were Farhi, Dichy Bey, Ovadia, and Stambouli.

In 1949–50 approximately 200 to 300 Jews immigrated to Israel. The majority of this group was composed of young or poor people. In Dr Attie's opinion there was no trend in the Jewish community toward a gradual migration to Israel. While many Syrian, Iraqi, Iranian and a few Turkish Jews has passed through Lebanon in transit to Israel, Lebanese Jews saw their future firmly within the Lebanese state. Only 500 Lebanese Jews had left.[30] This stood in stark contrast to the 96% of Arab Jews who were forced to leave,[31] revealing the true nature of the relations between Lebanon and its Jews.

In 1950 an *Alliance* school in Beirut was demolished by a bomb.[32] This, however, was an isolated incident. Indeed a report in the Israeli foreign ministry files makes it very clear that the community continued to live and travel freely and had the same rights as all other communities. The only problem, in fact, was the differing ideas on the construction of a new school. The community, to the chagrin of Israeli officials, was adamantly opposed to *Aliya*. The foreign ministry report even raised the concern that if Israel were to try to "force emigration", Lebanon's Jews would publicly demonstrate against Israel – a rather embarrassing situation. Thus the author of the report advised the adoption of a special position on the Jews of Lebanon, particularly if the case were to be raised in the forum of the United National General Assembly, especially since the Lebanese Jewish community had already prepared a memorandum on this subject.[33] As Marion Woolfson so poignantly stated, "what is not generally realized is the part played by the Zionists themselves in the troubles which beset the Jews of Arab countries . . . They encouraged emigration not because of the danger, but because Israel required new immigrants to tighten their claim over the land."[34]

In the same year the community reported a lack of Hebrew teachers for the Jewish schools in Lebanon affecting an estimated 2,000 children.[35] The rabbi was so concerned about the status of the Hebrew education that he sent a number of letters to international Jewish and Zionist organizations requesting teachers and books.[36] The main obstacle, it was claimed, was the impossibility of "obtaining entry permits to Lebanon for Jews, even those with French citizenship".[37] The recommendation to the Israeli government was that special effort should be made to supply Lebanon with three to five teachers, considering that these children might immigrate to Israel later on.[38] Part of the problem lay in the curriculum of the *Alliance*.

The *Alliance* was applying the complete educational program of the French schools with the minimum Arabic required by the Lebanese government. Not being able to reduce the Arabic classes and not wanting to reduce the French classes, it was forced to teach Hebrew in supplementary classes rather than as part of the curriculum. In February 1951 the situation still had not improved,[39] the Jewish Agency being preoccupied with clarifying whether any teachers would be paid by the community.[40] As opposed to the *Alliance* school, the 250 children attending the Selim Tarrab school received a thorough Hebrew education. Thirteen hours out of 38 were devoted to Hebrew, and at kindergarten level 32 out of 38.[41] This school, however, served only the poorer segments of the community, as well as providing education, food and clothes.

On 24 April 1950 there was a profound change in the community leadership. The outgoing community council consisting of Dr Joseph Attie, Toufic Attie, Murad Chayo, Raffoul Chalom, Maurice Costi, Isaac Elia, Moise Elia, Raffoul Farhi, Joseph Saadia, Emile Saadia, Jacob Safra, Isaac Sidi, Jacques Stambouli, Ezekiel Totah, and Dr Z. Veicemanas[42] paid tribute to its president from 1939 to 1950. Joseph Dichy Bey, who had spent 30 years of his career in the service of the community decided for health reasons not to stand again for the presidency of the Jewish community. His response to the honours accorded him was as follows:

> My friends and collaborators, thank you for your solidarity, your love of the good and your continuous devotion to the success of our efforts. I am entirely satisfied that I am leaving the community in very good hands. Its destiny today is with men of high standards . . . I am certain that (they will spare) neither their efforts nor their sacrifices to maintain and develop what we have built up together. I am convinced that you will continue to work for the greater interests of the community . . . I will take this occasion to extend my congratulations to all organizations on the magnificent work just completed . . . to obtain increasing radiance and prosperity.[43]

Dichy Bey was succeeded by Dr Joseph Attie, who was the chief medical officer and the chief surgeon of the government hospital in Beirut. He had often represented Lebanon at international conferences on neurology. His excellent relations with the authorities were an example for the rest of the community, and he remained community leader until 1976.

The community was still on the increase. In 1951 there were 9,000

Jews in Lebanon, 6,961 of which were Lebanese citizens. On 2 April 1951 the Lebanese government issued a set of legislation on the competence of religious jurisdiction. This legislation was specifically aimed at limiting the powers of all Christian communities and the Jewish community, and to regulate disputes between Lebanon's civil law and the communities' religious jurisdictions. The articles 15, 17, and 19, all on marriage were the only articles which provoked a lengthy response from Chief Rabbi Ouziel. The rabbi's comments throw some light on the issues of inter-marriage and polygamy in the community. The first comment voiced strong opposition to mixed marriages, which according to Lebanese law were permitted. It appears that the question of intermarriage was discussed at length as marriage lay within the realm of religious jurisdiction, thus effectively resulting in conversion in the case of mixed marriages. From the rabbi's statement one can surmise that there were few conversions to Judaism while there seem to have been some to Christianity. Moreover, Ouziel's condemning remark that the silence within the community on this issue was "like a tacit agreement for autho-rising mixed marriages" reflects that mixed marriages may have been more common than admitted.[44] The second lengthy rabbinical comment on the legislation addressed the issue of polygamy. Article 19 specified punishment from one month to one year imprisonment for bigamy but exempted Jewish husbands whose marriage to an additional wife had been authorized by the religious head of the Jewish community. Rabbi Ouziel's response to this article was a clear endorsement of the Sephardi accep-tance of polygamy. At the same time he stated that in Lebanon it was generally the case to only have one wife and "there have been only one or two cases of bigamy".[45] Yet it was acceptable for a Sephardi to take a second wife without the consent of the first, but only with the permission of the *Beit Din*.

On 10 June 1951 the community also celebrated the 25th anniversary of the construction of Magen Avraham. The ceremony was widely attended and reflected the solidarity and to some extent the religiosity of the community. Religious life was thriving. Itzhak Levanon remembers that at this time Beirut still had many synagogues.

> We were close to the Eddy synagogue. It was a small synagogue but it was where my father used to go. He was somebody in this synagogue, so this is why we used to go there on a regular basis. One of the characteristics of this synagogue was that it used to "export" Cohanim for the services of the other synagogues. Everyone who was a member was a Cohen on both sides of the family. Only on very few occasions did we go to Magen Avraham – for weddings and for *Yom Kippur*.[46]

In 1952 the Jewish community according to its president Dr Attie was composed of one per cent wealthy, 79 percent well-off, and 20 percent poor. Their economic activity fell into the following categories: 65 percent were in business, 28 percent were small wage earners, 4.5 percent were professionals, two percent labourers, and 0.5 percent were in government service.[47] The community was organized to safe-guard its overall interests. Although there were differing social, ideological, and economic views within the community, there were no important internal tensions. The *Conseil Communale* at that time consisted of Zaki Aliya, Joseph Saadia, Kamel Hilwani and Isaak Zeitoune in addition to Dr Attie. The community had a wealthy public fund supported by an affluent Jewish middle class.

This financial status was seen as the main reason by the Jewish Agency that Lebanon's Jews had so far not chosen to immigrate to Israel. The Agency saw the obstacles, on the one hand, in the unresolved question of transferring money and possessions, and, on the other hand, in the rumours of lack of opportunities for worthwhile capital investment in Israel.[48] Lebanese Jews emigrating from Lebanon during this period generally chose Italy, Belgium, and Switzerland as their destiny.

The general economic situation in Lebanon in 1953 and 1954 was not at its best. Unemployment was high and trade was slow. The Beirut market was characterized by a large supply of merchandise, but virtually no turnover and no cash-flow. Traffic of ships to Beirut port was reduced, partly as a result of Syria opening a rival port in Ladhakiya.[49] Despite this, the Jewish community was thriving.

> Life was nice because we had everything. We had our schools – the *Talmud Torah* and the *Alliance* – and most of the people were wealthy in terms of the times. In the 1950s to have a fridge, a radio, a car, a telephone, central heating when at the same we knew that in Israel they had no phones, no fridges – the situation was different. We were living in the Paris of the Middle East. We had everything. The clothes were fancy – we didn't have anything but Bally shoes, a designer tie; it was normal. It was unusual to see men or women whose outfits did not match, who were not coordinated. It was a fancy society. We had the possibilities, the money; it was not a poor society.[50]

The status of education for Jewish children had improved, in spite of the fact that the number of Jewish university students remained small. As one Jewish Agency emissary reported : "The state of education of Jewish children is good. Most of them receive elementary education – primarily at the *Alliance* and also the *Talmud Torah*. A small portion goes to high school. By contrast, the number of Jewish students in university is minimal. At the *Alliance* schools in Beirut they also learn Hebrew. Yosef

Sedaka was present at the *Hanukka* party at the *Alliance* school, a large beautiful party, with candle lighting and songs in Hebrew."[51]

Youth movements had been officially dissolved, but groups continued to meet in private homes to talk about current events and analyse news broadcasts from *Kol Israel*. The attitude of the Lebanese authorities towards the Jews was also beyond reproach. According to the Jewish Agency emissary, there was no open persecution or articles of incitement in the press.[52] The community remained vibrant and much of this vibrancy was reflected in the numerous celebrations, parties, and holidays. Itzhak Levanon recalls the festive atmosphere, which prevailed at the time:

> On the eve of the holidays everyone went to the synagogues – nicely dressed. The custom was that before a holiday you used to buy new clothes for the family, so everybody was walking in the streets, to the synagogues, and showing how fancy he was. It was part of the holidays. Less the services. It was a place to show off. Very few people used to work on holidays, this changed after 1958. People started to keep on working because of the economic situation. They could not be closed the whole of *Shavuot*. One day is enough. And they started to open the stores. Holidays were definitely felt in the street. *Pessach* was absolutely nice. *Yom Kippur* was something. The whole community was on the street, going from one synagogue to another. It was a big happening, not to go and *daven*, that was not the idea. It was to see people, meet your friends, chat, visit. We kept a high percentage of our traditions and customs. During the night of *Hoshana Raba*, the night we spent reading, all youngsters were in the streets or the *shul*, till six or seven in the morning – everybody, regardless of whether he was religious or not. A month before *Rosh HaShana* everybody went to *Slichot* at three in the morning – everybody was out. And after finishing the service at six we went to the sea and jumped into the water. That was life.[53]

In 1956 there were 5,382 Jews in Beirut, 95 in Mount Lebanon, 40 in North Lebanon, 1,108 in South Lebanon (Saida), making a total of 6,692 Jews in Lebanon.[54] In 1957 the US Ambassador to Lebanon reported that the Jews were well-off and enjoyed all the necessary freedoms. "In various branches of the business world they sometimes even hold leading positions." His observation continues with a rather curious statement. According to the Ambassador the Jewish community was offered a representative in parliament but they refused, out of fear of becoming the balancing vote between the Arab and the Christian population.[55] While no other evidence exists that such an offer was indeed made and refused, these remarks reveal a number of issues. Firstly, it affirms that the Jews were essentially non-political and held the middle ground. And secondly, it gives a glimpse into the deteriorating Christian-Muslim situation in 1957, which would result in a civil war only months later.

The First Lebanese Civil War

In March 1957 Lebanon embraced the Eisenhower Doctrine, designed to fight communist subversion in the Middle East and provide American economic aid. By so doing, Chamoun openly risked confrontation with Nasser. At the same time, Chamoun became a hero to many Christians and Jews, as a president who took no account of opposition and maintained traditional ties with the West, regardless of what "the Arabs" might have thought. Chamoun turned the 1957 parliamentary elections into an informal plebiscite on his foreign policy.[56] Charges of irregularities pervaded the political establishment as many of those patrons who had ensured Chamoun's victory in 1952 lost in the general elections of 1957. These had been cunningly manipulated by the partisans of the president who relied on the organized forces of his allies, the *Kata'ib* and the SSNP.[57]

Early in 1958 the United Arab Republic (UAR) was established, uniting Egypt and Syria. In May of that year tensions gave way to open rebellion. Lebanon's political existence was on the verge of collapse. In essence, the combination of domestic, regional, and international dynamics had plunged the country into a civil war. The crisis was the outcome of a number of key factors: firstly, President Camille Chamoun's intention to amend the constitution so that he could run for a second consecutive term; secondly, the irregularities of the 1957 parliamentary elections which had resulted in a land-slide victory for the government list; thirdly, the governments "excessive" pro-Western orientation, and, fourthly, the Nasserist–Syrian attempt to overthrow the government.[58] When Chamoun reissued his appeal for US intervention under the Eisenhower Doctrine on July 14, the very day the Iraqi monarchy was overthrown, America did not object. On 15 July US troops started landing on Beirut's beaches, but refrained from taking sides in the civil war. Discreet American mediation finally resolved the crisis with the election of Lebanese Army Chief-of-Staff Fuad Chehab to the presidency.[59]

On the eve of the civil war the Jewish community was at its largest in history: 9,000 according to Patai,[60] 10,000 according to Heskel,[61] 11,000 according to Schechtman,[62] and 15,000 according to de Bar.[63] They were a prosperous community which was not surprising since they constituted 1.9 per cent of the country's business leaders, while only constituting 0.4 per cent of the population.[64] But as the internal situation deteriorated many Jews started leaving the country.[65] After the war 1,000–2,000 left via Cyprus or Turkey to Israel.[66]

When the civil war broke out, and despite the opposition's incitement against the Jews, the authorities assigned soldiers to prevent any harm being done to them.[67] In 1958 Joseph Chader defended the Jewish community against charges of treason.[68] And, during the civil war the Maronites provided for their immediate security. Some Jewish families decided to move to the safer area of Kisrawan, but most stayed under *Kata'ib* protection in downtown Beirut.[69]

> In 1958 we collaborated with the *Kata'ib*. They used to come and protect us with arms during the night during the civil war – until the Marines came. This protection started with the cooperation between the youngsters. It grew later on and in 1975 and 1982 it became a cooperation between the State of Israel and the Maronite community. The Jews in the *Kata'ib* gave a boost. There was an armed wing of the party and this protected the Jewish community, and afterwards they started training us. We also went with Camille Chamoun. The Christians gave us self-defence training. They started in 1958 during the war. It was a war between Christians and Muslims, and we were caught in the middle of this fight. We used to go to Ashrafieh and have joint patrols. They trained us in our quarter where the *Maccabi* used to meet in the courtyard of the *Talmud Torah*. And women went as well. But during the night, only men patrolled.[70]

Nissim Dahan remembers a funeral during this time. The Jewish cemetery was partly in the Muslim quarter and the mourners, who had attended the funeral, had to cross through that quarter to return. They were stopped by a group of Muslims and detained. Pierre Gemayel personally rang one of the Muslim leaders and got the Jewish mourners released half an hour later.[71]

Moreover, during 1958 the relationship between the Jewish community and Camille Chamoun was so good that not only did Chamoun ensure for Lebanese Army protection of the Jews, but some Lebanese Jews were also actively involved in Chamoun's private militia.[72] As Toufic Yedid Levy recalls:

> We had armbands that had military assistant written on them. Many Jews volunteered for this service. The whole youth club volunteered. They took us to the secret service for clearance because we were not part of the army. In other words they issued us with a special permit to carry guns. We guarded the area where the president lived.[73]

Thus, while Lebanese soldiers were guarding Wadi Abu Jamil, Jewish militia members were guarding the Lebanese president. Apart from this contribution, the Jews did not really play much of a role within the overall context of the war. They remained inconspicuous and apolitical, stressing their aloofness from world Jewry and Israel.

Political and Cultural Identification

The end of the French mandate, Lebanon's independence in 1943, the creation of the State of Israel in 1948, and the first Lebanese civil war in 1958, all had a profound impact on the identity of the Lebanese Jews. During the mandate period they, more than any other minority in Lebanon with the exception of the Maronites, had considered themselves to be somewhat French; be it through the active advocacy of the *Alliance* that treated Oriental Jewry as French citizens, or be it through cultural and linguistic identification. The struggle for independence from 1936 onwards made a number of issues clear: first, Lebanon's Jews could not rely on French protection indeterminately, and, second, French political presence was not always desirable. Lebanon's Jews like many of Lebanon's Christians during this period started to exchange their "French" identity for a particular Lebanese identity. Lebanon for the Jews was synonymous with a multi-cultural, independent state, which had little "Arabness". They came closest to the *Kata'ib*'s political vision of Lebanoness.

Having opted for a strong Lebanese identity while remaining essentially francophile and retaining all cultural, educational, and linguistic links, Lebanon's Jews also had a strong Jewish identity. The latter was religious rather than ethnic or national. It expressed itself through a vibrant community life and traditional religious observance. Zionism as an additional political identity was able to co-exist, because Zionism in the Lebanese context had few practical implications. At a theoretical level there was some sympathy for the Yishuv and Israel, but not to the extent that Lebanon's Jews wanted to leave. While contacts with Palestine and Israel were maintained for religious and family reasons, there was always a certain degree of alienness about Zionist ideology, which clashed with the Jews' inherent Levantiness. Zionism, compared to the inclusive concept of a multi-national Lebanon, was inherently exclusive. Thus, Lebanon's Jews considered themselves to be Lebanese by nationality and Jewish by religion. Political affiliation, as far as it was expressed by an essentially apolitical community, lay between adherence to Maronite Lebanoness and pragmatic Zionism.

The most important source of identity, however, for the Jews as well as for most other Lebanese was still the family. Urbanization and economic modernization did not diminish its importance: it simply adapted to changing circumstances.[74] This becomes clear when considering patterns of social interaction. In Lebanon people were in daily contact with parents and grandparents, married children, and married grandchildren, with nephews, nieces, uncles and aunts. The extended family was more than an institution for intensive personal contact and relationships; it had economic significance. The majority of economic enterprises in Lebanon were family businesses, as were many joint-stock companies.[75] The Safra bank is a case in point.

In many ways the Lebanese Jewish family was like its Christian counterparts as it had distinct Middle Eastern features as well as those which would be considered more western. It was Middle Eastern in that it was essentially patriarchal, vesting the authority for all decisions in the oldest male, and virilocal, meaning that the family resided near or with the family of the husband.[76] Male heirs were desired, while female heirs were usually not celebrated. Lebanese Jews, and Middle Eastern Jews, in general, also shared some of their neighbors' norms of honour and shame. In this context it has often been noted that the lack of "resort to arms" in defence of the virtue of Jewish women against majority group males made maintenance of honour more difficult.[77] Here, it should however be said, that women were not an issue in the first Lebanese civil war, and that while "tactical" rape in order to shame communities occurred during the second civil war, it was aimed against Christian and Muslim women.

5

The Beginning of the Exodus

The first Lebanese civil war had awakened among Syrian, Iraqi and Lebanese Jews residing in Beirut the age-old question of Diaspora Jewry: to stay or to go? Unlike others faced with this decision, the Jews in Lebanon were not responding to anti-Semitism or persecution, but to the experience of civil strife in 1958, which had left them physically safe but emotionally affected. Syrian and Iraqi Jewish refugees took this opportunity to move on, leaving the safe-haven they had found in Lebanon, to go to Europe, South America, the United States, and, in a minority of cases, Israel. Lebanese Jewry felt more secure in its environs, not having the same historic baggage as their Syrian and Iraqi brethren. But as the security situation once again started to decline in the late 1960s and early 1970s, they, too, had to ask themselves, whether staying in Beirut or Saida was ultimately a wise choice. Many left at the first signs of trouble signaled by Palestinian-Lebanese clashes from 1969 onwards. Others stayed and got dragged into a war which was not theirs to fight; they stayed and watched the world they knew disintegrate before their eyes.

The Chehabist "Miracle"

The 1958 Lebanese crisis was brought under government control by September, and the new President Fuad Chehab, along with the new Prime Minister Rashid Karami, embarked upon a set of administrative reforms. They were intended to address Muslim grievances of powerlessness but within the framework of the National Pact. Chehab had remained relatively neutral during the crisis, not letting the Lebanese Army interfere on behalf of Chamoun because he feared that the army would disintegrate along confessional lines.[1] He was seen by some Christians as a traitor for not helping Chamoun and he was regarded by some Muslims as just another oppressive Christian president. Most Lebanese, however, welcomed him, his reforms, and the stability they provided.

Chehab did not propagate an openly pro-Western foreign policy.

Neither did he align himself with the UAR, paying no more than lip service to Nasser. His main goal was to keep Lebanon independent and non-aligned and to prevent a civil war from happening again. Yet, beneath this official line, he was perceived as pro-Western and anti-Nasser. The United States trusted his "sound reasoning" as "a rational Arab observer who looked at Middle East problems without the usual bitterness of an Arab towards the US".[2]

The following decade, from 1958 to 1967, confirmed the instrumental nature of the National Pact. It was a time in which Lebanon enjoyed security and prosperity. While preserving its relations with the West, the country opened up further to the Arab world to which it presented itself as a land of asylum and dialogue, where it was happy to play the mediator, with what Picard describes as the "hypocrisy of an ultra-laissez-faire political system that was more hospitable to great fortunes than to the poor, and to Christians more than Muslims".[3]

The Chehabist administration responded to these criticisms not so much with arguments as with a subtle policy of weakening its opponents. This was coordinated in the Office of Military Intelligence – the *deuxième bureau*. A large part of the notables' militias, village and suburban associations, and youth groups were given favours and subsidies, and increasingly controlled and manipulated.[4] Yet, on balance, the Chehab presidency remains impressive. He was able to restore peace after a civil war and apart from the 1961 SSNP coup attempt, Lebanon enjoyed six years without internal unrest. Chehab was the first president to grasp that the division of political power as agreed to in the National Pact could only survive if it was complemented by social and economic improvement.[5]

The remarkable dynamism of Lebanese merchants, bankers, and entrepreneurs enabled them to profit from the achievements of Chehabism. The opening to the underdeveloped outlying areas smoothed the way for the arrival of capitalism with its vehicles, machines, and also its agendas and mode of functioning. Enriched by exports to the Arab world, the big traders of Beirut, Tripoli, and Zahle bought back unused or underexploited land from absentee landlords.[6] Charles Helou, who succeeded Chehab in 1964, was unable to sustain both the political stability and the economic growth, illustrated by the crash of the Intrabank in 1966. The Intrabank, which was Palestinian owned, was brought down by a "clever operation of its Lebanese competitors". This affair showed the mistrust and even hostility provoked by the Palestinians' settling in Lebanon[7] as well as the increasingly unstable economic situation. Helou, compared to Chehab, was un-charismatic and had no political pressure group of his own to fall back on. In fact, his sole claim to fame was being the most educated of Lebanese presidents.

Jewish Emigration

The first wave

The first stream of Jewish émigrés left in 1958 at the start of the civil war.[8] In November, despite the end of the first civil war, a further 500 Jews left Lebanon, fearing that this was only the beginning of lasting instability. They immigrated to Mexico, Brazil and Argentina. Another 500 registered with the US Immigration Department to enter the United States.[9]

Emigration continued in 1959. Lebanese security sources estimated that half of Lebanon's Jews left the country "in a panic", traumatized by the conflict.[10] Jewish community president Dr Attie claimed that the majority of those left were, in fact, Syrian refugees who were understandably nervous about the situation given their past experiences. Another émigré component was the younger generation, which found it difficult to find work in fields other than those of their parents.

Emile Eddé, who was interior minister at this time, called upon Dr Attie and expressed his concern over the Jewish emigration. He said that the Lebanese of all confessions considered the Jewish community to be an element of stability and thus were not pleased about their departure. He even went as far as asking Dr Attie to plead with the Jews not to leave. Attie explained the situation to him, the Syrian Jewish fears, and the economic reasons, also stating that the Community Council had already tried to intervene but failed.[11] Emigration continued and it was not just the Lebanese and the Israelis who noticed the departures, but the neighbouring Jordanian press also took notice. In September 1959 an article on this subject appeared in *Filastin*, reporting that 32 Jewish businessmen were liquidating their businesses and property in Beirut and immigrating to Brazil. The newspaper noted that an estimated 400 Syrian Jewish merchants, who had found refuge in Lebanon, had already immigrated to South America. They were flocking toward Sao Paolo "a town which was established with Zionist capital".[12]

In March 1959 community president Attie travelled to Rome for a medical congress. He met up with Joe Golan in order to provide the latter with information about the community. This information was then passed on to Nahum Goldman in New York and then found its way to concerned parties in the World Jewish community and Israel. Attie told Golan that Beirut was the only Arab capital in which freedom of opinion and the press continued to exist. The political climate in Beirut was stable with the internal security assured and the economic situation was flourishing. With the insecurity in other Arab countries, capital investment was flowing towards Beirut. Lebanon's Jews, 7,000 in Beirut and 1,000 in

Saida, were going about their usual business and their situation in general was above complaint. The relations between the Jews and other communities, Christian and Muslim, were excellent. In the recent troubles of 1958, the community had maintained good relations with both sides. There were no attacks on the Jewish quarter or against Jews. In fact, during the crisis, Attie and a couple of other members of the Community Council had met with Muslim leaders, who had assured him that even if they were compelled to attack the part of the city that contained Wadi Abu Jamil, that the latter would not be touched.[13]

There were still six *Alliance* schools in Lebanon with a total number of 1,443 pupils. The largest school in Beirut was attended by 446 boys and 642 girls. The elementary school, maintained by *Ozar HaTorah*, had 100 pupils.[14] Fifty children were enrolled in the school in Saida.[15] The *Talmud Torah* was attended by 250 pupils in 1959, but that number declined to 193 in 1962.[16] In 1960, 28 students passed the Lebanese Government *brevet* examination and 17 passed the French *brevet*.[17] An estimated 50 passed the intermediate exams. Cohen surmises from these numbers that "few graduated from complete secondary schools or universities".[18] Yet the numbers of pupils signaled not only the existence of a younger generation, but also one that was as socially and religiously varied as its parents had been.

The community as a whole, and despite the onset of emigration, remained an active one, with a number of committees. An overview of these committees and serving members provides an interesting insight into the community, the breadth of activity and the families involved. It reflects the key personalities as well as the gender structure of the community. The committee in charge of the administration of Magen Avraham had nine members: Victor Isaac Dichy, Isaac Elie Diwan, Joseph Farhi, Joseph Helwani, Zaki Jajati, Henri Magnouz, Joseph Mouadeb, Nathan Vayezel, and Selim Zeitoune. The community also had a committee for religious endowments. Members of the *Waqf* were Joseph Attie, Zaki Elia, Moise Elias, Joseph Helwani, Selim Levy, Joseph Mouadeb, Albert Sidi, Joseph Zeitoune, and Ezekiel Totah. The education committee included Toufic Attie, Albert Abdallah Elia, Raffoul Farhi, Elie Helpern, Emile Saadia, Edouard Sasson, Carmen Tauby, and Edmond Totah. They were responsible for religious classes, adult and children's education. The *Arikha* committee was composed of Joseph Attie, Zaki Elia, Moise Elias, Selim Levy, Moise Mann, and Joseph Mouadeb. The committee responsible for the administration of the Selim Tarrab school had seven members: Jacques Ades, Ariel Doubine, Albert Abdallah Elia, Moise Elias, Elie Helpern, Desire Liniado, and Isaac Sasson. The members of the finance committee were Toufic Attie, Zaki Elia, Moise Elias, Selim Levy, Emile Saadia, Edouard Sasson, Jacques Stambouli, and Jacques Tarrab. The *Mattan*

Basseter committee included Mikhael Dana, Marco Farhi, Raffoul Kichik, Victor Magnouz, Joseph Mann, Selim Nahmod, Albert Obercy, Joseph Politi, Dib Saadia, Joseph Tauby, Selim Zeitoune, and Victor Totah. It was responsible for distributing chairity to the poor without elevating the donors to "sainthood" and without depriving the poor of their dignity. The *Bikhur Holim* committee was composed of Jacques Ades, Nissim Berzelai, Edouard Cattan, Joseph Costi, Isaac Victor Dichy, Raffoul Kichik, Joseph Mann, Moise Mann, Edouard Sasson, Isaac Sasson, and Jacques Tauby. Its members visited the sick and tended to the health care which was not a state responsibility. On the Dons committee were Viviane Bazbaz, Carmen Galante, Linda Hakim, Joseph Helwani, and Desire Liniado. The statutes committee had eight members: Albert Elia, Desire Liniado, Selim Moghrabi, Jamil Sasson, Jacques Stambouli, Edmond Totah, and Joseph Zeitoune. These members dealt with the bylaws of the community. The *Abbatage Rituel* committee, composed of Rabbi Lichtman, Rabbi Attie, Ibrahim Chaya, Issac Victor Dichy, Kamal Eskenazi, David Tauby, and Nathan Vayezel, observed *shehita* and issued *kashrut* certificates. The *Hevra Kadisha* included Ibrahim Chaya, Zaki Elia, Moise Elias, Eliahu Levy, Dib Saadia, and Nathan Vayezel. This committee took care of the dead, washed and prepared bodies for burial. The members of the *Keter Torah* were Rabbi Attie, Khalil Balayla, Rabbi Chreim, Ibrahim Kayre, Nissim Tawil and Chehade Zeitoune. On the cultural and social committee were Toufic Attie, Albert Elia, Ariel Doubine, Marco Farhi, Joseph Helwani, Desire Liniado, Emile Saadia, Ernest Sasson, and Jacques Stambouli. The youth committee was composed of Charles Abadi, Nino Behar, Nissim Dahan, Moise Kamhine, Joseph Khodri, Moise Mann, Victor Magnoz, Albert Obercy, Isaac Stambouli, and Jacques Stambouli. The coordination committee had eight members: Albert Abadi, Toufic Attie, Ariel Doubine, Marco Farhi, Joseph Helwani, Emile Saadia, Jacques Stambouli, and Joseph Zeitoune. The committee responsible for the upkeep and administration of the synagogue in Aley was composed of Mikael Dana, Selim Dayan, Victor Dichy, Marco Farhi, and Moise Mann,while the committee responsible for the synagogue in Bhamdoun included Kamel Ajami, Khalil Balayla, Nissim Berzelai, Kamel Mbazbaz, Joseph Mouadeb, Edmond Sasson, Edouard Sasson, Chehade Zeitoune, and Selim Zeitoune.

Dr Attie had excellent relations with the Maronite Patriarch Boulous Meouche. Meouche had given Attie the guarantee that the Maronites would continue to protect the Jews in Lebanon when needed. In fact, it had been the Maronites who had obtained the necessary travel documents for many of the Syrian refugees. He also was held in high esteem by Lebanese government officials for raising Lebanon's profile in international medical circles. Further, he was a personal friend of *Kata'ib* leader

Pierre Gemayel, and had good contacts with Israeli diplomats, often serving as a go-between for the rather unstructured *Kata'ib*-Israeli relations.[19]

In the summer of 1959 the community, which was still keeping a low profile after the war, came under attack in parliament during the debate of Prime Minister Rashid Karami's bill which allowed persons who had emigrated from Lebanon and non-Lebanese Arabs to own land in Lebanon. Deputy Kamel el-Assad argued that this bill would make it possible for Lebanese Jews who had left to buy large tracts of land for Israel. Deputy Takieddine Sulh then raised the issue of loyalties once again, claiming that he did not believe that the Jews' allegiance lay with Lebanon but rather with Israel.[20] And Emile Boustani, instigator of similar troubles in 1952, proposed an amendment which would have explicitly banned the purchase of real estate in Lebanon by Jewish residents of Arab states. The proposal, however, lacked the support of the other delegates.[21] *Kata'ib* deputy Joseph Chader came to the defence of Lebanon's Jews. He stated that it was the right of every Lebanese without distinction as regards religion or race to purchase property in Lebanon.[22] He pointed out that no Lebanese Jew had been convicted of spying for Israel. Indeed, the Jewish community was more loyal than most other communities in Lebanon.

The departure of Rabbi Lichtman

At the end of 1959, Chief Rabbi Ben Zion Lichtman also left Lebanon. It was a sad day for the community. Rabbi Lichtman, who had been born in Brailov (Lithuania) into a Hassidic family, had moved to Beirut in 1932. Before moving to Beirut he had lived in Jerusalem and Tel Aviv. He had immigrated to Palestine in 1923/4 from Russia where he had been a young militant, active in the ultra-religious *Agudat Yisrael,* and had devoted much of his free time to researching rabbinic literature, with a specific interest in the *Shulchan Aruch.*

He had not wanted to leave Palestine, but the economic situation was very bad, and he needed to find a way to support his family. From a relative who travelled in the region he heard that the Beirut community was looking for a *shohet.* So he went. After his arrival in Beirut, he went to the main synagogue on *Erev Shabat.* He was immediately spotted as a "foreigner" and invited for *kiddush.*

Among the predominantly Sephardi community there were some Ashkenazim who had come to Beirut from Safed after the First World War. The Safed community had dispersed because of the famine. Part of it had gone to Haifa, others to Jerusalem and Beirut. Rabbi Lichtman, whose wife was from Safed, relaxed once he had found someone to relate to in this strange city. After making these first contacts he returned to Jerusalem and gathered his wife and two sons to move to Beirut. He became the *shohet* of the community, despite being overqualified. The community took to him, and gradually he started taking on more and more rabbinic duties, eventually becoming the head of the rabbinic tribunal. By the late 1930s his reputation had grown to such an extent that in 1940 he was appointed chief rabbi of Lebanon and Syria.

Lichtman liked Beirut and he was fond of the Sephardi community whose customs he found strange. "He thought of them as 'Turks' and learned to appreciate their qualities."[23] Rabbi Lichtman's son Joseph remembers the community he grew up in as "quite ignorant but traditional". These comments illustrate some of the Ashkenazi–Sephardi tensions which, however, did not surface very often.

The Lichtmans lived in Wadi Abu Jamil, not far from Magen Avraham. They had Palestinian passports and maintained their connection with relatives in Jerusalem. After the establishment of the State of Israel, the situation for them became more difficult. Yet the rabbi did not even contemplate leaving the community which needed him.

The Lichtman sons attended the *Alliance* school, followed by the *Lycée Français Laïque*. The one memory Joseph Lichtman has of his years at the *Lycée* concerns a fellow student, a certain Rabinovich, who was very bright. At one point, in 1936, Rabinovich's mother came to the *Lycée* and was apparently boasting a bit that her son was a genius. So the French director trying to take her down a few pegs, said: "Well, you know, among all this rabble, no wonder a Jew excels." Unperturbed she retorted: "Well, in France, among all the rabble, no wonder a Jew is prime minister (Leon Blum)." The director got the message.

Being the rabbi's sons and since the *Alliance* offered no formal religious education, they received their religious education at home. Joseph later started a university degree at the *Université St. Joseph*, but in 1950 decided to immigrate to Israel and continue his university education at the Hebrew University of Jerusalem, seeing "no future for youngsters who were not tradesmen" in Lebanon. In 1952 he started working for the Jewish Agency.

Joseph Lichtman remembers the Beirut community as one where most people observed *Shabbat*, not always very strictly, but definitely in their hearts. There were Jews who lived outside the quarter and came to the services in their cars. They wanted to be with the community. When car-ownership became more widespread in Lebanon, they all owned cars – and changed the model regularly. They bought expensive designer clothes, and after wearing them a few times gave them to poorer members of the family. This was a sign of success. The older generation was very

Levantine in its attitude; the children were more European, completely assimilated into Western culture.

Lebanese Jews liked to live well. They spent time in the mountains, went skiing, and in the evenings to casinos. They used to have weddings on Sundays because the business community was then free to attend and shops did not have to be closed for the occasion. "This community did not produce Einsteins or Trotzkis, but it was a good and open community. Lebanon was like a dream – there was never anything like it and there will never be anything like it."[24] Joseph Lichtman, who has maintained close contacts with other Lebanese Jewish émigrés, asserts that many of these very Levantine customs were maintained abroad. The Paris community, for example, has kept up the "tradition" of inviting politicians to weddings and including them in their businesses. Relations with other minorities in Lebanon came mainly through business. Joseph Lichtman estimates that 60–70 percent of the Beirut Jewish community were merchants or bankers, and that inter-communal relations in this context were very good. Inter-communal relations were also, to some extent, a sign of status. When the son or daughter of a well-off Jew got married, the prime minister, or the president, or the speaker of the house were invited – "for a fee".[25] According to Lichtman, big businesses like the Safra Bank generally had the "prime minister, the director of the secret service, and the head of police on their payroll and made them members of the board of directors. It was good for business."[26]

Rabbi Lichtman dealt with all the marriages and divorces in the community and often consulted his wife on relationships. One of Rabbi Lichtman's major humanitarian contributions to the community was his relentless pursuit of helping European Jewish refugees during the Second World War. His son Joseph recalls the house always being full of refugees, first those who had fled Nazi persecution, then those from Syria. The rabbi always had food and a place to sleep for any refugee passing through Beirut. His greatest mark on the community, however, was of a religious and literary nature. In Beirut, Lichtman began his six-volume work, examining the commentary on the *Shulchan Aruch* since Joseph Caro,[27] four volumes of which were published during his time in Lebanon.

Lichtman was ready to retire at the age of 69 and decided that he wanted to return to Israel and join his family there. His Palestinian passport had long expired, so he contacted the Interior Minister Eddé. They exchanged polite phrases and then Rabbi Lichtman said : "As the religious head of the community I would like to take part in an international religious symposium." Eddé replied: "Of course, for religious purposes even to Israel." Then Rabbi Lichtman said that he would never place Lebanon in that position. But Eddé continued: "Now rabbi, we need to plan for your departure to Israel in such a way that no damage will be done to us, the government and the Jewish community." They planned it in such a way that Rabbi Lichtman went to Istanbul, while all his luggage went in a container to Cyprus and then to Haifa.

He joined his family in Jerusalem and devoted his retirement to the last two volumes of *Bnai Zion, Beur Rahav al Shulkhan Arukh Orakh Khayim*. He died only three years later, at the age of 72.

The new Chief Rabbi

The community Rabbi Lichtman left behind still boasted eight synagogues in Beirut – the grand synagogue of Magen Avraham, and seven smaller houses of worship. The community was still prosperous and active, especially during the Chehabist regime. When Lichtman left, the community was faced with a grave problem – finding a new chief rabbi. The post as it was "advertised" required French but not Arabic language skills. It would pay 1,400 salary, plus provide for an apartment in the city and another in the mountains. The chief rabbi would also receive presents on the occasion of marriages and *briths* as was customary in the Middle East, which would essentially double his salary. Dr Attie voiced requests for help to a number of personalities in the World Jewish community. His contact, Joe Golan, approached Dr A Steinberg of the World Jewish Congress in London, hoping that he could suggest a suitable rabbi for this post. Attie himself also planned on travelling to London to discuss this subject with Chief Rabbi Brodie.[28]

The search for a chief rabbi to keep the community spiritually together had become particularly urgent since twelve Jewish girls had become involved with Christian and Muslim men, causing commotion in the community. The rabbi would thus have to play a particularly active role with the youth. At this time facilities for the youth included a youth center which offered athletics. It also boasted a lecture hall where there was a phonograph, classical music, and a television. Dr Attie requested help in this domain as well. He requested books, classical and Jewish music records but no Israeli songs, and financial assistance.

Lichtman was finally succeeded by Chaoud Chreim in 1960. Rabbi Chreim was from Halab, born in 1914 and married in 1940. He had six children: Moshe-Nissim, Shlomo, David, Celly, Chouly and Rosy. He served the community until 1977 as Lebanon's last chief rabbi. At the same time he was also the president of the rabbinic tribunal, was a member of the synagogue commission, the *Bikur Holim* and the *Mattan Basseter*, and was involved in the Hebrew teaching at the *Talmud Torah*.[29]

The rabbi's son Shlomo remembers that during this period the relationship between the Jewish community and the *Kata'ib* continued to flourish.

The earlier integration of the youth movements meant that from 1965 onwards the Jewish youth, along with Maronite youngsters, started training with weapons, including attending a summer camp which was specifically set up for this purpose. Wadi Abu Jamil continued to support the *Kata'ib* in elections and to turn to *Kata'ib* deputies as well as Sheikh Pierre himself when they needed something. There was a growing ideological affinity in a society in which the sectarian divide was becoming increasingly pronounced.[30]

On 4 October 1966 the Michkan Moche synagogue was inaugurated. Speeches on this occasion were given by president Attie, Chief Rabbi Chreim and Selim Eliahu Zeitoune, on behalf of the Zeitoune family. The synagogue was established by Malake Zeitoune who wanted to replace the *midrash Tikun Hassot* founded by Mrad Zeitoune and his son Hakham Eliyahu. Hakham Eliahu had always wanted to found a yeshiva but circumstances never permitted it. Chief Rabbi Chreim expressed his appreciation to Mme Zeitoune for the family's religious and humanitarian contributions to the community. The synagogue committee, which had endeavoured to realize this project, included Eliyahu Youssef Levy, Salim Mrad Zeitoune, Moise Chehade Zeitoune, Salim Mikhael Skaba and Hay Mrad Zeitoune, as well as the already mentioned Selim Eliahu Zeitoune.[31]

The religious life of the community continued unencumbered by the political situation. There was no great difference between religious and non-religious Jews. Everyone went to a synagogue, most to Magen Avraham. Some people were more observant and some less. "There was not this big gap the way it exists today between religious and non-religious Jews. We all went to the same synagogues and the same schools. The Jews who were originally from Halab learned more than the Beirutis, but they were not more observant."[32]

A Jewish spy

The dormant issue of questionable loyalties came to full force with the case of Shula Kishek Cohen. She was the only Jew residing in Lebanon who was convicted and sentenced for spying for Israel. Her story embodies personal tragedy and courage while also revealing some of the underlying currents within the Jewish community and Lebanese society.

Shula Kishek Cohen was not of Lebanese origin. She had come to Lebanon from South America via Palestine at the age of 16 through marriage to a much older Lebanese Jew in 1936. She and her husband had a large home next to the synagogue, and once she learned enough Arabic to communicate, she became active at the *Alliance* school. "It was difficult to make friends and I had to do what my mother-in-law or sister-in-law wanted – until I started teaching. That was after my fourth baby."[33] She taught Hebrew, but took care not to be too Zionist. She also started taking care of the paperwork between the Jewish community and the Lebanese government.

> Little by little I got government contacts because we needed permits for the school and because somebody had to go. I was young and did not think too much, so I offered to go. I was not afraid. It was a little adventure. I went to the Prime Minister and he sympathized with me. Later he invited me home and I became good friends with his youngest daughter. From then onwards every Jew with a problem came to me.[34]

The Prime Minister Riad as-Sulh introduced her to other government officials. At an official Christmas party in 1947 she overhead Lebanese officers discussing military plans against Israel. "I heard them planning actions against Israel, and I thought I was going to die. I started shivering and trembling and the prime minister saw me and sent me home."[35] As she never felt particularly Lebanese, her loyalty to Judaism motivated her to pass on the information to the *Haganah*. The borders were already closed, and she knew no one in Israel. But then she kept on imagining how many were going to die if the operation went ahead.

> I had been a girl guide and had learned to write in invisible ink, but I wasn't sure I remembered. I sent my children to the garden. I sent the servants out. I prepared the liquid and everything was fine. I wrote a letter in English with real ink and in between the lines I wrote the information in invisible ink. I finished it and addressed it to Jerusalem. I went to South Lebanon where my husband was on business. He was upset that I showed up – it was not acceptable to show up at your husband's business. I cried and told him a story about a cousin in Jerusalem. He said: "You're lucky there's a Druze here who's going, he'll take it." He was friendly with some *Haganah* soldiers and passed it on. The next day I got the answer. They sent me a letter asking me to do something for them. I was invited to Metullah and the work began seriously.[36]

A working relationship developed. Shula Kishek Cohen started nurturing her government contacts. Her comings and goings caused the community to assume she was having a string of affairs – after all she was married to a much older man! She conveyed intelligence to Israel until 1961 when she was caught. " I was caught without evidence. I was tortured and my husband was forced to pay bribes. They searched my home, but did not find anything." Many of the Lebanese officers she had known quite well, left for Europe when she was caught, fearing that she might implicate them. She received a life sentence and was tortured, but did not reveal anything. At the time of imprisonment she had seven children, all of which were being shunned by the community in an attempt to dissociate itself. But Cohen recalls the friendly gestures by her non-Jewish friends: "The officers from the jail tried to help my family. They helped me more than my husband's relatives. . . . Pierre Gemayel used to come and visit me." Her sentence was reduced and in the run-up to her release the Syrians offered a lot of money for the seizure of Shula Kishek Cohen once she had been set free. Convinced that she was related to Israeli spy Eli Cohen, who had been executed in Syria in 1967, they wanted to hang her as well. In the face of this threat, the Lebanese authorities decided to release her three months early. They covertly transported her across the Lebanese-Israeli border at Rosh Hanikra, and she has lived in Israel ever since.

The Six-Day War and Beyond

On the eve of the Six-Day War the Sofer family knew there was going to be trouble. Nathan Sofer remembers his father and mother leaving for Paris on 15 May. There was tension along the Syrian-Israeli border. "Nobody wanted war, but they all were pushed by their speeches and could not go back. And then the Straits of Tiran were closed, providing the famous *casus belli*."[37] His father had left before that. He had got plane tickets without telling his wife. On the day of departure he got up in the morning, told her to pack their belongings, and that they were going to France. Unlike the Sofers who left before the war, most Lebanese Jews did not leave until the Palestinian presence became a problem two years later.

When the Six-Day War broke out in June 1967, Lebanon's president Charles Helou took great care not to entangle the Lebanese army in the fighting, and not to allow the other Arab armies to utilize Lebanese territory in their war efforts.[38] As Shlomo Levitan recalled:

> In 1967 there was some tension. There were some demonstrations. One was next to Wadi Abu Jamil. The army came and stayed for a couple of days. But the Muslims understood very quickly and stopped. Proper protection came from the *Kata'ib*. The Christians were very good. They understood that if the Israelis lost the war, the Muslims would kill them after they had finished with us.[39]

The war itself had almost been a non-event. However, Lebanon did express formal solidarity with the Arab side and it has been claimed that had the war lasted any longer, it would not have been spared from getting involved.[40]

Despite Lebanon's non-involvement, Lebanon and Lebanese Jewry were affected irreversibly. The war, more than anything, politicized the Palestinians in Lebanon,[41] increasing both the Palestinian refugee popu-

·lation and guerrilla activity.[42] If before they could have been regarded as a more or less settled community, they were now a revolutionary movement, a community in transition, a people at the center of Arab support to regain their country. Commando operations, which had been launched from Lebanon and Jordan into Israel since 1965 became a regular feature after the war. They resulted in an Israeli reprisal policy aimed at "convincing" Lebanese authorities that they should prevent the commandos from operating out of their territory.[43] However, the Israelis were not alone in having to counter the new militarization of the Palestinians: Lebanese forces and Palestinians clashed increasingly over the issue of political and military freedom, which threatened the fragile Lebanese system. In search for stability, which the authorities failed to provide, each Lebanese sectarian community started arming itself and looking for an outside protector.[44]

The Jewish community in 1967 was estimated at between 5,000[45] and 6,000.[46] During the Six-Day War, in anticipation of trouble from Arab nationalists or Palestinians, the Jewish community was once again protected by the *Kata'ib*.

> They used to send us people to take care of us, as we didn't have arms. We were all afraid that the Palestinians would make trouble. So they came to us and used to stay for the night. During the day there was no problem, but during the night . . . a hundred of the *Kata'ib* came all armed and they guarded us for two or three weeks. . . . The same happened in 1973.[47]

After the Six-Day War only 3,000 Jews remained.[48] Until the 1967 Arab-Israeli War, the Jewish community maintained a fairly high profile. The prime minister and several members of parliament continued to visit the synagogue. There were still a few officers in the army and the security services. In 1967 they were advised to resign, as "the government said that it could not deal with mounting Arab and Palestinian pressure".[49] In 1968, 150 Jews were still living in Saida. There were still two Jewish banks in Lebanon at that time: the Safra Bank and the Zilkha Bank which had changed its name to *Societé Bancaire du Liban*. Some limitations were put on non-Lebanese Jews. They now needed to get work permits, and this led to emigration of those few Syrian Jews who were still residing in Beirut.[50]

The general security situation started to decline rapidly. The Beirut raid of December 1968 was as characteristic of the decline of Israel's basic security as it was of the destabilization of Lebanon. On 28 December 1968 eight Israeli helicopters attacked Beirut airport, destroying thirteen civilian aircraft, in retaliation for an attack by two Arabs on an El Al plane at Athens airport two days earlier.[51] The Popular Front for the Liberation of Palestine (PFLP) had claimed responsibility for the attack. But since the

PFLP had been operating openly in Lebanon from 1967 onwards, with the knowledge and acquiescence of the Lebanese government, Israeli policy makers decided to strike against Lebanon. At the United Nations Security Council meeting following the Beirut raid, Israel charged Lebanon with "assisting and abetting acts of warfare, violence, and terror by irregular forces and organizations against Israel",[52] referring to actions which Lebanese Prime Minister Yafi had described as "legal and sacred".[53] Rather than getting the Lebanese authorities to clamp down on the Palestinians, the events surrounding the Beirut raid only showed up the inability of the Lebanese to counteract the growing Palestinian influence and the ineffectiveness of Israeli retaliatory policy in the Lebanese arena. A mere three days after the raid, the PFLP bombarded the northern Israeli town of Kiryat Shmonah as an act of counter-retaliation, killing two Israeli civilians.

The initial clashes between the Palestinian resistance and the Lebanese army attempting to impose its authority took place in 1966. But it was not until 1969 that clashes between the Lebanese population and Palestinian commandos occurred. In defiance of a government ban a demonstration in support of Palestinian guerrillas killed in battle was staged on 23 April 1969. Violent clashes between the security forces and pro-commando marchers in Beirut, Saida and in the Beqaa ensued. A state of emergency was declared and a curfew imposed.[54] This was only one of the incidents, which provided a glimpse of what was to come: the collapse of Lebanon under weight of the Arab-Israeli conflict into 15 years of sectarian warfare.

The Cairo Agreement: The Road to Disintegration

Violent clashes erupted in 1969 between the Lebanese army and Palestinian fighters while Prime Minister Karami argued that Palestinian commando activity on Lebanese territory could easily be made compatible with the sovereignty and security of the country by introducing what he called *tausiq* (co-ordination) between the Lebanese army and Palestinian Armed Struggle Command (PASC).[55] The Maronites outrightly opposed this idea, upholding their view that the best defence would be to curb Palestinian activity so as not to give Israel a reason for attacking. Pressure from Lebanon's Arab neighbours, however, left no room to manoeuvre and finally resulted in the Cairo Agreement, which most Lebanese Christians saw as the betrayal of Lebanese sovereignty.[56]

On 3 November 1969 the Cairo Agreement, negotiated by Chief of Staff General Emile Boustani,[57] formalized the Palestinian military presence in Lebanon under pressure from Syria, Saudi Arabia, Jordan and

1 Chief Rabbi Shabtai Bahbut, 1920–1950. (Courtesy of the Ben Zvi Institute)

2 Selim Zeitoune in traditional Druze dress. (Courtesy of the Ben Zvi Institute)

3 Rabbi Benzion Lichtman leading a Maccabi parade through Beirut, 1947. (Courtesy of Joseph Lichtman)

4 Joseph Attie, Sami Sulh, Rabbi Benzion Lichtman and Habib Abi Chahla, 1946/7. (Courtesy of Joseph Lichtman)

5 Nino Behar, Joseph Attie, Pierre Gemayel, Rabbi Benzion Lichtman, Yacob Safra, Rabbi Obersi, Isaac Sutton and Murad Chayo. (Courtesy of Joseph Lichtman)

6 The Community Council and Chief Rabbi Benzion Lichtman and his wife. (Courtesy of Joseph Lichtman)

7 Traditional commemorative dinner, 1946/7.

8 Wedding at Magen Avraham, 1947. (Courtesy of Salomon Sfinzi and Camille Cohen Kishek)

9 Wedding in Bhamdoun synagogue, 1950s. (Courtesy of Joseph Mizrahi)

10 Public lecture at Magen Avraham, 1951.

11 Wadi Abu Jamil, 1955. (Courtesy of Salomon Sfinzi and Camille Cohen Kishek)

12 Summer in the mountains. Bhamdoun 1964/5. (Courtesy of Salomon Sfinzi and Camille Cohen Kishek)

13 A Bar Mitzva in the Spanish Synagogue in Wadi Abu Jamil, 1967. (Courtesy of Salomon Sfinzi and Camille Cohen Kishek)

14 Magen Avraham, Summer 1995.

15 The Jewish Cemetery, Summer 1995.

16 View of the gallery of Magen Avraham, Summer 1995.

17 The main entrance to Magen Avraham, Summer 1995.

18 Inside Magen Avraham, before the rubble of the war was cleared, Summer 1995.

19 Inside Magen Avraham, 1996. (Courtesy of the Beirut Jewish Community Council)

Egypt. Nasser, as the champion of the Palestinian cause, saw the Cairo Agreement as one more act to ensure Egypt's hold over the Palestinians and, more importantly, as an act that would take away attention from his own defeat in 1967.[58] Instead, he would be seen as solving the problem and he would gain an additional base from which to attack Israel. Neutral Lebanon had been effectively transformed into a confrontation state with the support of its Arab neighbours. For instance, Jordan saw the Palestinianization of Lebanon as a way to take pressure off its own situation in which the Palestinian population was threatening the Jordanian monarchy with a "state within a state".

The Cairo Agreement provided the Palestine Liberation Organization (PLO), as an umbrella organization, with the legitimate means to attack Israel from Lebanon with complete freedom of movement while it assured the Lebanese that their integrity and sovereignty would not be jeopardized. It further legitimized the presence of command centers for the PASC inside the camps which were to cooperate with the local authorities and guarantee good relations. These centers would later handle arrangements for the carrying and regulating of arms within the camps, taking into account both Lebanese security and the interests of the Palestinian revolutionaries.[59] It was agreed to facilitate operations by the commandos through assisting access to the border, mutual cooperation between the PASC and the Lebanese army, and appointing PASC representatives to the Lebanese High Command.

Many of the existing problems were exacerbated by the Cairo Agreement, and it served as a catalyst to the disintegration of Lebanon and foreign intervention. Most Maronites and Jews saw the agreement as signalling capitulation to Palestinian pressures, made effective by the support of Arab states.[60] They became more and more suspicious of other Lebanese, especially those who were sympathizing with the Palestinian cause. Mutual distrust resulted in all Lebanese political and confessional groups – bar the Jews – establishing their own paramilitaries for protection. Lebanon's Jews, once again, came under the protection of the *Kata'ib*.

The open access to Israel's border allowed for more successful Palestinian attacks and South Lebanon increasingly became a target of Israeli punitive raids.[61] By March 1970, Israeli raids on those parts of South Lebanon from which the commandos were operating were beginning to lend substance to the misgivings voiced by most Christians. Hope for change was placed in the election of a new Lebanese president, Suleiman Franjieh, who was expected to take similar measures as Jordan had against the Palestinians,[62] meaning a military clampdown. By that time, more than 240,000 Palestinians were living in Lebanon in 1970, growing by another 100,000 expelled from Jordan as a result of Black

September. The Lebanese Jewish perception of events was captured by journalist Yaakov Gal, telling the story of Shaul Fayena:

> With the arrival of the autumn of 1970, the wheel of success began slowly to reverse. Shaul F., son of one of the Jewish families in Wadi Abu Jamil and pupil at the Talmud Torah . . . remembers those days well. That was the month which would later be called Black September. Palestinian terrorists escaped from Jordan, where Hussein's soldiers were massacring them. Thousands of them arrived in Beirut and settled in the city. The refugee camps were too small to hold the thousands of "guests" and so the terrorists slowly started to take control of every possible building in the city. The fact that precisely in the "Wadi" there were many empty homes of Jews, who had immigrated to Israel, turned the Jewish neighbourhood into a desirable destination for Palestinians. They started to take control of the dwellings opposite the Jewish quarter. Relations with their Jewish neighbours were cool but not hostile. The only troubles were caused by Palestinian children who frequently threw stones at worshippers on their way to the synagogue or simply quarrelled with the Jewish children. The adults were more restrained, but the children found expression for all the hate they were brought up with by plotting against Jewish children.[63]

Black September had been the turning point for Jordanian-Palestinian relations with a clear Jordanian victory. It was also a turning point for Lebanon. The Lebanese army was no longer united when acting against the Palestinians once the Palestinians had become a symbol of the Muslim Lebanese aspirations to ascend politically and socially to the level of the Christians who were commanding them in every sense of the word. The struggle had begun.

In December 1969 community president Attie published an article in the *Toronto Telegram* which was a response to the editor Reuben Slonim's articles on the latter's visit to the Middle East. Attie in his article described Lebanon's Jews as "loyal to the Lebanon where we live peacefully, with our fellow citizens, enjoying all rights and privileges with no discrimination whatsoever against us".

> At no time had we any concern about the faith of the Lebanese soldiers who guard our synagogue, many of whom are Muslims. We feel exactly the same safety with Muslim and Christian military and police forces.
>
> I would like to confirm that Jewish businessmen are free to undertake any commercial activity without having to go into any partnership with a non-Jew. Mr Slonim is perfectly right in reporting that I am not pessimistic about the community so long as there is a democratic republic in Lebanon.[64]

In the 1960s the community began to dwindle. By 1969 there were fewer than 2,500 Jews, almost all in Beirut.[65] Some sources claim that by 1970 the community had even decreased to 1,000.[66] Confessionalism in the country had started to erode to a considerable extent, owing to inter-marriage between members of different religions and sects, making increasing use of the civil marriage facilities provided by neighbouring countries such as Turkey or Cyprus. Strong personal and family friend-ships were elevated above sectarian differences, and secular education as well as common social, business and cultural associations of various kinds[67] reflected a degree of integration when Lebanon was truly a "Switzerland in the Middle East".

Yet despite these social developments which seemed to bridge communal differences, Lebanon's fragile political system was unable to stand up to the widening gaps between the wealthy and the poor, especially if the poor were also those with the least political and social power – the Shi'a Muslims. In addition, the population explosion of the Palestinian refugee community after their expulsion from Jordan increased not only the poverty belt around Beirut but also revived the fear among many Christians that they were becoming a minority, and thus started to reverse the integrative trend. The PLO's disregard for its host country's problems by creating a "state-within-a-state" contributed to the de-legitimization of the Lebanese government. And finally, Syrian and Israeli concerns over the lack of stability and control threatening their own security led to the political vacuum left by warring Lebanese factions being filled by foreign powers.

In 1970 Suleiman Franjieh was elected president of Lebanon. Franjieh was a traditional leader, a *za'im* from Zghorta in northern Lebanon. He saw himself as an Arab, but nevertheless a Christian, and viewed Lebanon as part of the Arab World but with a special role to play. His family's friendship with Syrian President Hafez al-Asad's family underlined his view of Lebanon's closeness to Syria. He was elected as a candidate acceptable to both the Christian and Muslim communities – a compro-mise candidate who was not chosen on the basis of strong leadership, but the lack of offence he caused.

Franjieh represented Lebanon's traditional political culture. About two thirds of the seats in his parliament were held by independents, nota-bles, and *zu'ama'*. In pre-war Lebanon the *zu'ama'* were the most important intermediaries between individuals and the state. Ideology oriented parties such as the SSNP, *Ba'th* or the Communist Party did not receive much support.

In the absence of real political parties with national followings among the masses, political life in the Lebanese Republic became the preserve of shifting alliances among politicians who formed parliamentary or extra-parliamentary fronts or blocs. In each constituency, candidates for elections belonging to different religious groups formed rival lists, political alliances were normally temporary, reflecting interests of the moment among the politicians concerned. In parliament and the government, the discipline of the blocs and fronts was loose, and politicians changed sides whenever it suited them. The electorate was only remembered at election time. This naturally led to a high degree of political alienation of people from the government, and impeded the development of national allegiance to the state.[68]

Franjieh's presidency started smoothly, mainly because of the cooperation of his Prime Minister Saeb Salaam. However, as time went on, he found it increasingly difficult to get his Muslim partners to cooperate in forming cabinets and maintaining a political majority. The repercussions of his slow loss of control were twofold: First, it led to increased support of single-community parties, and second, to a further decline in the security situation. Politically this meant increased support for the *Kata'ib* from both Maronites and Jews, mirroring that community's fundamental orientations.[69] The *Kata'ib*'s ideology was protectionist in the sense that it aimed at preserving Lebanon from the forces of disintegration. During this period in history the party did not have a structured ideology, but "during every event, in every crisis, the *Kata'ib* was there . . . ; against unionist projects, against our neighbours' schemes and intrigues; against the 'Fertile Crescent' and 'Greater Syria' projects; and against all projects of union or federation".[70] In every event and crisis, the party was also there for Lebanon's Jews.

Lebanon's Jews, for obvious reasons, sympathized with the *Kata'ib*, although few formally joined the party. They did, however, lend their full electoral support to the party's candidates. Since Lebanon's Jews voted as a block in Beirut's first electoral district, they were courted by many parties. In the 1968 parliamentary elections, 4,329 Jewish voters were registered.[71] In 1969 Jews made up two per cent of the *Kata'ib* membership.[72] In 1970 the *Kata'ib* had 70,000 members, 82 per cent of whom were Maronite.[73]

The decline in security was particularly crucial for the Jewish community. In December 1970 a bomb exploded in the Selim Tarrab school.[74] This was the first such incident since the turbulent time of 1947/8. It was seen as such a departure from the co-existence between the Jews and the other communities that the Minister of Interior Kamal Jumblatt publicly apologised. Yet this bomb was a sign for what was to come as the security situation in the country deteriorated, the government of Suleiman Franjieh increasingly lost its credibility, and inter-communal tension rose.

Changes were becoming evident in the community. The *Alliance* was still open in 1970, but the numerous synagogues that had flourished had been closed. Only Magen Avraham remained. The year 1970 also signalled the end to the yearly pilgrimages to Saida to the tomb of Ben

Abisamak and the mausoleum of Zebulon.[75] On 6 September 1971 the community's secretary Albert Elia was kidnapped as he left his home. Initially, it had been suggested that he had been abducted by Palestinians. Later, however, it was reported that Elia had been taken to Syria.[76] Syrian involvement cannot be dismissed, especially since it was Elia who had gone to investigate the deteriorating position of Syrian Jews earlier that year,[77] a situation the Syrian regime did not wish to highlight. His fate remains unknown to the present day.

In 1972, it was time for the next parliamentary elections. They have been described as the freest and cleanest in Lebanese history, despite discreet Syrian intervention.[78] Traditional patronage flourished again. Franjieh and Prime Minister Salaam decided to smash the *deuxième bureau*, which had become too independent. This, however, opened the floodgates to an unprecedented militarization of Lebanese political groups and factions, beyond the control of the state. The Palestinian National Movement as well as the Christian resistance and Shi'a Imam Musa al-Sadr's *Amal* militia grew in this environment.[79]

In many ways these parliamentary elections were another turning point in Lebanese foreign and domestic politics. They signified the replacement of Cairo with Damascus as the external center of allegiance for Lebanese Muslims. Damascus acquired virtual veto power over major decisions concerning Lebanon's domestic and foreign policy: it now became customary for Lebanese politicians to go to Damascus.[80]

Since the beginning of the seventies and after its defeat in Jordan the PLO had transferred its headquarters to Beirut. Lebanon became, by the mid-seventies, the main operational basis for the Palestinian quasi-state, with its bureaucracy, armed forces, institutions and activities. It is estimated that by 1981, the Palestinian economy generated more than 15 per cent of the gross domestic product in the Lebanese territory.[81]

At the same time, during 1971–2, Lebanon was faced with the establishment of the PLO on its territory. Up to September 1970 the guerrilla movement had been based in Jordan, which shared the longest border with Israel. From there the PLO had pursued a policy of eroding the strength and will of Israel by using guerrilla operations to show up Israeli failure to maintain effective control and provide protection within the country.[82] Israel, in return, had a policy of retaliation not only disproportionate to the original attack, but also aimed at punishing the country hosting the guerrillas. The combination of attracting unwelcome Israeli military strikes against Jordan and the fear of losing control of Jordan to the Palestinians who had set up a "state-within-a-state", shaped the decision of the Jordanian military and political elites to stop the erosion of their state's authority by force. Taking advantage of the PLO's mistakes and provocations, the Jordanians precipitated a confrontation with the

Palestinian organization and drove it out of Jordan.[83] During what is known as Black September, the Jordanian army attacked refugee camps, forcing those who were lucky enough to escape, over the border into Lebanon. Lebanon, now was the only state left that shared a border with Israel and had insufficient means to control the PLO.

Imposing control over Palestinian actions in Lebanon was not an easy task for the Lebanese government. The Palestinians received much support from Lebanese Muslims and this, in return, caused disunity within the political elite. Nevertheless, in June 1972, a Commando-Lebanese Accord was drawn up. It temporarily suspended attacks on Israel to spare Lebanon from reprisals. Some Palestinian groups, however, did not feel bound by that accord. Commando operations against Israel continued, as did Israeli strikes against Lebanon. On September 16, Israel launched a major ground and air attack against 16 Arab villages, destroying 150 houses and killing 35 Palestinians, 18 Lebanese soldiers and 35 Lebanese civilians.[84] Despite the high casualties, Israel saw such operations as necessary. Moreover, this action was condoned by the United States. Secretary of State William Roger endorsed Israel's contention that priority should be given to combating the current wave of "Arab terrorism" and expressed no reproach for Israeli attacks on Palestinian bases in Lebanon.[85]

The Lebanese government responded by ordering the commandos to leave all Lebanese villages, confining them to the refugee camps and only allowing them to carry weapons in those camps. The Palestinians acceded; but the Israelis were not satisfied. On October 15, the IDF spokesman announced Israel's new policy: "We are no longer waiting for them to hit first. This is the operative phase of our pledge to hit the terrorists wherever they are and they are in Lebanon."[86] Israeli President Chaim Herzog elaborated on this statement, saying: "We are not engaged in reprisal, but in a war against terrorism. The very presence of terrorists in the area between the border and the Litani River is a provocation."[87]

In spring 1973 the situation had not changed much. The Lebanese army was trying to restrain the Palestinians without any tangible results. In April, Israel staged raids on Palestinian targets in Saida and Beirut.[88] An Israeli commando unit landed in Beirut and killed three PLO leaders in the Verdun quarter. Domestic and external developments were converging into a crisis that Franjieh and the groups he represented were incapable of coping with. Prime Minister Salaam had resigned over the Israeli raid on Beirut. He had asked the Commanding Officer Iskander Ghanim to step down, but when this move was not endorsed by President Franjieh, he resigned himself.[89] His resignation brought forth another political crisis, sparking clashes between the Lebanese army and the Palestinians. Heavy fighting ensued with the Palestinians firing rockets at

Beirut airport and the Lebanese Air Force bombing Burj al-Barajne.[90] Palestinians and the leftist-Arabist Lebanese National Movement accused the Lebanese security forces of complicity.[91] The subsequent outburst of PLO violence in Beirut led to a direct Lebanese-Palestinian confrontation. Syria then closed its border as a threat to Lebanon, openly denouncing what it described as Lebanese complicity in a foreign inspired plot to complete liquidation of the Palestinian commando movement.[92] The message was clear: Lebanon had to come to an understanding with the Palestinians.

This understanding came in the form of the Melkart Agreement. The Agreement was concluded on 17 May 1973. It reaffirmed Lebanon's support for the Palestinian cause, but banned commando presence and weapons from the camps. Further, all commando operations from Lebanese territory were suspended according to the decisions of the Joint Arab Defence Council. Lebanon's sovereignty was to be respected. Additional aspirations were to re-establish the atmosphere before the clashes, the reduction of suspicion and the cancellation of the emergency situation.[93]

Lebanon's political crisis, however, was not solved. The influence of political and militant Islam was growing throughout the Arab world, and with it grew the assertiveness of Lebanese Muslims. Franjieh was no longer seen as the candidate of compromise. Shi'a deputy Mohsin Sulim described him as follows: "Suleiman Franjieh is an extremely nice person, but not a great intellect. He has chosen assistants of the same cast and surrounded himself with sons of old families. In doing so he is paralysing Lebanon for these families have not the slightest interest in progress."[94]

The Middle East oil revolution further added to social and economic tensions in Lebanon. Socio-economic gaps were widening with the influx of oil revenues. Soaring prices, political and administrative corruption, labour demands, student unrest and protests, and the growing political demands of the Shi'a community contributed to the disintegration of society. Governmental authority was challenged not only by domestic constituencies demanding a reallocation of power but also by Israel's raids on the South and Syria's renewed claim to Lebanon. As time went on, the Maronites and Jews increasingly perceived the events of the 1970s as moving against their interests.[95] The clashes had convinced the Lebanese Christians more than ever that Lebanon would not regain its sovereignty until all Palestinians left. The country, in which the Jews had felt perfectly at ease, was coming apart at the seams. From 1973 onwards, led by the *Kata'ib*, President Franjieh, and former president Chamoun, the Christian community prepared for its own show-down with the Palestinians.[96]

In October 1973 another war between Israel and its Arab neighbours broke out. Once again, Lebanon managed to remain uninvolved. In the wake of the war, Lebanese Christians advocated settlement with Israel. Radicals among the Lebanese Muslims denounced this as a "surrender plan",[97] highlighting inter-communal tensions. The seeds of mutual suspicion sown earlier were beginning to grow.

In the meantime, Beirut's Jews had learned to live with their new Palestinian neighbours. The proximity of the Palestinian refugees did not make the Yom Kippur War an easy time. For many Jews it meant days of fear and prayer, staying glued to the radio. While their Maronite friends openly displayed joy over Israel's victory, Lebanon's Jews mostly just felt relieved.

In 1974 hardly a week passed without some villages in South Lebanon being hit by Israeli raids. Between June 1968 and June 1974, the Lebanese army counted more than 30,000 Israeli violations of their national territory.[98] Clashes between Palestinians and Lebanese Christians were also increasing while the political situation was deteriorating rapidly. The Palestinians declared the Melkart Agreement invalid, no longer feeling bound to restraint against Israel or respect of the Lebanese establishment.[99] Not surprisingly Lebanese Jewish emigration was also on the rise.

Jewish emigration was not directly related to discrimination, anti-Semitism or inter-communal hostilities. Rather it was the result of the onset of a subtle economic decline from the presidency of Charles Helou onwards. Stringency in the country's economic life led many Lebanese, predominantly Christians and Jews, to transfer their business interests abroad.[100] Moreover, Jewish emigration should be seen within the context of overall emigration from Lebanon. Between 1959 and 1962, 14,700 Lebanese left in the aftermath of the first civil war. During the period of stability which followed, the number was considerably lower. Between 1963 and 1972 only 5,200 emigrated. The onset of the second civil war essentially meant that everyone who had the means left or sent his family abroad. The number of emigrants between 1975 and 1979 was 53,000, between 1980 and 1983 it was 33,000, and between 1984 and 1987 it was 68,400.[101]

Just as communal priorities changed over time, so did the assumptions and conditions, which gave rise to the 1943 Pact. By 1975 there was little room for a swap between Christians and Muslims regarding the external dimension of the Pact. The 1969 Cairo Agreement and the 1973 Melkart Accord, signed between the Lebanese government and the PLO, following two ministerial crises, exhausted Christian tolerance of Palestinian excesses.[102] Relative deprivation grew and was increasingly articulated in the discourse of "rich Christians" and "poor Muslims".

The Second Civil War

The event, which is generally considered to have triggered the Lebanese civil war, was the inauguration of a Church in 'Ayn al-Rumana attended by Pierre Gemayel. Shots were fired from a passing car into the congregation, killing one of the *Kata'ib* leader's body guards. The attack was traced back to the Palestinian Democratic Front. Later in the day a bus carrying guerrillas of the Palestinian Arab Liberation Front was passing through the same suburb. The bus was fired at by *Kata'ib* militiamen, killing twenty-seven.

Soon every neighborhood and village had its militia. Lebanon was being torn apart by sectarian conflict and foreign intervention becoming what Henry Kissinger in *Years of Upheaval* described as a "prostate body" over which all "factions and forces of the Middle East still chase their eternal dreams and act out their perennial nightmares".[103] The Switzerland of the Middle East had fallen prey to the inability to uphold its neutrality in the face of the sweeping currents of the Arab-Israeli conflict. From 1975 onwards Lebanon became Palestine's surrogate battlefield.

For many Lebanese, the matter appeared self-evident. The resistance organizations were pursuing their struggle on Lebanon's home territory, and the neighbouring Arab countries were in turn brandishing threats and interventions, while the Israeli army was escalating its retaliatory operations in contempt of national sovereignty. Lebanon succumbed to a state of war, the victim of conspiracy; if the country had not deliberately been saddled with the Palestine issue by regimes only too happy to be relieved of it, and perhaps even pleased to see the ruin of Lebanon's prosperity and political equilibrium, it would have had enough resources to deal with the changes within its society.[104]

> Every combatant was convinced he was defending his Lebanon from an outside threat, since the enemy was mentioned only obliquely, the goals presented with all kinds of detours, and explanations reduced to the claim of the "plot." The gunmen poised for ambush were anonymous, murderers remained undiscovered, and kidnapping victims disappeared for good.[105]

The internal dimension of this war pitted Shi'a, Sunnis, Druze and various Lebanese and Palestinian left-wing forces against the Maronites. It was their goal to establish greater political and economic equality and a more Arab identity for Lebanon. However, the "left" was by no means reducible to a uniform political, social, economic or ideological structure. Indeed, it was not easy to delineate or trace the "left" within the Lebanese context, where the situation presented itself as a juxtaposition of forces that were products of very uneven social, economic and regional developments.[106]

While most Lebanese up to the present day tend to shrug off responsibility and cling to the notion of having become the victims of some greater plot, others, such as social scientist Theodor Hanf, have suggested that it was, in fact, the irresponsibility of the Lebanese political class which prepared the ground for disaster. An appalling social policy had raised social tension to breaking point. This was compounded by the regional dimension. "All of them underestimated the external threats, clung to unarmed neutrality in a region bristling with arms, and undermined the already limited powers of the state in perilous time."[107]

The problem underlying the war was one of minority-majority integration. Instead of the political leaders balancing the different communities and creating a basis for a wider Lebanese identity, the communities were mutually suspicious of each other. They did not trust the formal institutions to be powerful or impartial enough to protect their local interests.[108] Thus, sectarian allegiances emerged as the primary affiliation even before the 1975–6 war when the political system was suffering from the strains of national development. Increasing pressure for fairer representation and equitable distribution of wealth and status came to be supported by the various sectarian militias. Invoking the issue of legitimacy or illegitimacy of an entity was one way of declaring this civil war, for the issue was the nature of the state and at the root the "debate" was aimed less at convincing the other party than in silencing it.[109]

The Maronite status quo forces formed the Lebanese Front comprising the *Kata'ib*, Chamoun's NLP, Franjieh's Zghorta party, the Organization of Maronite Monks, as well as more extremist groups such as the Guardians of the Cedars, the *Tanzim*, the Kisrwan Front, and the Zghorta Army of Liberation. The Christians who were united in their hostility to the Palestinians and their defence of "Lebanoness" started training in the mountains with weapons supplied by Israel.[110]

Over 100,000 Palestinians had taken refuge in Lebanon after the 1948 war, a total swollen mainly by natural increase to about 270,000 by the mid 1970s.[111] It was this large number which caused the fear of power-sharing within the Maronite community. If these refugees had been absorbed into the Lebanese system as citizens it would have threatened the uneasy political balance, depriving the Maronites of their dominant position in the government. As it was, their presence had already tipped the military balance numerically against the Christian establishment.

The Palestinians thus reinforced the Maronites' fear of being surrounded by a "Muslim sea", exacerbating the sectarian split. This feeling of vulnerability made the Maronite *Kata'ib* appeal to Israel as the fighting started in 1975. They approached the Israelis not only as common enemies of the PLO but also appealed to Israel as a kindred minority vulnerable to the pressures of the Muslim world.[112] They looked towards Israel as an important factor of equilibrium in the region, one with which they already had a certain affinity.[113]

Israel, at that time, was more than willing to help anybody as it had surplus revenue from the wars of 1967 and 1973 as well as Russian weaponry. To Israeli decision-makers it was cheap and made sense politically to help the Maronites.[114] Israel's response, however, was limited to military aid under the policy of "helping the Maronites to help themselves".[115]

During the war and the following years the Palestinians succeeded in taking control of virtually all of South Lebanon. In order to maintain this control and operational freedom against Israel, the PLO had a vital interest in a weak Maronite government at the worst, and a strong Muslim government at the best. Israel, conversely, had a strong interest in maintaining the status-quo and even strengthening the Maronite position in order to create a friendly, anti-PLO government. In terms of security, this would have meant the extension of Lebanese government control over the South and the disarming of the Palestinians.

Israel was not the only country trying to protect its interests by intervening in the Lebanese civil war. Concerned about the establishment of a military cabinet and the possibility of future military rule in Lebanon, Syria intervened in 1976 in order to restore peace.[116] Syrian intervention, however, made everything worse; all militias started fighting with partition in mind.[117] Moreover, Syrian President Hafez al-Asad's real aims were to preempt an Israeli invasion and to gain control over Lebanon, never having relinquished Syrian territorial claims from the mandate period. By intervening in Lebanon and resolving the crisis, Asad would not only end a situation that threatened Syrian interests but would also demonstrate that Syria was the most effective Arab power in that part of the Middle East.[118] Further, the Syrian military feared that Israel could attack Syria by advancing either through Jordan or Lebanon. In order to create strategic depth and keep Damascus protected, it was necessary for Syria to have control over the Beqaa Valley in east Lebanon. However, Syria's deliberate policies of destabilisation were aimed at preventing a strong Maronite government which could lead to secession and the creation of a pro-Israeli Christian state.[119]

Lebanon thus became an important factor in the Syrian-Israeli deterrence dialogue. Israel felt threatened by the intrusion of the considerable Syrian forces into Lebanon and their deployment in the vicinity of Israel's northern border.[120] According to this logic, both states needed to be in Lebanon, in order to deter the other from advancing. Both states were vying for strategic depth and proxy armies. Syria had been using Palestinian factions such as *as-Saʻiqa* to carry out a war by proxy against Israel. From 1976 onwards, the Israelis set up their own proxy arrangement, with mainly Christian forces in South Lebanon, in order to protect its northern border.

The first two years of the war may be seen as a sequence of conflicts between changing opponents and allies, each of them characterizing one phase of the war. Syrian intervention in 1976 returned the country to a relative normality between 1977 and 1981. A fourth of the population had taken refuge abroad, reducing domestic needs, and thus the war had not yet made a major impact on the national economy.[121] After 1978 the situation became more complex: conflicts ran congruently or overlapped; instead of one war, there were now several.[122] Syrian-Christian confrontation as well as Israeli intervention in the South had become added dimensions. Over the years it became a war of the Christian Lebanese Forces against the Syrians, the Palestinians and the Druze; an Israeli–Palestinian–Syrian conflict; a Christian–Christian battle for control; and a war between the Shiʻa and the Palestinians in the South – all before the Israeli invasion of Lebanon in June 1982. Among the small number of non-combatants were the Jews.

Decline of the community

When the civil war broke out there were between 2,000 and 5,000 Jews in Lebanon.[123] Most of the expensive shops in the fashionable Hamra district were still owned by Jews.[124] One Jewish family had actually been in ʻAyn al-Rumana to visit friends on that fateful Sunday in 1975 when the war began. The change in atmosphere was obvious even to the most unobservant. Vehicles suddenly disappeared from the road and guns and automatic weapons became prominent. When the family returned to their home right on the front line between the Christian quarter and the Palestinian neighbourhoods, the street had become a battlefield between the *Kataʼib* and Palestinian fighters – the Jews caught in the middle.

Community life and economic activity in Wadi Abu Jamil virtually came to a standstill, with the exception of the prayers, which did not cease. Public prayer was moved from Magen Avraham to a less dangerous area in one of the smaller alleys.[125] During the autumn of 1975, in several weeks of extremely violent fighting, Beirut's port and its financial, touristic, and commercial center were destroyed. So, too, was a large part of Wadi Abu Jamil – all being essentially in the same area – at the crossroads between East Beirut and West Beirut.

Wadi Abu Jamil had become a battle field between the pro-status quo mainly Christian forces and the anti-status quo coalition of Sunni, Shi'a, Druze and Palestinian forces early on in the war – as had most interface areas of the city. The schools were closed, and economic activity was severely restricted.[126] Jewish lives were, for the first time, in serious physical danger – not from Palestinian radicalism, Arab nationalism or anti-Semitism, but from an ethnically divided society at war with itself. An estimated 200 Jews were killed in the cross-fire between warring factions in 1975–6.[127]

The first Jewish death in the war occurred in October 1975. The victim was an old man who had been the *shammash* at the "Srour" synagogue and the "El-Man" *Beit HaMidrash*. He had found his place in history as the companion of Joseph Trumpeldor, the hero of Tel Chai. His name was Yousef Salem, but he was better known as Abu Raffoul. He had been a popular figure in Beirut, who loved to laugh and to make children laugh. Charles Mizrahi, in an article published in *La Voix Sepharade*, recalled that Abu Raffoul used to spend the second *seder* with his family every year between 1970 and 1975.

In October 1975 the Jewish quarter bore the calm of an area under siege. It was under the protection of the *Kata'ib*. But that autumn, Muslim Kurds started appearing in the quarter and the Jewish families took up arms. On the last Friday of October 1975, the main street of Wadi Abu Jamil was deserted. No one crossed the road except for the cats. Abu Raffoul, who was a man of habit, rose early and decided to go to the bakery to buy bread. For that he had to cross the besieged road, and thus Yousef Salem "became the first martyr in a war which didn't concern him".[128]

He was shot by a sniper from one of the roofs. His body lay in the street for some time until some Kurds sought to retrieve it. The sniper shot at them as well. Unwilling to risk their own men, the Kurds sent three Jews out to retrieve the body. Among those who had been "volunteered" were Joseph El Man and Isaac Fayena. "With the guns in their backs, the Kurds forced them to cross the Jewish quarter, beneath the gaze of their wives and children, who cried and begged, and to walk to the road where Abu Raffoul lay."[129]

The Kurds promised that if the two Jews did not return alive from their mission that they would eulogize their deed in all Beirut newspapers and even photographed them before their departure.[130] Their trembling family members in the meantime were desperately trying to call the Jewish family living near the location of the sniper. Finally, one young woman got through and soon the Christian gunman knew that there were three Jewish men approaching with a white flag in order to recover the body of Abu Raffoul which still lay in the middle of the road. Isaac Fayena muttered prayers all the way to the body. They collected the body and

carried it to an ambulance, which took it to the morgue until the situation had clamed down.

"In Wadi Abu Jamil they would say that Abu Raffoul didn't want his
friends to be killed for his sake, and above all not Isaac Fayena, who used
to invite him to *kiddush* and to dinner every Friday. And that for Isaac
Fayena, he had intervened from heaven."[131] That evening many of the
remaining Jews left Wadi Abu Jamil amidst the fear that there would not
be a *minyan* for the *kaddish* for Abu Raffoul's funeral. The Fayenas
remained, but not for long. The Syrian intervention in the civil war in
1976 and consequent Syrian control of the city triggered their migration
first to Bhamdoun and later to the home of friends in the vicinity of the
port. Not far from the Holiday Inn where the *Kata'ib* fighters embedded
themselves and were fiercely attacking the Syrians, the Fayenas made the
painful decision to leave Lebanon. Making use of good relations Isaac
Fayena had with Palestinians before the war, he asked one of the comman-
ders for help in getting his family out of the city. After a "donation" and
under cover of darkness the Fayenas left Beirut on a vehicle belonging to
what some would call terrorists.[132]

At the height of the civil war, the Palestinians and Muslims were
advancing and the Jews took shelter in Magen Avraham. Wadi Abu Jamil
had become caught in a fierce battle between the PLO and the *Kata'ib*.
The Christian militias, headed by Bashir Gemayel and Dani Chamoun,
attempted to occupy Wadi Abu Jamil in order to rescue the Jews. The
PLO, however, and its left-wing Muslim allies got there first.[133] Rabbi
Chreim, concerned about the welfare of his community, phoned Prime
Minister Karame and Interior Minister Jumblatt for help. At that point
there still was a Lebanese government and the army had not completely
disintegrated along sectarian lines. Before the government troops arrived
to rescue the community, PLO leader Yasser Arafat took the opportunity
to make a humanitarian gesture. He sent his men with food and water for
the Jews trapped inside the synagogue and ensured that they were not
harmed.[134] It has been claimed that "largely because of Israeli retaliation,
and also motivated by thoughts of gaining political advantage, the
Lebanese left-wing forces supplied the Jews with food and water."[135] But
the further development of this incident proves otherwise. The PLO
placed guards on the premises of the synagogue in order to protect it from
vandals.[136] And then Druze warlord and Minister of Interior Kamal
Jumblatt, one of the leaders of the Lebanese Nationalist Movement, evacuated Chief Rabbi Chreim and his family to Bhamdoun.[137] From
Bhamdoun he travelled to Beirut on a daily basis to tend those members
of the community who had not left.

In 1978, Rabbi Chreim left for Sao Paulo to head the Lebanese Jewish
community in that city. His son, Shlomo, who opted to immigrate to Israel

instead, believes his father's decision to go to Brazil was based on the fact that between 1968 and 1978 many Lebanese Jews had gone to Sao Paulo. "They needed him and he felt that going to them was the right thing to do."[138] Though the main synagogue and two other smaller houses of worship remained open until 1984, the spiritual life of the community declined rapidly. The synagogue in Bhamdoun became inactive in 1975.

As the situation became almost unbearable, most Jews fled to the mountains. They found temporary shelter in the mountains and in the resort of Aley, south of the city. When they returned they found that their homes had been looted. Many of the Jews whose property was destroyed or stolen left the country. About 1,000 who tried to restore their businesses were discouraged by a renewal of hostilities between Muslims and Christians, and they decided to go too.[139] Toufic Yedid Levy opted to leave Lebanon:

> After 1975 there were hardly any people left – about 150. Only the doctors stayed. We had no problem with the government. Personally, during the 1975 War, I had to travel because the square where I lived was an important center. There were bombardments and I had to leave. . . . I left Beirut for two years and went to Milan. I have a niece who lives in Milan. After that I stayed with my nephew in Sao Paulo, in Brazil. My sister lives there as well. I stayed six or seven months with her, but wasn't able to get a residence permit. So I returned here. . . . My house, my work were all in Beirut.[140]

The civil war caused a sizeable segment of the community to emigrate, leaving the community without a rabbi and a *shochet*. A rabbi had to be brought in from Italy or Syria. By the end of the first phase of the civil war in 1976, only some 2,000 Jews were left in the country.[141] By the end of 1976, 4,500 had emigrated to Cyprus, the United States and Western Europe,[142] leaving a very small community of between 400 and 500. It was often difficult to find a *minyan* as the war had taken its toll on the Jewish quarter, which was situated right on the greenline. Most Jews had fled the area and dispersed. The wealthier members of the community had fled to East Beirut or the safety of the mountains. The few remaining Jews who lived in West Beirut were old, poor and sick.

In 1978 a tourist who had met with members of the Beirut community reported that it had become difficult to get a *minyan* on *Shabbat*, with only 60 Jews left in downtown Beirut and another 450 spread throughout the mountains, unwilling to leave their refuge for religious services. The school had been closed, along with most of the other infrastructure in the country such as the banks and post offices. Jewish merchants, who were now more or less unemployed due to the circumstances, stated that they did not believe that "Beirut would ever again be what it was in the past". Every evening the electricity was cut off and only in a few areas on the

Muslim side did life resemble normality.[143] They also reported that two weeks earlier Muslims had watched the Christian quarter being bombed as if it had been a theatre performance. Syria had taken control of Beirut and *as-Sa'iqa* had set up a number of checkpoints.

Wartime responses are generally a good indicator of underlying communal hostilities, as "official" fighting is often abused to settle scores. During the Lebanese civil war many such scores were indeed settled, mainly between Druze and Maronites dating back to the war of 1860 – none with the Jews. Neither during the Arab-Israeli wars, nor the two civil wars, were the Jews victimized for their religious affiliation.

The appearance of Israeli aircraft over the city stopped the shelling of Christian Beirut. But fear continued to pervade with armed men being the only ones on the street. Between the Muslim and the Christian quarter was no-man's land, Wadi Abu Jamil, the greenline, which was haunted by snipers. The prevalent feeling was that the Muslims and their Syrian allies were only waiting for the right moment to eliminate the Christian minority.[144]

In July 1980, journalist Yoel Dar gave an equally depressing description of the community, one which, in many ways, summed up the silent despair of the uninvolved victims within a war-torn country. If imaginable, the situation had deteriorated further.

> Lebanon's once prosperous Jewish community, one of the oldest in the world, has nearly disappeared. Lebanese Jews who have left the country have reported that only a few dozen remain, most of them poor or too old or too sick to move, and who look to Jewish relief organizations to help. All others have left in recent years because of the tense situation and the fear of a renewal of the civil war between Muslims and Christians.[145]

There were only 200 Jews left by 1980 and most were suffering because of the bad economic situation. Lebanon's economy, which had survived above and beyond the first years of conflict, was starting to collapse under the strains of the war. The majority of the Jews had fled to the mountains, leaving only 20 in Beirut for whom Syria permitted a *shochet* to visit Lebanon from Damascus periodically.[146] While Jews were not harmed for their religious affiliation it was reported that four Jews were killed solely for this reason.[147] Yet most Lebanese Jews still preferred to stay in Lebanon.

In an article published in *La Revue du Liban* Dikran Tosbath asked what was left of the once flourishing community in 1980.

> Where are those who organised active community life? Those who voted as a constituency of thousands of voices as one for Joseph Chader? Who is still here from among the Atties, the Bercoffs, the Mizrahis, the Anevis, the

Romanos, the Mograbis, the Albarenes, of the Farhi tribe, of the Dichys, the Heloinis, the Benjamins, the Ben Judas, the Stamboulis, the Sidis, the Liniados, the Delbourgos, and the Grunbergs, the Doubines, the Berakhas, the Danas, the El-Nekaves, the Chayos, the Browns, the Olchaneskis, the Manns, the Kouguells, the Israels, the Doueiks, the Lawis and Levys, the Cohens, the Abrahams, the Elias, the Mandils, the Srours, the Saades, the Hazans, the Matalons, the Saadiyas, the Safras and Totahs (some vague poor cousins?). The Tarrabs, the Hararis, the Telios, the Spigels, some Yedids, some Danas, have not budged.[148]

For Tosbath the community has already become history – a history of names which are slowly escaping Lebanon's memory.

Of those who fled, not everyone went to Israel. And those who did, often left when the time came for their children to go to the army.[149] Lebanese Jewry preferred emigrating to Europe and to the United States where they often settled among other Lebanese expatriates – Muslim and Christian – to making *Aliyah*. With them they took a deep feeling of regret and the memories of a prosperous and uncomplicated life.

6

The Israeli Invasion and Beyond: Renaissance or Decline?

The Israeli invasion of Lebanon in 1982 "discovered" the "lost" community of Lebanon's Jews and raised its profile within Israel and world Jewish organizations. Few had known about the existence of a functioning and thriving community in Lebanon; most had vaguely assumed that Jews living in Arab countries had all left in and around 1948. Moreover, the lack of persecution kept Lebanon's Jews well out of world attention. In 1982 this situation changed as first Israeli soldiers and then Israeli and American Jewish journalists came to talk to Lebanon's "last" Jews. For the small community which like other Lebanese had been living in a war-torn country since 1975, the Israeli invasion came as a mixed blessing. The benefits of the Israeli presence were the newly opened avenues which brought with them relatives now living in Israel, increased mobility, friendships, a boost to Jewish life, and an increase in basic security and living standards. The Israel Defence Forces were hailed as the liberator of Lebanon – an end to war and a return to the *status quo ante bellum*. But as the invasion increasingly failed to achieve its aims hopes for Lebanon and then hopes for Lebanon's Jews began to dwindle. When Israeli forces redeployed in 1984, they left behind shattered dreams – Maronite, Jewish, and Israeli. Above all, however, the invasion of 1982 managed to achieve what decades and even centuries of Lebanese political struggles failed to do: it transformed the apolitical Jewish community who had been friendly with everyone into a combatant – a combatant without arms.

Operation Peace for Galilee

On 6 June 1982 Israel invaded Lebanon. Operation Peace for Galilee's official objective was security. In the broader sense, this included peace with Lebanon as well as the Palestinian issue, which encompassed the future of the Israeli Occupied Territories of the West Bank and Gaza Strip, the Israeli–Syrian deterrence dialogue and Israel's position in the Middle East. Accordingly, the goals of the war can be summarized as: firstly, the elimination of all Palestinian presence and influence from Lebanon; secondly, the creation of a new political order in Lebanon by establishing a Maronite government that would, in effect, be a protectorate of Israel; thirdly, the expulsion of Syrian troops from Lebanon; fourthly, a peace treaty with Lebanon; fifthly, the destruction of Palestinian nationalism in the West Bank and Gaza Strip and, finally, the freeing of Israel from past national traumas such as the 1973 war.[1]

The Israeli aims were the result of Israel's deepened commitment to the Lebanese Christians and the changed position *vis-à-vis* the Syrians. The Syrian role was no longer perceived as convenient to Israeli security interests, and therefore the Syrian military presence needed to be removed. The notion emerged that once Israel acted in Lebanon, but on a wider scale than South Lebanon, it could crush the Palestinians and neutralize the Syrians. It would then place Lebanon in the hands of its Maronite allies and sign a peace treaty. In terms of security, this would establish a more comprehensive security arrangement than the limited version in South Lebanon. In a way it was like substituting a proxy-militia with a proxy-government so that a new order could be created. A blow to Syria could even set in process a domestic disintegration of that state as well.[2] Regarding these broader aims of General Ariel Sharon's "grand plan", it becomes clear that peace for Galilee in fact was not the main objective of the war. Rather, the main and indeed the joint Maronite-Israeli objective of the war, supported by Lebanon's Jews, was attaining a basic change in the politico-strategic situation in Lebanon, requiring the destruction or neutralization of all military elements which might inhibit the election of a Lebanese president who was allied with Israel.[3]

It took six days for the Israeli army to reach Beirut in June 1982, which was then besieged for three months. The Shouf was occupied for a year (until September 1983), and the western Beqaa and the south for three years (until June 1985). The expansion of the war from the initially approved 40 km incursion to the entering of Beirut can be regarded as a manifestation of the change from decades of clandestine aid to the Maronites to a full alliance with them. If dealing a major blow to the PLO as a political force was the *raison d'être* of the entire operation, it would require the occupation of the western part of Lebanon all the way to Beirut.[4] The confrontation with the Syrians was deliberately provoked as part of the implementation of Sharon's "grand plan". The IDF on June 9 attacked Syrian troops and maintained the attack for four days.[5] The rationale for the expansion of the war on this level was that a review of

Israel's security status ordered by Sharon in 1981 had indicated that Syria would probably attack Israel in late 1983 or early 1984.[6] Thus, the expansion was justified on preemptive grounds.

However, the expansion of war aims was not as well thought-out as it seemed. The premises on which the "grand plan" was based, namely, the cooperation of the Maronites and the capabilities of military force, had been grossly overestimated. When Sharon unleashed the war in 1982, his strategic calculations proved correct. However, his erroneous interpretation of the Lebanese situation was to make a military victory a political disaster for both Israel and Lebanon.[7] Indeed, the war mirrored faithfully both Sharon's personality and his worldview. It was his belief that Israel should use military power to change the face of the Middle East, extending its margin of security to offset any possible negative change in the balance of power between Israel and its neighbours in the future.[8]

The last family in Saida

In 1962 the *Alliance* school in Saida closed as the community started to shrink, but it was not until the *shohet* left in 1972 that it became clear that the Jewish presence in Saida dating back a thousand years or more, was coming to an end. Life for the community, of which 3,500 Jews who can still be found on today's electoral roll, was good. It was safe, relations with other Lebanese were friendly, and as the community was small everyone knew everyone else. The religious and spiritual leader was Rabbi Habib, who also carried out the role of *shohet*. The head of the community had been Yosef Politi, who had been a successful textile merchant, owning houses in Saida, Beirut and Bhamdoun as well as orchards and a shop.[9] When he immigrated to Israel he was succeeded by Yosef Levy. Saida's families were very traditional. Shops closed for *Shabbat* and holidays; *kashrut* was observed. But when the civil war started, Beirut's *shochet* left, and kosher meat could only be obtained under difficult circumstances. Passover *matzot* were another problem. They came from Holland via Beirut until the war. Since the fighting broke out, however, the remaining Jews in Saida had become increasingly isolated.

In 1975 only one Jewish family was left in Saida – the family of Yosef and Jamila Levy, with their children Michel, Malka, Itzhak, Golda and Justine, a grandmother and Yosef's brother. Jamila Levy had come to Saida from Beirut, but her family had originally been from Deir al-Qamr. Yosef Levy's family was originally from Hasbaya but had moved to Saida 150 years ago.[10] Yosef Levy worked as a tailor. He made uniforms for the Lebanese army and consequently had good relations with the local and national administration.[11]

In 1975 when the civil war broke out Zaki Levy was finishing his secondary education. He had gone to the Frères Maristes school and had to travel through the troubles to Beirut to the French Embassy in order to take his final exams. "When I came back from Beirut the whole city was on strike and shut down." He then left for France to study pharmacy. He had been studying for two years when his father suddenly died; he had to return and, as the eldest, take charge of the family. In 1980 his uncle also died and Zaki had to work in the family-owned orange groves on the road along the Awali river.[12]

His sister Malka soon married and she and her husband left for Brazil, while the other four siblings continued their education. Yitzhak, at that time, was enrolled in an advanced computer course and his sister Justine was in her first year of a French and Arabic literature degree. Their younger siblings, Michel and Golda were still attending the local Christian high school.

On 5 June 1982 the Israeli Airforce dropped leaflets over the city asking the population of Saida to leave, but the Palestinians prevented everyone from leaving as Zaki Levy distinctly remembers. "From Friday until Monday we stayed in the home. On Wednesday more leaflets were dropped because the IDF was on the verge of entering Saida. I took my mother and aunt and left for Marjaoun. On the road I saw my first Israelis at a roadblock. I went to a soldier and spoke to him in English and told him I was Jewish. After the IDF had entered Saida we returned to our house."[13]

Later, when Israeli troops were claiming the streets of Saida one after the other, they were taken by surprise by a lone woman, shouting in broken Hebrew: "Don't shoot – we're Jewish." The woman was Jamila Levy. The soldiers were surprised to find her and her family.

The family had decided not to leave as people had started looting homes. The Israeli soldiers went through all the streets and started rounding up all males between 18 and 50, ordering them to assemble at the sea shore. Zaki Levy, who did not want to leave his family, went to one of the officers. The soldier ordered him to go to the sea shore along with the rest. So Zaki told him that he was Jewish. The officer was taken aback and asked for proof. So Zaki Levy took the officer back to the family home with the *mezuzzot* and other religious articles. The IDF let the Levy family stay in their home, supplying them with food and water.

When asked about his life in Lebanon as a Jew, eighteen year old Michel Levy, gave the following impression:

My friends include Christians and Muslims, Palestinians and Lebanese. After the Israeli invasion, all of my friends were in shock. But none of them was ever politically minded. Or if they did talk politics, it never affected our relationship. I was never looked on with suspicion. I was never viewed as a Zionist agent. Everybody, of course, knew that I was Jewish, but it never mattered to anybody.[14]

Zaki Levy recalls that relations with Lebanese neighbours were always very good, and there were no political tensions until the Palestinians arrived in 1970. The Syrian intervention in Lebanon in 1976 added to the problems. "Everyone knew how badly Jews were treated in Syria."[15]

The Levys were the last family of the once thriving community in Saida. When the others left because of the civil war, the keys to the shuttered synagogue were put into their hands.[16] The Levys lived in a spacious second-floor flat on the edge of the area in Saida referred to as the *casbah*, located on the seashore across the street from the customs building and above a fish-mongers and barbershop. In fact, the two shops were owned by Palestinians who were good friends of the Levy's.

When *Jerusalem Post* journalists visited the Levy family on a Friday they found the house freshly cleaned for *Shabbat*.

> The tiled floors shone, the flowered chair and sofa covers were crisp and bright. Family portraits loom down from the high walls. The salon has a beamed ceiling and a tiny balcony, which affords a view of the Crusader port. Cracks in the walls indicate the age of the house, but the place is comfortable. The Levys have a large tv set and kerosene heaters. *Mezzuzot* are fixed to every doorpost. And the pride of the salon is the large *hanukkiah*, which Mrs. Levy says was made in Damascus many years ago.[17]

The Levy's reaction to the Israeli invasion is reminiscent of others among Lebanon's Jews. They were pleased to see Jews and happy to receive kosher meat from Israeli soldiers. Jamila Levy also had relatives in Israel who had left Lebanon years earlier and had settled in Holon, a Tel Aviv suburb, which has a sizeable Lebanese community. The Israeli presence enabled Michel Levy to travel to Israel to visit his relatives. When asked whether he would contemplate making *Aliyah*, Michel was not so sure. He did not believe that there was much of a future for himself and his family in Lebanon. But he still needed to finish his last year in school before any decision could be made in any case. Characteristic of the early days of the Israeli invasion of Lebanon was the hope the Levys and the community as a whole placed in the possibility of an Israeli–Lebanese peace.

The *Jerusalem Post* journalists described the Saida synagogue as follows:

> The electric lights on the peeling blue walls are working, as are the old-fashioned long-bladed fans in the domed ceilings. The place has been cleaned

and brightened somewhat, and the IDF Chaplaincy Corps has left some prayer books, *Shabbat* candles and prayer shawls in the cabinet. Mrs. Levy attended the *Tisha B'Av* services, which the army held the previous week. She says she was thrilled to see a *minyan* here again, and reminisced about the happy times here when she was a girl, especially the holidays like *Simhat Torah*, *Hannukka* and *Pessach*. . . . But even a non-observant Jew feels the sadness inherent in an abandoned synagogue of a vanished community.[18]

The synagogue is said to date back to the period of the second temple. It is expansive, its ceiling vaulted, and its floor is made of white marble imported from Italy. The ceiling was decorated with 12 large oil lamps made of silver, and a crystal chandelier. Four study halls, two sanctuaries and a magnificent women's section were also part of the structure. Legend holds that many years ago one of Saida's governors planned to turn the synagogue into a mosque. When he went to the synagogue to discuss his project with the Jews, a poisonous snake suddenly appeared and wrapped itself around the neck of the governor. Only after the governor declared that he was renouncing his plan, did the snake release him. A more recent story tells of an Arab who sought shelter in the synagogue during Operation Peace for Galilee. He broke in through one of the windows. When he returned home at the end of the fighting and proceeded to light a kerosene lamp with a match, his clothes caught fire. He was seriously burned and died.

Former leader of the community Yosef Politi watched the IDF entry into Saida on television from his new home in Israel. One of the pictures shown was of a Torah scroll bearing the name of Yosef ben Menachem Politi – a scroll he had donated to the synagogue 30 years earlier. He recalled that there were a total of 18 scrolls in the Saida synagogue. "Seven scrolls I sent to Israel. Five scrolls were taken by Jewish families to whom the scrolls belonged, two scrolls I sent to the synagogue of the Saida community in Rio de Janeiro. One silver-crowned scroll was sent with a magnificent ark to the community in Sao Paolo. Two scrolls were sent to Brooklyn in the USA. And the last, which remained in Saida, was the Torah scroll found by the IDF soldiers."[19] The dispersion of the scrolls parallels the emigration pattern of the Saida Jews. The removal of the last scroll to Israel signals the conclusion of a long history.

With the IDF withdrawal from Saida, the remaining members of the Levy family also left. Representatives of the Israeli administration had advised the family to leave for fear that they would become victims of "terrorism". The Levys locked their house, shut windows and doors, took a few personal belongings, photographs and mementoes. They had told their neighbors that they were moving to Brazil to join their co-religionists there, but in fact they left their home for Israel, crossing at the Rosh

Hanikra checkpoint. The younger children, Justine, Golda and Michel began their new life on the religious kibbutz of Be'erot Yitzhak, between Lod and Petah Tikva. The eldest Yitzhak and his mother joined relatives on the outskirts of Tel Aviv.

Renaissance in Beirut

The Israeli invasion became the backdrop for numerous very personal stories and encounters, which are recounted here to give an impression of Beirut Jewry in 1982, the atmosphere of renaissance, and a fleeting breath of Jewish life. These accounts encompass all the nostalgia of Lebanese Jewry today, without the bitterness caused by the collapse of Israel's plans. The contacts that were reopened between families in Lebanon and their relatives in Israel, and the rediscoveries of Israeli soldiers with Lebanese roots provide a glimpse of the richness of Lebanese Jewish life.

One such personal encounter with the past was that of Raphael Sutton, who was the young man who had fled Halab in 1947 on the day of his *bar mitzvah*. He had emigrated from Lebanon to Israel in 1948, convinced he would never return to the place which had provided him with a second *bar mitzvah* and refuge from Syrian persecution. In 1982, Rafi Sutton returned to Lebanon as an IDF colonel. It had been 37 years since the *bar mitzvah* when he once again entered the synagogue in Bhamdoun. The town had been captured by the Israelis in July after intense Israeli–Syrian fighting along the Beirut–Damascus highway.

When Sutton first visited the synagogue as an adviser of the IDF civil administration in the area, the town was humming with holidaymakers. After their departure, only 4,000 local residents remained – among them three Jewish families.

> As he entered the synagogue vestibule, Col. Sutton immediately spotted the three plaques, which he remembered from the old days, paying tribute to those who had contributed to the building of the synagogue in 1945. Three beautiful chandeliers were still hanging down from the vestibule ceiling. But as he entered the sanctuary itself, he noticed that the 12 crystal chandeliers, which were once there, were no more. The Ark was wide open, with no scrolls in it. For a moment Sutton feared that the synagogue had been vandalized by Syrians or terrorists who had occupied the town before the Israeli army ousted them. He did, however, notice that the furniture was in perfect condition, the *mikvah* was in good order, prayer books were intact in their racks. The soldier even found the list allotting seats by names.[20]

The Muslim and Christian residents of Bhamdoun who had shared their summers with the Jews from Beirut for decades, had watched closely over the building in their absence. Thus the building, for which no effort or money had been spared, despite the fact that there was no permanent Jewish community in Bhamdoun, did not fall victim to sectarian warfare or foreign armies.

Another story stumbled upon by journalists was that of Susie Assalan, who had used the open border to visit her brother in Jerusalem. In his home she told of her life in Lebanon, as a Jewess married to a Greek Orthodox. Originally from Alexandria, Egypt, she had been studying at the American University of Beirut when she met her husband, Victor. They made their home in East Beirut, where everyone knew that she was Jewish and her husband Christian, commenting that mixed marriages were actually quite common in Beirut. Her husband was a prosperous investment banker. At the beginning of the civil war their three children were 16, 12 and eight. She recalls the war as follows:

> The last seven years have been a nightmare. . . . Only armed men dared be out on the street after dark, and even for them it was dangerous. My elder son was injured when a bomb was tossed into the lobby of a cinema at two in the afternoon. Thank God he wasn't badly hurt. . . . The PLO have practised terror for terror's own sake. There is no military objective to be achieved by that kind of thing. It got to the point that a trip to the supermarket had to be planned like a sortie into enemy territory.[21]

She had prayed for the Israeli invasion to happen.

David Frank's account of the couple the *Jewish Times* refers to as Jules and Jocelyn is similar. Frank met them during his month IDF reserve duty in Lebanon. Jules, a lawyer and member of one of Lebanon's distinguished Maronite families was married to Jocelyn, a Lebanese Jew. They had met when they were in their late twenties, had fallen in love and decided to get married. "There was some opposition to the intermarriage on both sides, but they resisted it. At one point Jules' father asked him to confer with a priest." He went to see Boulous Neeman, head of the Maronite church and a friend of the family. Neeman told him: "Have no fear, my boy. When her forefathers could already read and write great literature, your ancestors and mine were still pagans living in caves."[22]

According to a Lebanese Jewish businessman with close contacts in West Beirut, some 40 Jews lived through the Israeli siege of the city. "He said that prior to the arrival of the Israelis, some 150 Jews had been living in the western part of the city and about 100 in the east. With the outbreak of the fighting, most of those in the west fled. The 40 who remained were mostly elderly, he added."[23] A different source estimated that in July 1982, at the height of the battle between Israeli forces and the PLO, there were an estimated 300 Jews in Beirut.[24] Nobody was killed, but there was considerable damage to Jewish property.

In what Robert Fisk described as one of the cruellest ironies of the war, Israeli shellfire raked across the Jewish quarter of Wadi Abu Jamil. It destroyed the roof of Magen Avraham, the very building which had been under *Kata'ib* protection as well as guarded by the PLO. When the Israeli bombardment swept over the quarter, the 50 elderly Jews who had not for one reason or another left their homes, were sent fleeing to other parts of the city.

> Only 15 remain in the narrow streets, where militiamen of the Shi'a *Amal* movement patrol past rubble and garbage heaps. The pretty little synagogue of white and yellow stone had already had its windows smashed by a car bomb, which exploded a quarter of a mile away. But two Israeli shells – apparently fired by a gunboat off the coast – punched two huge holes in the roof of the building some days later. . . . As is the custom in Sephardic synagogues of the Middle East, the pulpit is in the centre of the building surrounded by a rectangle of chairs. At the back, the Torah Ark appears to be untouched although several glass shards hang from the ceiling.[25]

One of the remaining Jews in Wadi Abu Jamil during the Israeli invasion was 70-year-old Yacob Eskenazi. He was joined in the battletorn neighborhood by Muslim and Christian refugees. During the fighting most of the remaining Jews fled to the east to the Israeli occupied area or the Christian enclave around the port of Jounieh.

The open border to Israel created opportunities for Lebanese Jews to visit relatives and the Jewish state. Israel offered citizenship to them in July 1982, but none were reported to have responded to this overture.[26] Lebanon's Jews, despite the experience of prolonged war, were happy to visit but were ultimately committed to their life in Lebanon. One account tells of a group of well-dressed men, women and children who "sat on the terrace of a coffee house in Rosh Hanikra, Israel's border point with Lebanon, enjoying the view of the coastal plain stretching all the way to the gulf of Haifa".

> The group, which seemed like typical tourists who visit the scenic border town, chatted in a mixture of Arabic and French and occasionally in Hebrew. They were indeed tourists but hardly typical. They came from the north, from Lebanon. Speaking in Arabic and French marked them as Lebanese nationals. But their usage of Hebrew indicated that they were members of the small Jewish community of Lebanon, a minuscule, almost non-existent community. . . They said they came to see Israel, visit relatives and then go back home. They said their life in Lebanon was good, business was good and they would do a lot of thinking before they would decide to immigrate to Israel.[27]

Another example was Elie Kalache's two teenage sons who were among those who took advantage of the increased mobility and the open border to Israel. Kalache was the director of the social services for the *Kata'ib* for the Hazmiyeh area. He had been to Israel earlier and now wanted to send his sons to see the country and attend school. He found them a place at Hadassim boarding school, away from the fighting in Lebanon.[28]

One evening in 1983, Toufic Yedid Levy received a phone call from a friend telling him that he had someone with him who wanted to see him. Levy was surprised to come face to face with his nephew who had left Lebanon at the age of 16.

> When he returned he was 40. I didn't recognize him at first but I recognized his voice. He stayed only one hour. I wanted him to spend the night, but they wouldn't let him. He came with the *Kata'ib*. The *Kata'ib* had met him in Tel Aviv. They said they would take him to Beirut. But they did not want trouble so he had to sleep at a *Kata'ib* member's house in the East, while I lived in the West near the Italian Embassy. He came and we talked. I asked all about the family.[29]

Among the Lebanese Jews who returned to Lebanon in the context of Operation Peace for Galilee, was also Joseph Lichtman, son of Chief Rabbi Ben Zion Lichtman. He was working for Israeli military intelligence in 1982 and met with representatives of the Maronite Guardians of the Cedars in July. During this meeting Lichtman asked to see Pierre Gemayel. The Maronite representatives "looked at him as if he was crazy". He repeated his request: "Call Pierre Gemayel and tell him the son of the ex-chief rabbi wants to meet with him." They made the call and the next day, a Saturday, Lichtman was invited to Bikfaya. "You should have seen the leaders taking a step back and the body guard driving me to Bikfaya. Amin received me and we began to talk. We waited for 15 minutes and Pierre came. When I showed him the photographs I had brought along, he cried."[30]

Shaul Fayena, whose family had left Lebanon only a few years earlier during the early years of the civil war, and whose father had been forced by the Kurds to retrieve the body of Abu Raffoul in 1975, had volunteered for the Golani brigade. In 1982 he, too, got the opportunity to return to the city of his birth. The images of war torn Beirut from which his family had fled with Palestinian help, had not changed. In the central mountains Druze militiamen controlled the area; *Kata'ib* soldiers were on the streets in Beirut. Artillery battles took place between the two, the Israelis often caught in the middle. Shaul all of a sudden found himself in the position of a mediator. His Beirut accent opened the way for him to talk to both sides and the conflict was regulated temporarily. At the end of his tour in Lebanon Shaul Fayena returned to the yeshiva he attended, taking with him the memories of "a beautiful and brutal land called Lebanon, a community yearning for life in Wadi Abu Jamil. A distant world, which the blood of a civil war brought to its end".[31]

A *failed peace*

The extent to which dreams, hopes and expectations of Lebanon's Jews were tied to "Operation Peace for Galilee" becomes clear when former Beiruti Jews who had left because of the civil war, started returning in anticipation of the restoration of their 'old' life. They believed that there was going to be a genuine peace between Israel and Lebanon and the Jewish community would regain its former vibrancy and glory.[32] Hopes for peace were plunged into darkness with the assassination of Bashir Gemayel on 15 September 1982, when the *Kata'ib* headquarters were bombed. With him Israeli hopes for a peace treaty and Jewish Lebanese hopes for peace and prosperity died. For the position of Jews in Lebanon as for Israeli–Maronite relations, Bashir Gemayel's death was a crucial turning point. No other Maronite leader combined the ability to govern Lebanon in these difficult circumstances with a political orientation acceptable to Israel, let alone a pro-Israeli one.[33] His assassination left his supporters without a leader; it left Israel without the foundation for its plans. Until today many Maronites and Jews, as well as some Israelis, believe the fate of Lebanon, the Maronite-Israeli alliance, and the Lebanese Jewish community would have been quite different had Bashir not died. Lebanon would have been a free place for all communities. It would have been a rough beginning, but the Muslims and the Druze would have stayed behind Bashir through peace with Israel. Bashir's plan to incorporate the Lebanese Forces into the Lebanese army and all other militias would have resulted in a national army under his control.[34]

His brother Amin was elected to succeed him as president of Lebanon. He not only had a different vision for the country but also failed to inspire Israeli enthusiasm. Amin Gemayel's aim was to consolidate his power throughout all of Lebanon, not just within the Christian community. To help him the IDF evacuated Beirut, Israeli soldiers being replaced with a multi-national peace-keeping force.[35] In many ways Amin's administration was a return to the traditional pattern of Lebanese politics, an alliance between a Maronite president and the Sunni *zu'ama'* of Beirut. Amin did not want an alliance with Israel. He had to accept Israel's massive presence in Lebanon and realized that it could also be used to counter-balance Syria and the remaining PLO.[36]

After Bashir Gemayel's death, Israel started to discover that Bashir Gemayel did not fully represent the *Kata'ib*, that the *Kata'ib* did not represent the whole Maronite community, that the Maronite community did not speak for all Lebanese Christians, and that Lebanon's Christians were no longer assured of their ascendancy.[37] It soon became obvious that Amin Gemayel was more interested in keeping good relations with the Arab states than becoming an ally of Israel. Israelis were realizing that they were no longer dealing with the Lebanon as represented by the Maronites. They were becoming painfully aware that Lebanon was based on a coalition of communities. The new President Amin Gemayel did not agree to a single word without first having the approval of the Sunni prime minister.[38] During the negotiations for the 17 May 1983 Agreement, the president insisted on having Muslim backing for everything as he did not want it to be seen as yet another Maronite agreement with Israel. The Israeli negotiating team could only accept the dwindling results of the talks as domestic pressure in Israel from the public outcry over the Sabra and Shatila massacres, made it paramount that a treaty be produced to justify the war.

The agreement fell short both of Israel's security and Lebanon's political requirements. The treaty terminated the war without installing peace. At the same time, the Lebanese were threatened by Syria with the renewal of civil strife if the treaty were ratified.[39] Seen from Damascus, Israel had got from the Lebanon war what it wanted – a political deal with the Beirut government, an enfeebled PLO and a broad band of Lebanese territory on its northern border under its direct control.[40] It was this conclusion that led Syria to pressure the Lebanese not to ratify the agreement, in order to prevent the growth of Israeli influence. On 5 March 1984, following talks between Asad and Gemayel, the Lebanese Cabinet decided to abrogate the 17 May Agreement, leaving Israel without any political gains.

The War Continues, 1985–1989

The Jews who had hoped that Israel's presence in Lebanon would lead to a revival of the community were disappointed. Wadi Abu Jamil once again, in 1984, became caught in the cross-fire due to its greenline location. This renewed round of fighting was between the army of president Amin Gemayel and *Hizb'allah*, which had emerged in response to the Israeli invasion. After the fighting, in 1985, came the kidnappings which paralysed the community. And in the summer of 1985 Israel decided to withdraw its troops from Lebanon.

The failure of "Operation Peace for Galilee" had disastrous consequences for the Jews and the Maronites in Lebanon. The Maronites lost their preferential political standing which had, by extension, protected the Jews and the Jews, as a result, lost their neutrality and security. Syria alone remained the arbitrator of their future, and the equilibrium among the

various communities comprising Lebanon had been upset in their
disfavour. The Maronite community had split into the Lebanese Forces
still loyal to Bashir Gemayel's ideas and now under the leadership of Samir
Geagea and Elie Hobeika, and the *Kata'ib* led by Amin Gemayel and
Karim Pakradouni, advocating a pro-Syrian orientation. The Jews, as far
as they were political, sided ideologically with the first but continued to
maintain relations with all Maronite politicians. Above all, however, they
kept a low profile.

Attempts at bringing the civil war to an end were embodied in the 1985
Tripartite Militia Agreement. The time seemed ripe as most Lebanese
actors were war weary and weakened. Palestinians, Druze and Shi'a forces
had reached a stalemate situation, while the Lebanese Forces were weakened by internal strife. Hobeika had managed to topple Geagea and
opened the path for possible Syrian arbitration. Thus, in September 1985,
the leaders of the three most powerful militias – Druze warlord Walid
Jumblatt, *Amal* leader Nabih Berri, and Elie Hobeika representing the
Lebanese Forces – met in Damascus to negotiate a comprehensive settlement for Lebanon.[41] The envisioned settlement rejected all forms of
partition, federalism, confederalism, and cantonization, but did not
attempt to reform the confessional system. The powers of the president
would be curtailed while those of the prime minister would be increased.
Christian-Muslim confessional parity was to be instituted in parliament
and the civil service. But the agreement went further, revealing that Syria,
in fact, was not an independent arbiter but hegemon. The agreement
stated that "Lebanon's Arabism found its true expression in its distinctive
relationship with Syria." History and geography were central to these
relations. These relations had to be translated in each of the countries into
legal frameworks above the whims of any political faction. Syria would
define Lebanese foreign and domestic policy, and Lebanon would effectively consent to Syrian military deployment on its territory.[42]

The draft of the agreement provoked massive outcry, which Hobeika
unsuccessfully tried to suppress. Many Maronites and Jews felt that if
Lebanon was going to lose its independence to Syria, then the last ten years
of fighting had been in vain. For Lebanon's Jews Syrian hegemony was
the worst option available. Hobeika continued to push for the agreement,
while fighting ensued within the Lebanese Forces. Hobeika was then
forced to resign and the change of command invalidated the Militia
Agreement.[43] The agreement had been "Syria's second attempt to impose
a settlement of the conflict in Lebanon by treaty. The first agreement, the
Damascus Agreement of 1976, foundered on the opposition of the
Lebanese Left and the PLO, the second on that of the Christians."[44]

In 1986 fighting in the Palestinian camps around Beirut broke out.
Lebanese politicians, such as Nabih Berri, who was intent on not letting

the "state within a state" reemerge, accused all Palestinians of "wanting Lebanon back and not Palestine". The war of the camps turned into a war of *Amal* against the Palestinians, followed in 1987 by *Amal*'s war against the Druze, Sunnis and the Left. Later on that year another enemy was added to *Amal*'s wars: *Hizb'allah*. The Lebanese civil war between 1986 and 1988 was characterized by fighting within the respective camps.

Hostage-taking

Between 1984 and 1987, 11 leading members of the Jewish community were kidnapped by the Organization of the Oppressed of the Earth which claimed links with *Hizb'allah*. Only four bodies have been recovered to date. The Lebanese government, lacking central authority in the on-going civil war, was impotent. The kidnappings of Lebanese Jews were subsumed within the kidnappings of Lebanese Maronites, Shi'a, Sunnis and foreigners, becoming just another statistic within the context of sectarian warfare, ethnic cleansing, intra-communal strife for leadership, and a country unable to extricate itself from the spiral of violence, which had taken on a life of its own.

The Organization of the Oppressed of the Earth in all cases demanded that Israel cease its operations in South Lebanon, withdraw from the security zone, and release all prisoners from Khiam prison. They stated that if their demands were not met other Israeli spies would be executed.[45] On a different occasion they claimed that they had killed all the prisoners, but made the release of their bodies conditional on a total Israeli withdrawal from South Lebanon and the release of all Lebanese and Arab prisoners from Israeli jails. The three bodies that were found, all bearing the evidence of torture, left little hope for any of the eleven victims still being alive.

The first victim of the spate of kidnappings by the Organization of the Oppressed of the Earth was Raoul Mizrahi. He was the owner of a small electrical tool shop and was abducted from his home on 10 July 1984. He was in his early 50s and lived in the West Beirut district of Sanayeh. He died on 25 July 1984. When his body was found on a deserted beach near Beirut's airport, the incident did not receive much attention in the local press.

His disappearance was followed shortly after by that of Selim Mourad Jamous, the then secretary of the Jewish community. He was kidnapped on 15 August 1984 and nothing has been heard of him since.

In 1985 Haim Hallala Cohen, a department store accountant, fell victim to the Islamists. He was kidnapped on 29 March 1985 and killed on 26 December of the same year. He was only 39 years old. His body was found 48 hours later in the center of old Beirut near the Cappuchine Church Saint-Louis near the entrance to Wadi Abu Jamil. He left behind his wife Sheila and three young children.[46] At a memorial service held for him in Los Angeles, his sister-in-law Dr Rosemary Cohen noted the tragic irony that her "brother-in-law was given the opportunity to go to Israel. But he did not want to go so as not to face the possibility of killing his Arab friends. He chose to stay in Lebanon."[47]

Only a day later 52-year-old Dr Elie Hallac was kidnapped on 30 March 1985. He had been the vice president of the community, and a prominent Beirut paediatrician. Hallac was known as the doctor of the poor because he treated patients without distinction to background,[48] and he provided free consultancy for non-Jewish children. Toufic Yedid Levy remembers Hallac's kidnapping vividly.

> At eight o'clock that night someone came that I knew. He tapped at the door, gave his name, and I recognised his voice. It was Dr Hallac's chauffeur. He said to me: 'They have taken Dr Hallac – *Hizb'allah* or *Amal*. They've taken Hallac and I'm searching for him.' I said: 'Where are you going to search for him? Leave this until tomorrow morning. Who is going to leave their home now?' There was fear all over Lebanon. I was afraid. He agreed to leave it. I was awake all night. I didn't sleep. I didn't let myself sleep. I got up the next morning at seven o'clock. I went down to his house. I had to see what he wanted me to do, because I was the secretary (of the community). He said to me: 'At nine we are going to Nabih Berri.' He was the head of *Amal* in our sector. So we went to ask him to help us. We didn't know this was only the beginning of the kidnappings. He was their doctor. He gave them treatment for free. . . . We were told to go away and not come back for a while. I went to the house of the wife of the community secretary who had been kidnapped earlier. As soon as the poor thing saw me she went white. 'What are you doing? Your name is at the top of the list.' . . . I went to my cousin's and called the community president. He wasn't there . . . I waited an hour, I was trembling, I was afraid. I kept on asking myself: 'I'm at the head of the list – am I indispensable?' I phoned Joe (the community president) – he told me three had been kidnapped.[49]

Dr Hallac's wife Rachel proclaimed the innocence of her husband and in a desperate appeal demanded that the kidnappers produce proof of her husband's crime. "My husband stayed in Beirut to tend to the ill at 'Ayn al-Mreisseh . . . where the majority are Muslim."[50] There were some initial reports that Dr Hallac was being held together with Isaac Sasson. These were followed by claims that he was working as a doctor among his captors.[51] Hostage Michel Seurat as well as the journalist Jean-Paul Kaufman claimed to have encountered him during their detention.[52] He died on 18 February 1986, but the community has not been able to recover his body. His wife and children moved to France soon afterwards.

Elie Youssef Srour was kidnapped on the same day, on 30 March 1985. He was a 68-year-old merchant and had also been in charge of preparing the dead for burial according to Jewish law. He died on 30 December 1986. His body, too, has not been returned.

Sixty-five-year old Isaac Sasson disappeared the following day on 31 March, raising the number of hostages to four in three days. He was the community president and the director of the pharmaceutical company Fattal. He had been kidnapped while travelling to the city from Beirut International Airport. He was returning from a business trip to the United Arab Emirates on behalf of Fattal & Fils. When the news of the kidnapping of three other Jews earlier in the weekend spread, friends warned Sasson not to travel to West Beirut. The company sent a car with police guards to take him to East Beirut. But eyewitnesses reported that when armed men stopped the car, the guards offered little resistance.[53] He died on 19 June 1987. The location of his body remains unknown.

A month later Isaac Tarrab, an internationally recognized retired mathematics professor aged 70 was kidnapped. He was taken on 18 April 1985 and killed on 1 January 1986. His body was returned to the community.

Yehuda Beniste was kidnapped on 15 February 1986. He was 70 and a former manager at the Safra Bank. The Organization of the Oppressed of the Earth confirmed on 12 January 1987 that Yehuda Beniste "a Mossad agent" had been executed for "the aggression of the Zionist entity against our oppressed people in Jebal Amal, Saida, the western Beqaa, the Golan and Palestine". They did not intend to release his body or those of the others in order to set an example. His son Ibrahim had been taken with him and killed the same day. Their execution coincided with a large Israeli operation in South Lebanon aimed at finding two soldiers who had been taken hostage by the Islamic resistance.[54] His body was returned. The tragedy for the Beniste family was further compounded when Yehuda's other son Youssef, a merchant, was also kidnapped on 18 August 1985. He was 33 when he died on 30 December 1986. The location of his body remains unknown.

Henri Mann was the eleventh victim. He was 40. The date of his kidnapping is not known. He died on 30 December 1986 and his body has not been recovered.

None of those kidnapped had been involved in Lebanese politics or in the Arab-Israeli conflict. They had stayed because of their commitment to Lebanon – as Lebanese. Yet there is no doubt that they were seen as Zionist agents by their kidnappers. This becomes quite clear when years later in 1993 Israeli Prime Minister Yitzhak Rabin told representatives of the families of terror victims that when he served as defence minister in the unity government eight years earlier, he had received a message from a Shi'a organization threatening to kill three prominent members of the Lebanese Jewish community if the IDF did not withdraw from the security zone. Rabin had not given in to the ultimatum, and the three were killed.[55]

The Jewish community repeatedly approached the Lebanese government, the embassies of the United States, Great Britain and France, as well as the United Nations in an effort to obtain information about the unrecovered bodies. Little hope remained that the victims were still alive. Unfortunately for Lebanon's Jews, they were not high on anyone's list when it came to discussions on prisoner release and hostage negotiations. So all the Jewish community council could do was to condemn the assassinations and equally the silence of the Muslim religious authorities in the face of such "falsification of Islamic precepts".[56] Appeals continued to be made to the Pope, the United Nations, the Islamic Conference, the League for Human Rights, and the International Red Cross.

Those Muslim Lebanese politicians who did try were also unable to make an impact. Shi'a *Amal* leader Nabih Berri condemned the kidnappings. On 4 April 1986 he declared that the kidnappings "falsify the image of Beirut which is built on co-existence. . . whoever kidnaps a Jew just because he is Jewish only helps Zionism and has nothing to do with patriotism or the struggle". Druze warlord Walid Jumblatt repeatedly called for the hostage question to be disassociated from the political problems[57] – but also to no avail. In 1989 the murder of US soldier William Higgins, brought the situation of the kidnapped Jews back into the international arena.

In 1991 a Swiss Jewish organization demanded that the Jewish hostages should be included in the list of hostages discussed in the broader framework of Middle East hostage negotiations.[58] In December of that year the *Conseil Communale* again called for the release of the remaining seven Jews. In a statement they stressed that it was important to determine the fate of the hostages while progress was being made of the issue of Western hostages. "We call again on the captors, on states, and organizations who can influence them, on Lebanese officials and international organizations, to reopen this case and to work to return our captives."[59] In 1993, UN Deputy President for Political Affairs, Bennon Saban, sent a letter to the International Commission for Jewish Communities in Distress, stating that the UN efforts to obtain any reliable information about the hostages had failed.[60] Until today, no movement on this issue has been made.

The End of the Civil War

The end of the civil war finally came in 1990. With it two separate but interconnected peace processes began, the first being internal national reconciliation and the second being the external, regional Middle East peace process. Both processes were welcomed by Lebanon's remaining Jews as they ultimately were seen as leading to a decline in inter-communal and regional tensions. The optimistic scenario could even lead to a normalisation of relations between Lebanon and Israel, bringing with it the possibility for the Beirut Jewish community not only to live in peace and security but also to flourish and grow. The most obvious political change that came about with the end of the civil war was in the reduction of the powers of the Maronite president *vis-à-vis* the Sunni prime minister, the cabinet and the parliament.

Important for both peace processes was the 1989 Ta'if Accord which, upon ratification in 1990, proclaimed Lebanon's second republic. The accords contained two key elements, the first dealing with the specific constitutional arrangements in Lebanon, and the second addressing Syro-Lebanese relations.[61] The Ta'if Agreement did not significantly alter the power-sharing arrangement of the 1943 National Pact in the sense that confessionalism is still the basis for coexistence in Lebanon, despite the claim that ultimately confessionalism will be abolished. If the end to confessionalism means a simple majoritarian democracy, such a move would be disastrous for Lebanon's remaining Jews as well as Christians who would all become a religious minority in a Muslim state.

The reconstruction of nation and community

The reconstruction of Beirut has in recent years increasingly become synonymous with national reconciliation or arguably even replaced it. The continued Syrian presence, unofficially sanctioned by the international community with the 1991 Gulf War and officially sanctioned with the Syro-Lebanese Treaty of Friendship and Brotherhood, has made genuine reconciliation an improbability. As long as those who fled the country during the civil war are unable to return for political or economic reasons, any reconciliatory process will remain incomplete. In the absence of such reconciliation, politicians and the business community have become transfixed on the reconstruction of the city, symbolizing at least an architectural healing of wounds.

Jewish money has not been insignificant in the reconstruction project and has provided the disunified Lebanese polity with ammunition to continue its traditional power games. In the summer of 1995 a debate was sparked when Deputy Najah Wakim claimed that Israel held a number of shares in Solidère. This debate found its way into the media where, for example in *an-Nahar*,[62] a lengthy article was published in defence of Lebanese Jewry, explaining that Jewish shareholders of Solidère had received their shares in return for property in Wadi Abu Jamil which would be demolished as part of the reconstruction of Beirut. Lebanese Jews holding shares were not the same as Israel holding shares. The Jews were loyal citizens and were innocent of the charge implied by Najah Wakim.

While the state was on a clear path of reconstruction the individual Lebanese minority communities also embarked upon a path to recovery. The Maronite community, the Jewish community, and the Palestinian refugee community, were, in many ways the worst afflicted. The main problem for the Maronites, as the real losers of the war, was of a political nature evolving around their future within the state. The Palestinians were faced with further dislocation, a state which did not want them, neighbours who blamed them for the war, and the end of work permits and benefits. It was clear Lebanon was intent on trying to recover from its 15-year-long trauma, and it was going to do so without the Palestinians. The Lebanese Jews were even worse afflicted. They were dispersed and had numerically shrunk to under 100. Most of those who remained were old – they were literally dying as a community.

In 1991 only a brother and a sister were still living in Wadi Abu Jamil. The quarter instead had become home to Shi'a refugees and Kurds. The rest of the Jewish community had all found safety in East Beirut and the mountains. Being dispersed, the community has almost ceased to function. It has been difficult to get a *minyan* for high holidays, never mind *Shabbat*. There was no functioning synagogue.

In 1992 Lebanon staged its first parliamentary elections since the end of the war. The electoral roll revealed that there were still 6,326 Jews registered to vote. At the polling station at the Anglican School in Qantari 400 Jewish voters were registered. But the electoral officer at the time said that none of them had voted nor was he expecting them to.[63] The oldest voter on the list was born in 1881 and the youngest in 1971.

In 1993 it was reported that 50 Torah scrolls which had served the Jewish community in Beirut were being brought to Israel via a third country. Guardianship over these Torah scrolls was accepted by Chief Rabbi Eliahu Bakshi-Doron, who promised to grant the first Torah scroll to the synagogue of Kibbutz Ein Gev.[64] In 1994 five *Sifrei Torah* were smuggled out of Syria and deposited for safekeeping in Beirut. These, too, were eventually destined for transfer to Israel. The Syrian Jews were in the process of leaving as Syrian president Hafez al-Asad, as a concession within the framework of the Middle East process, had decided to lift the travel and emigration ban for Syrian Jews.

A Dutch journalist that year conveyed a sad picture of the remnants of the once vibrant Lebanese community: "The Jewish cemetery, in West Beirut on what was until now the Green Line, is rather abandoned and in the last three years there were only two funerals, attended by no more than six people. The situation of the large synagogue . . . is no better."[65]

As the political situation in the country stabilized and the reconstruction of the city got underway, the state of the cemetery and the synagogue were also improved. Mines were removed from between the graves, barrels and sand bags which had served as protective barriers for the fighting militias were dismantled, and almost fifteen years worth of overgrowth and weeds were cleared in stages.

> We had to go to the army and they sent twenty soldiers to clear it of bombs that had been put there during the war by the Christians and Muslims. One side of the cemetery was Muslim, the other Christian. So each laid mines and we could not enter the cemetery until it had been secured. For six months the army disarmed the mines. . . . We could not even bury our dead there during some periods of the war. Neither the army, nor the Christians or Muslims would let us pass. We had to take our dead to Saida. . . . When the Israelis were here, the army rabbi said the prayers and performed the necessary rituals for the funeral.[66]

In 1996 the *Conseil Communale* had the graves sufficiently cleared to order a survey. The grand synagogue of Magen Avraham also had years of rubble removed in 1995/6, from parts of the collapsed roof and from debris squatters had left on the floor. Graffiti on the walls was removed. The next step for the community in the preservation of the synagogue was to fight for the building to be officially recognized as a historic landmark. While the majority of the houses in Wadi Abu Jamil were uninhabitable and earmarked for demolition, the synagogue had become the symbol for the survival of the community – even if only as a historic monument, a fleeting memory of Lebanon's Jewish and indeed multi-communal past.

Community life has virtually disappeared. Toufic Yedid Levy, who in his eighties spent most of his life in Beirut and took on the role of the executive secretary of the *Conseil Communale,* lamented the state of the community:

> We do not even have a synagogue. All of them have been destroyed. And although many Jews live in this part (East Beirut), nobody goes there (West Beirut). All has been occupied by Muslims. So we have meetings in the house of Mr Joseph (the community president). For *Rosh Hashana* and for *Pessach*. The big families make their own arrangements, we say our prayers at home. Everyone lives so far from the others. One is in Broumana, another in Bikfaya, others in Jounieh. How can they come for prayer? So to get a

minyan is difficult. . . . I cannot even get a *minyan* at the cemetery. I go on
my own and say lots of little prayers. What can I do? I cannot arrange for
people to come.[67]

Those Jews who have remained still exhibit their deep attachment to the
community and have no plans to leave. "The way of life that we have here
cannot be found anywhere in the world. . . . Age is also a factor for many.
The easy life, habit, fear of the unknown – all convince them to stay."[68]
While the remaining community is generally an old one, the average age
being 65, there is a small number of younger people. Some are studying
at the university, some are in still in high school – none are planning on
leaving. Indeed, not all is death and decay, in 1988 a baby boy was born
into the community and the Syrian authorities permitted the Damascus
rabbi to travel to Beirut to perform the *brith mila*. In 1994 one of the
youngsters celebrated his *bar mitzvah*.

Conjectures, Considerations, and Conclusions: A Sentimental Journey

The Community in History

The Jewish minority in Lebanon historically has been integrated into Lebanese economic, social, cultural and political life. Lebanese Jews have been described as "Arabized", and, in the 20th century, were as Levantine as their Christian and Muslim Lebanese counterparts. Yet, despite being fully integrated unlike Jews in many other Middle Eastern countries, they were not assimilated like many Western European Jews. Rather, they maintained their own religious and communal identity, cherishing customs and traditions.

This integrated but non-assimilated position of the Lebanese Jews was a result of Lebanon's political system and ethno-religious composition. The history of providing refuge to persecuted minorities, the tradition of tolerance, the consociational political system in which minorities were represented on a proportional basis, and the retaining of personal status laws within the separate communities created a formula according to which Lebanon's 23 minorities were able to interact on friendly terms without losing their distinct identity. The two civil wars of 1958 and 1975 did not change this. Indeed, an argument could be made that the civil wars reinforced the system as both times the same formula – with demographic amendments – was revived for national reconciliation.

The history of the Jews of Lebanon as one characterized by the absence of major anti-Jewish hostilities and the commitment of the state and its people to protect the Jews during times of instability, proves that the monolithic view that Jews in the Middle East were all second-class citizens suffering from severe restrictions, discrimination and persecution, does not hold true. This assertion is not intended to diminish the persecution that did take place in other Arab states. Rather, it serves to highlight the special political and social dynamics of Lebanon, which made Lebanon different, placing the history of Lebanese Jewry in stark contrast to that, for instance, of Syrian Jewry.

During the time of the French mandate, life for the Jewish community was culturally vibrant. Many of the community structures were laid down during this time, such as the committees, the community council, and some of the charities. New synagogues and schools were built. Youth organizations – Lebanese, Jewish and Zionist – flourished, and the community as a whole was well off and active in finance and commerce. The community had its own newspaper and an economic journal; the youth had two journals of their own. This period in Lebanese Jewish history saw numerous hardships ranging from Christian-Muslim tensions, economic depression, the Second World War, Jewish refugees, and the Vichy government, to the emerging conflict in neighbouring Palestine. Yet it was exactly these upheavals, the communal solidarity and the inter-communal friendships, which provided the space for some of the communities greatest leaders to emerge: Joseph David Farhi, Joseph Dichy Bey, Rabbi Ben Zion Lichtman, and Moshe Kamhine.

The post-independence period until the first civil war was one of almost carefree existence in a Lebanese state, which had emerged as the Paris or the Switzerland of the Middle East. The community had increased to its largest ever in history as a result of Syrian and Iraqi refugees after the 1948 Arab-Israeli war. The war itself did not have a lasting impact on the community. Lebanese Jews had and retained equal rights and enjoyed life in Lebanon, which is why they did not immigrate to Israel in 1948, or in significant numbers any time later. By this time the original Lebanese Jews who had resided in Wadi Abu Jamil, had become thoroughly middle class in attitude and lifestyle. They started leaving the traditional quarter, moved to more fashionable neighbourhoods, acquired designer clothes, cars, technological gadgets, and spent money on lavish entertainment, while, at the same time remaining socially conservative. Jewish youngsters were better educated than in the past, they were enjoying a life where going to the beach and skiing on the same day were not an exception.

With the first civil war in 1958, the community started to decrease. Syrian and Iraqi refugees who had never intended on staying, and had not been granted citizenship in any case, saw the political instability as a signal to move on. Some Lebanese Jews joined the stream of émigrés who left as a result of the war. Others, many of the younger generation, left because the increased education had theoretically opened avenues other than their parents' occupations. Lebanon did not have much to offer for those who did not wish to be merchants or bankers.

The Six-Day War in 1967 was another turning point for Lebanese Jewry. The war itself had not threatened the Jews, but the consequent influx of Palestinian refugees into the country overburdened Lebanon's economic and political stability. Politics were becoming increasingly sectarian and polarized, while the middle ground – the traditional place of the Jews – was being eroded. Lebanese-Palestinian clashes, Israeli operations against Lebanon, and Christian-Muslim tensions were a sign for the troubles that followed. Many Lebanese Jews left in 1970, 1971 and 1972 when it started becoming clear that the tensions would not "just pass". Thus, by the outbreak of the second civil war in 1975, the community consisted only of Jewish Lebanese nationalists who refused to leave, optimists who did not believe the situation would deteriorate into a full-blown war, families who did not wish to uproot school-aged children or move elderly relatives, and the old and infirm who could not leave even if they had wanted to.

The power vacuum created by the civil war attracted the intervention of both of Lebanon's stronger neighbors Syria in 1976 and Israel in 1982. Both turned out to be a mixed blessing for the remaining Jewish community. The initial stability provided by Syria was superseded only months later by Syria becoming a fully-fledged actor, aligning itself with the Muslim forces. The Israeli presence provided a comparatively longer respite and triggered a Jewish renaissance. But open borders, better living standards, and hopes for an Israeli–Lebanese peace were brutally shattered with the death of Lebanese president-elect Bashir Gemayel. The history of Lebanese Jewry from the redeployment of Israeli forces to the security zone onwards plunged into the depth of darkness with the beginning of the kidnappings. Lebanon's Jews, who had been essentially apolitical, had become the enemy in the eyes of many Islamists. The community was forced to leave the Jewish quarter, which bordered on Muslim Beirut and dispersed within the Christian enclave. Life as a community had effectively ceased to exist.

Nevertheless, it should be stressed, that Lebanese Jews throughout the twentieth century unequivocally considered their home to be Lebanon, defined themselves as Lebanese nationals of Jewish religion, and when the political situation in Lebanon disintegrated they immigrated to places with existing Lebanese expatriate communities such as Paris, New York, Montreal or Sao Paulo. In the end, the place that the Jews occupied in the history of Lebanon, was not that of the enemy within, but as one minority among many.

The Arab-Israeli Conflict

Regional dynamics and especially the Arab-Israeli conflict have played a not insignificant role in Lebanese Jewish history. The proximity of first

Palestine and later Israel to the Lebanese community meant that there had always been strong religious and family ties. These did not break off with the creation of the State of Israel. The closed borders made the connections more difficult, but religious, cultural and family contacts continued via third countries.

Lebanon and Lebanon's Jews occupy a curious place within the dynamics of the Arab-Israeli conflict in the sense that the former was no more a "real" combatant than the latter were "real" victims. Despite the fact that Lebanon had been officially at war with Israel, its military actions against Israel were minimal. Moreover, certain sections within the Maronite community saw Israel as an ally in the region, and thus had continuous connections with the Jewish State dating back to the mandate period. The Jews were more aligned with this pro-Israeli element than with any other Lebanese political constituency. This should not, however, be interpreted as an expression of Zionism, but rather as an ideological affinity between the Jews and those very Maronites as both supported the political project of a multi-cultural, multi-confessional, independent and modern Lebanese state.

The Jewish community in Lebanon had equal rights and was not victimized or restricted by the state during or following any of the Arab-Israeli wars. In fact, the opposite is evident: the Lebanese state actively protected its Jews and treated them much the same as any of the other 23 minorities. This does not mean that there was no anti-Jewish sentiment expressed by individuals, and that there were no anti-Jewish incidents. Rather, it illustrates that there was a clear distinction between government and private actions just like most Lebanese differentiated between anti-Zionism and anti-Semitism.

Unlike Jews in other Middle Eastern states, Lebanon's Jews were neither expelled nor did they leave their homes in 1948. This provides a different dimension to the Arab-Israeli conflict which is often approached from the simplified premises that while the creation of the State of Israel triggered the Palestinian refugee situation, Israel's Arab neighbors immediately proceeded to expel their Jewish citizens, resulting in an *quid pro quo* situation.

Lebanon's Jewish community grew after 1948, and the exodus did not begin until after the Six-Day War in 1967, as the result of the increasing Palestinian presence, the onset of economic decline, and the increasing political instability of the state. It was not a case of unbearable tensions between Palestinian refugees settling in Lebanon and the country's Jews, despite the fact that they lived in close proximity to each other and could easily have used the turbulent Arab-Israeli history as a pretext for violence. The reason why Lebanon's Jews started to leave lay in the clashes between Palestinian guerrillas and the Lebanese army, followed by

Palestinian-Christian clashes, the loss of state control, and the descent into civil war in 1975.

This is not to say that the history of the Jewish community in Lebanon was not unequivocally linked to the history of the Arab-Israeli conflict. There is no doubt about that, as Lebanon's political history cannot be separated from the conflict either. But the story of Lebanese Jewry throws light on some of the other currents evident in the regional dynamics, which may not fall quite so clearly into a simple cause-effect analysis. It thus contributes to the on-going historiographical debate on Israel, Palestine, and the Arab-Israeli conflict.

Conceptually, it presents a clear departure from the state-centered discourse and essentialist idea of the nation as advocated by Israel. Lebanese Jewish-Israeli tension over the attempts at "forced immigration", in addition to already existing similar evidence from Egyptian,[1] and Iraqi Jews, provides an insight into more complex identities and loyalties. The relative alieness of Zionism, the lack of immigration to Israel, the existence of a strong Levantine, and, indeed Lebanese identity, raises the overarching question Joel Beinin has already asked in the context of his research into Egyptian Jewry, of whether an inclusive, pluralist, multi-ethnic, communitarian Middle East can ever be compatible with the exclusiveness of the one nation-state.[2]

A History of Lebanon

Historical accounts in highly heterogeneous societies such as Lebanon vary greatly across the communal divide. Historical "fictions" during prolonged periods of ethnic conflict are even more polarized as they are generally created for political purposes, to legitimize one community at the cost of another. Events of the past are not only interpreted through the present, but are consciously selected or omitted to prove an "objective truth". For example, Maronite histories of Lebanon, especially those written before and during the war, tend to dwell on the past of a people synonymous with the mountain, a proud people who did not surrender and were not defeated, despite numerous occupation armies passing through the region. It was a history aimed at justifying the status quo of Maronite hegemony. Sunni historical accounts were less directed, but clearly had their own set of national myths of integration in a broader region with a glorious Arab and Islamic past. Historical evidence was used to "prove" the injustice of partition, colonialism, and imperialism, the "artificiality" of state boundaries, and to justify policies ultimately aimed at reunification. Along similar lines, Shi'a history invokes a golden Islamic past but, in addition, is often presented through the political awakening in the late 1960s as well as traditional Shi'a rather than Lebanese concepts of martyrdom, struggle, and salvation, marking its difference from Sunni Islam. Druze, Armenian, Nestorian, and Greek-Orthodox histories also tell different Lebanese tales.

The Jewish history of Lebanon has been comparatively less marked by state-oriented political projects, yet also has a "fiction" of its own. As the Jews tied their fate to the multi-confessional image of Lebanon, the refuge for persecuted minorities, and the modern liberal democracy, their history is one that was constructed around the vision of Lebanon as the Paris or Switzerland of the Middle East. It is an account of economic vibrancy and tolerance, of playing down inter-communal tensions in a century of two civil and four Arab-Israeli wars; it is a history of the middle ground, stressing what existed in common rather than divided, the story of a community which truly did have good relations with all its neighbours.

Given the position of the Jews in Lebanon as a minority that was never large enough to warrant a parliamentary seat of its own, neither the lack of overt political activity nor the account itself are surprising. What is important is what it says about Lebanon. It is a story told from the center, not Christian not Muslim, not from the perspective of those in power and not from the position of the powerless in their eternal struggle. In essence, it reveals an underlying layer of social, political and economic dynamics beneath the Christian-Muslim struggle paradigm. This layer was one of every day cooperation, bargaining, compromise and, ultimately, coexistence. Thus, the Jews' history of Lebanon illustrates a functioning inter-communal discourse, one which ultimately was the basis for the ideal of the National Pact in 1943, the settlement after the 1958 civil strife, and the national reconciliation from 1990 onwards. Above all, it provides recognition that Lebanon does have a social and political foundation which distinguishes it from its environs and upon which the nation can be reconstructed, providing that, as Kamal Salibi phrased it, the past "ceases to be a question of political rights and wrongs, of outstanding tribal or quasi-tribal scores to be settled, and acquires more meaning with the respect to the present – and even more with respect to the future".[3]

Nostalgias and memories

For those who left the land of the cedars, the images of the mountains, Aley and Bhamdoun represent a different life, an existence now confined to photoalbums, personal memory and statements such as these:

> They called it Wadi Abu Jamil, but the residents . . . preferred the nickname
> 'Jews' Street' for the Beirut street which descends the mountain ridge

towards the sea. In this street and the nearby alleyways . . . for hundreds of years (lived) of one of the most flourishing communities in the East: the Beirut community. The vast majority of the city's Jews resided there . . . along with the beautiful synagogue Magen Avraham, the pride of the Jews of Beirut.[4]

Or:

Charles Helou was good, Camille Chamoun was great, Sami Solh was very good to the Jews. The truth is, life in Lebanon was good. If it was hot in the summer you went to the sea. There were the mountains. People had two houses, one in Beirut and one in Bhamdoun. All the summer we spent in the mountains. You didn't feel the heat there and the humidity.[5]

Or:

The life in Lebanon did not exist anywhere in all of the world. There was nothing like it. The work was easy. Here (Israel) you go at 8 a.m. and return at 10 p.m. In Lebanon it was ten minutes walking. At six in the evening we were home. In the summer it was like four months holiday. Every evening we went out, met friends, went to movies, sat in cafés. You could see the lights from the mountains.[6]

Like other Lebanese émigrés, the Jews often idealize the period before the second civil war, editing out unpleasant events or censoring the accounts told to an outsider fearing a violation of the emotional history so closely connected. It is thus difficult to reconstruct an all-encompassing picture of what Jewish life was like from these memories.

Many of the personal stories do not dwell on or even mention incidents such as the bombs in 1947 or Emile Boustani's anti-Semitic rhetoric, while the memories of Pierre Gemayel's, Sami Sulh's or Joseph Chader's regular visits to the community and grand holiday celebrations loom large. In contrast, newspapers articles from the same period suffer from the opposite, focusing on tension, violence, and hatred, much of it related to what tends to be perceived as "news." Both present a discourse on the Jews in Lebanon, neither more accurate than the other.

Narratives constructed from personal memories and nostalgias are often dismissed because they are not objective. Oral history is sometimes perceived as inaccurate as the telling and retelling of events from one generation to another may have distorted the "original facts." Yet history is not, and never will be objective. It is a selection and interpretation of "events", "facts", and "sources" by a "narrator", more often than not to fit an agenda or to prove some theory.

Personal recollections are not just stories, which add flavour or colour to a chronological account of "facts" and "truths". Rather, they function

as critical commentary on understanding human existence, in this particular case the existence of Lebanese Jews within their own confessional
group, within Lebanese society, and indeed, within the region and Jewish
history. Much lies in the way these recollections are read and understood,
as they, beyond the obvious story, reveal assumptions and aspirations of
the individual and the collective. One of the assumptions which so clearly
stands out in this history is that Lebanese Jews constructed their identity
within a particularly Levantine framework. Their whole existence was
based on the premise of inclusive multi-culturalness and co-existence. The
community flourished over centuries until the forces of nationalism
turned the tide towards the search for exclusivity as represented by the
Zionist, the Arabist, the Maronitist, and the Islamist political projects,
ultimately leading to regional conflict and the community's decline.

Appendix

---

1 *Jewish Community Presidents, 1910–1999*

	Ezra Anzarut
1910–1924	Joseph D. Farhi
1925–1927	Joseph Dichy Bey
1928–1930	Joseph D. Farhi
1931–1934	Selim Harari
1935–1938	Joseph D. Farhi
1939–1950	Joseph Dichy Bey
1950–1976	Joseph Attie
1977–1985	Isaac Sasson
1985 –	Joseph Mizrahi

2 *Chief Rabbis, 1908–1978*

1908–1909	Rabbi Danon
1910–1921	Jacob Maslaton
1921–1923	Salomon Tagger
1924–1950	Shabtai Bahbout
1932–1959	Benzion Lichtman
1949–1966	Jacob Attie
1960–1978	Chaoud Chreim

Notes

Introduction

1. Saul Friedman, *Without Future* (New York: Praeger, 1989), p. 6.
2. Quoted in Tudor Parfitt, "Jewish Minority Experience in Twentieth-century Yemen", in Kirsten E. Schulze, Martin Stokes and Colm Campbell (eds.), *Nationalism, Minorities and Diasporas: Identities and Rights in the Middle East* (London: I.B. Tauris, 1996), p. 121.
3. Maurice Roumani, *The Case of the Jews from Arab Countries: A Neglected Issue* (Tel Aviv: World Organization of Jews from Arab Countries, 1978), p. 24.
4. Daphne Tsimhoni, "Jewish–Muslim Relations in Modern Iraq", in Schulze, Stokes and Campbell (eds.), *Nationalism, Minorities and Diasporas*, p. 107.
5. Morroe Berger, *The Arab World* (London: Weidenfeld & Nicolson, 1962), p. 251.
6. Gudrun Krämer, "Political Participation of the Jews in Egypt Between World War I and the 1952 Revolution", in Shimon Shamir, *The Jews of Egypt: A Mediterranean Society in Modern Times* (Boulder, Co: Westview Press, 1987), p. 69.
7. *The Jerusalem Post Magazine*, 20 August 1982.
8. Ibid.
9. Friedman, *Without Future*, p. 14.
10. *An-Nahar*, 27 June 1995.
11. *Encyclopedia Judaica* (Jerusalem: Keter, 1972), p. 1543.
12. Ibid.
13. Itzhak Ben Zvi, "From a Discussion with Salim Hasbani", 18 March 1929 (in Hebrew), File 1/3/4/18, BZA.
14. *Encyclopedia Judaica*, p. 1543.
15. Luc Henri de Bar, *Les Communautés Confessionelles du Liban* (Paris: Edition Recherche sur les Civilisation, 1983), p. 155.
16. *Encyclopedia Judaica*, p. 1543.
17. *An-Nahar*, 27 June 1995.
18. Jewish Easter in Lebanon, AMLEGATION, Beirut 576, 2 May 1951, R 59, Box 5448, National Archives and Records Administration (NARA).
19. Ibid.
20. Interview with Fuad Abu Nader, Commander of the Lebanese Forces under

Bashir Gemayel, Beirut, 28 June 1995.

21 For a detailed account of this relationship see Schulze, *Israel's Covert Diplomacy in Lebanon* (Basingstoke: St Antony's/Macmillan, 1998).

22 Interview with Fuad Abu Nader, Beirut, 28 June 1995.

23 *Encyclopedia Judaica*, p. 1545.

24 *An-Nahar*, 27 June 1995.

25 Ibid.

26 *Israel Nachrichten*, 25 July 1978.

27 *Jewish Chronicle* (London), 14 November 1978.

28 The exact numbers are unknown. Estimates vary from one report to another. The *Jewish Chronicle* (14 November 1978) cites 1,000 Jews remaining out of 5,000. *Israel Nachrichten* (25 July 1978) cites 450 out of 6,000 as remaining, with only 60 still living in Beirut proper.

29 *The Jerusalem Post*, 29 October 1980.

30 *Jewish Chronicle* (London), 2 July 1982.

31 *The Jewish News* (Detroit), 2 July 1982.

32 Helena Cobban, *The Making of Modern Lebanon* (London: Hutchinson, 1985), p. 26.

33 Elizabeth Picard, *Lebanon: A Shattered Country* (New York: Holmes & Meier Publishers, 1996), p. 11.

34 de Bar, *Les Communautés Confessionelles du Liban*, p. 161.

35 Walter P. Zenner, "Jews in Late Ottoman Syria: External Relations", in Shlomo Deshen and Walter P. Zenner (eds.), *Jewish Societies in the Middle East: Communities, Culture and Authority* (Washington, DC: University of America Press, 1982).

36 Joseph Schechtman, *On Wings of Eagles: The Plight, Exodus and Homecoming of Oriental Jewry* (New York: Thomas Joseloff, 1961), pp. 168–9.

1   A Voyage through History

1 As quoted in Friedman, *Without Future*, p. 15.

2 Cohn-Sherbock, *Atlas of Jewish History* (London: Routledge, 1994), p. 20.

3 *Hamodia Supplement*, 18 June 1995.

4 Marion Woolfson, *Prophets in Babylon: Jews in the Arab World* (London: Faber and Faber, 1980), p. 33.

5 *Yediot Aharonot*, 21 January 1983.

6 Raphael Patai, *Tents of Jacob: The Diaspora Yesterday and Today* (Englewood, NJ: Prentice-Hall, 1971), p. 231.

7 Woolfson, *Prophets in Babylon*, p. 43.

8 Hayyim J. Cohen, *The Jews of the Middle East, 1860–1972* (Jerusalem: Israel University Press, 1973), pp. 1–2.

9 de Bar, *Les Communautés Confessionelles du Liban*, p. 156.

10 *Shearim*, 12 November 1982.

11 *Encyclopedia Judaica*, p. 1543.

12 de Bar, *Les Communautés Confessionelles du Liban*, p. 156.

13 Ibid.

14 Raphael Patai, *The Vanished Worlds of Jewry* (London: Weidenfeld & Nicolson, 1981), p. 139.
15 Shlomo Goitein, *A Mediterranean Society: The Jewish Communities of the Arab World as Portrayed in the Documents of the Cairo Geniza*, Vol I, Economic Foundations (Los Angeles: University of California Press, 1967), p. 48.
16 *Encyclopedia Judaica*, p. 1543.
17 de Bar, *Les Communautés Confessionelles du Liban*, p. 156.
18 Patai, *Tents of Jacob*, p. 231.
19 *Shearim*, 12 November 1982.
20 *Hamodia Supplement*, 18 June 1995.
21 Youssef Courbage and Philippe Fargues, *Chrétiens et Juifs dans l'Islam arabe et turc* (Paris: Fayard, 1992), p. 182.
22 Kamal Salibi, *House of Many Mansions: The History of Lebanon Reconsidered* (Los Angeles, University of California Press, 1988), p. 14.
23 Stephen Hemsley Longrigg, *Syria and Lebanon under French Mandate* (Beirut: Libraire du Liban, 1958), p. 21.
24 Salibi, *House of Many Mansions*, p. 16.
25 Picard, *Lebanon*, pp. 21–2.
26 Longrigg, *Syria and Lebanon under French Mandate*, p. 23.
27 Nicola Ziadeh, *Syria and Lebanon* (Beirut: Libraire du Liban, 1968), p. 34.
28 Norman Stillman, *The Jews of Arab Lands: A History and Source Book* (Philadelphia: Publication Society of America, 1979), pp. 109–10.
29 Ibid.
30 W. P. Zenner and Shlomo Deshen, "The Historical Ethnology of Middle Eastern Jewry", in Deshen and Zenner (eds.), *Jewish Societies in the Middle East*, p. 21.
31 *An-Nahar*, 27 June 1995.
32 *Encyclopedia Judaica*, p. 1543.
33 Ibid.
34 Leila Tarazi Fawaz, *An Occasion for War: Civil Conflict in Lebanon and Damascus in 1860* (Cambridge, MA: Harvard University Press, 1983), p. 37.
35 de Bar, *Les Communautés Confessionelles du Liban*, p. 156.
36 Ibid.
37 *Encyclopedia Judaica*, p. 1543.
38 *Yediot Aharonot*, 21 January 1983.
39 Woolfson, *Prophets in Babylon*, p .94.
40 de Bar, *Les Communautés Confessionelles du Liban*, p. 156.
41 *Hamodia Supplement*, 18 June 1995.
42 Woolfson, *Prophets in Babylon*, p. 96.
43 J. J. Benjamin, *Acht Jahre in Asien und Afrika von 1846 bis 1855* (Hannover: Selbstverlag des Verfassers, 1859), p. 38.
44 *Encyclopedia Judaica*, p. 1543.
45 Itzhak Ben Zvi, "From a Discussion with Salim Hasbani", 18 March 1929 (in Hebrew). File 1/3/4/18, BZA.
46 *An-Nahar*, 27 June 1995.
47 de Bar, *Les Communautés Confessionelles du Liban*, p. 156.

48 *Shearim*, 12 November 1982.
49 This description of Beirut is based on Fawaz, *An Occasion for War*, pp. 8–13.
50 Walter Fischel (ed.), *Unknown Jews in Unknown Lands: The Travels of Rabbi d'Beth Hillel, 1824–1832* (New York: Ktav Publishing House, 1973), p. 64.
51 Ibid., p. 63.
52 Patai, *Tents of Jacob*, p. 231.
53 Heskel Haddad, *Jews of Arab and Islamic Countries: History, Problems, Solutions* (New York: Shengold Publishers, 1984), p. 59.
54 Fischel, *Unknown Jews in Unknown Lands*, p. 63.
55 Courbage and Farques, *Chrétiens et Juifs dans l'Islam arabe et turc*, p. 182.
56 Patai, *Tents of Jacob*, p. 231.
57 Courbage and Farques, *Chrétiens et Juifs dans l'Islam arabe et turc*, p. 187.
58 Ibid.
59 Fischel, *Unknown Jews of Unknown Lands*, p. 63.
60 Report by M. Angel, Beirut, May 1902, Liban I.C.2., AIUA.
61 Woolfson, *Prophets in Babylon*, p. 43.
62 Zenner and Deshen, "The Historical Ethnology of Middle Eastern Jewry", p. 22.
63 S. Klein, "Das tannaitische Grenzverzeichnis Palästinas", Palästina Studien, II, p. 1.
64 *Hamodia Supplement*, 18 June 1995.
65 *Hamodia Supplement*, 18 June 1995.
66 Schwartz as quoted by Ben Zvi, "The Settlement of Hasbaya" (n.d.), BZA.
67 Ibid.
68 *Hamaggid*, No. 5 (Kislev 5619), 1859, pp. 197–8.
69 Conversation with Salim Hasbani, 18 March 1929, BZA.
70 Fawaz, *An Occasion for War*, p. 49.
71 Conversation with Salim Hasbani, 18 March 1929, BZA.
72 Conversation with Salim Hasbani, 18 March 1929, BZA.
73 *Encyclopedia Judaica*, p. 1543.
74 Haddad, *Jews of Arab and Islamic countries*, p. 59.
75 Shlomo Goitein, *Jews and Arabs: Their contacts through ages* (New York: Schocken, 1955), p. 7.
76 Longrigg, *Syria and Lebanon under the French Mandate*, p. 10.
77 Norman Stillman, *The Jews in Arab Lands in Modern Times* (New York: The Jewish Publication Society, 1991), pp. 20–1.
78 P. C. Sadgrove, "The Beirut Jewish-Arab Theatre: A Question of Identity", in *Democracy in the Middle East*, BRISMES Conference Proceedings, July 1992, p. 173.
79 Ibid., p. 170.
80 Niqula Fayyad, "Dhikrayat Adabiyya", *Muhadarat al-Nawda al-Lubnaniyya*, Nos. 3–4, 25 June 1954, p. 48.
81 Sadgrove, "The Beirut Jewish Arab Theatre", p. 170.
82 Aaron Rodrigue, *Images of Sephardi and Eastern Jewries in Transition: The Teachers of the Alliance Israélite Universelle, 1860–1939* (Seattle, University of Washington Press, 1993), p. 18.

83 "Appel à tous les Israélites", *Alliance Israélite Universelle* (Paris, 1860), p. 39.

84 See André N. Chouraqui, *Cent Ans d'Histoire: L'Alliance Israélite Universelle et la Renaissance Juive Contemporain (1860–1960)* (Paris: Libraire Arthème Fayard, 1965) for a detailed history.

85 Rodrigue, *Images of Sephardi and Eastern Jewries in Transition*, p. 8. See also Aaron Rodrigue, *French Jews, Turkish Jews: The Alliance Israélite Universelle and the Politics of Jewish Schooling in Turkey, 1860–1925* (Bloomington: Indiana University Press, 1990), pp. 1–8.

86 Michel Abitbol, "The Encounter between French Jewry and the Jews of North Africa: Analysis of a Discourse (1830–1914)", in Frances Malino and Bernard Wasserstein (eds.), *The Jews of Modern France* (Hanover, NH: University Press of New England, 1985) pp. 31–53.

87 Rodrigue, *Images of Sephardi and Eastern Jewries in Transition*, p. 10.

88 *The Jewish Chronicle* (London), 2 July 1982.

89 Zenner and Deshen, "The Historical Ethnology of Middle Eastern Jewry", p. 11.

90 Conversation with Salim Hasbani, 18 March 1929, BZA.

91 Zenner, *Jews in Late Ottoman Syria*, p. 172.

92 Zenner and Deshen, "The historical ethnology of Middle Eastern Jewry", p. 25.

93 Erster Bericht des von der Jahres-Konferenz 1906 eingesetzten Palästina-Comites, Z2/647, CZA.

94 Letter to Chief Rabbi Nahoum, Constantinople, 24 December 1909.

95 Ibid.

96 The Chief Rabbi of Beirut, 25 August 1910 to the President of the *Alliance Israélite Universelle*, Paris.

2 Lebanese Jews under the French Mandate: Liberty, Fraternity, and Equality

1 Salibi, *A House of Many Mansions*, p. 20.

2 Longrigg, *Syria and Lebanon under French Mandate*, p. 111.

3 Yehuda Nini, *Yehudei Agan HaYam HaTikhon nokhah Hitbolelut ve Imut im Tarbut HaMaarav (Assimilation and Westernization among the Jews of the Mediterranean Basin)* (Jerusalem: Institute of Contemporary Jewry, Hebrew University, 1979), pp. 11–12.

4 Longrigg, *Syria and Lebanon under French Mandate*, p. 82.

5 "The Mandate for Syria and Lebanon, 24 July 1992", *League of Nations Official Journal*, August 1922, cols. 1013–17.

6 Longrigg, *Syria and Lebanon under French Mandate*, p. 118.

7 Decree No. 1307, 10 March 1922.

8 Longrigg, *Syria and Lebanon under French Mandate*, p. 127.

9 Ibid.

10 Salibi, *A House of Many Mansions*, p. 35.

11 Farid el-Khazen, *The Communal Pact of National Identities: The Making and Politics of the 1943 National Pact*, Papers on Lebanon, No. 12 (Oxford: Centre for Lebanese Studies, 1991).

12 Theodor Hanf, *Coexistence in Wartime Lebanon: Decline of a State and Rise of a Nation* (London: I.B. Tauris/Centre for Lebanese Studies, 1993), p. 69

13 Salibi, *A House of Many Mansions*, p. 27.

14 Walter Laqueur, *Communism and Nationalism in the Middle East* (London: 1956), p. 234.

15 Michael W. Suleiman, *Political Parties in Lebanon: The Challenge of a Fragmented Political Culture* (New York: Cornell University Press, 1965), p. 78.

16 Salibi, *A House of Many Mansions*, p. 165.

17 Pierre Rondot, *Les Institutions Politiques du Liban* (Paris: Institut d'Etudes de l'Orient Contemporain, 1947), pp. 28–9.

18 *Encyclopedia Judaica*, p. 1543.

19 Albert Hourani, *Syria and Lebanon: A Political Essay* (London: Oxford University Press,1946), p. 121. See also John P. Entelis, *Pluralism and Party Transformation in Lebanon: Al-Kata'ib 1936–1970* (Leiden: E.J. Brill, 1974), p. 26.

20 Hanf, *Coexistence in Wartime Lebanon*, p. 63.

21 Patai, *The Vanished Worlds of Jewry*, p. 140.

22 Cohen, *The Jews in the Middle East*, p. 101.

23 Longrigg, *Syria and Lebanon under French Mandate*, p. 144.

24 Ibid., p. 205.

25 Caroline Gates, *The Historical Role of Political Economy in the Development of Modern Lebanon* (Oxford: Centre for Lebanese Studies, 1989), p. 14.

26 Laura Zittrain Eisenberg, *My Enemy's Enemy: Lebanon in Early Zionist Imagination, 1900–1948* (Detroit: Wayne State University Press, 1994), p. 82.

27 Abraham Elmaleh, "Une Grande Figure de Judaisme Oriental", in Abraham Elmaleh (ed.), *In Memoriam: Hommage à Joseph David Farhi* (Jerusalem: La Famille Farhi, 1948), p. 9.

28 Schechtman, *On Wings of Eagles*, p. 168.

29 Interview with Toufic Yedid Levy, Beirut, 28 June 1995.

30 Kisch to Jewish Agency Executive (London), 19 October 1930, L9/350b, CZA.

31 Profile of Joseph David Farhi, Jacques Stambouli Private Papers (JSPP).

32 Cohen, *The Jews of the Middle East*, p. 141.

33 Hanf, *Coexistence in Wartime Lebanon*, p. 63.

34 Report of Maurice Sidi, director of the Alliance School for Boys (Beirut) to Alliance Headquarters (Paris), 25 March 1926, Liban I.C.1, AIUA.

35 Jewish Community President to His Excellency the High Commissioner of the French Republic in Syria, Greater Lebanon, 10 February 1926, Liban I.C.1, AIUA.

36 Joseph Saadia, "L'Amé de la Communauté de Beyrouth", in Elmaleh (ed.), *In Memoriam*, p. 25.

37 Passover 1932, 21 April 1932 (in French) JSPP.

38 La paque à la synagogue, clipping from an unidentified newspaper, 9 April 1936, JSPP.

39 Ibid.

40 Ibid.
41 Speech of Joseph Farhi on the visit of Msgr. Pierre Arida (in French), 1 April 1937, JSPP.
42 Stillman, "The Jewish community of Beirut receives the Maronite Patriarch", *The Jews in Arab Lands in Modern Times.*
43 Ibid.
44 Joseph Dichy Bey, Allocutions, Pacque, 1943, JSPP.
45 Interview with Stella Levy, Haifa, 16 August 1995.
46 Joseph David Farhi, JSPP.
47 Eisenberg, *My Enemy's Enemy*, p. 83.
48 John P. Entelis, *Pluralism and Party Transformation in Lebanon: Al-Kata'ib 1936–1970* (Leiden: E.J. Brill, 1974), p. 36.
49 *Connaissance des Kataeb: Leur doctrine et leur politique nationales. Dans les declarations, messages, articles et lettres officielles, depuis 1936 de Pierre Gemayel, chef supérieur des Kataeb* (Beirut: Imprimerie Jeanne d'Arc, 1948), p. 79.
50 Eisenberg, *My Enemy's Enemy*, p. 83.
51 Tofic Attie, "Joseph David Farhi", in Elmaleh (ed.), *In Memoriam*, p. 27.
52 Schechtman, *On Wings of Eagles*, p. 167.
53 Saadia, "L'Amé de la Communauté de Beyrouth", p. 22.
54 Profile of Joseph David Farhi, JSPP.
55 Elmaleh, "Une Grande Figure de Judaisme Oriental", p. 14.
56 Ibid., p. 5.
57 Profile of Joseph Dichy Bey, JSPP.
58 Jacques Stambouli, "Hommage à Joseph David Farhi", in Elmaleh (ed.), *In Memoriam*, p. 79.
59 *The Times*, 16 August 1982.
60 Profile of Joseph David Farhi, JSPP.
61 Stambouli, "Hommage à Joseph David Farhi", p. 48.
62 Abraham Elmaleh to the Sephardi Federation (Jerusalem), 26 December 1927, Archives of the Sephardi Communal Council, as published in Stillman, *The Jews of Arab Lands in Modern Times.*
63 Ibid.
64 Patai, *The Vanished Worlds of Jewry*, p. 141.
65 Cohen, *The Jews in the Middle East*, p. 135.
66 Attie, "Joseph David Farhi", p. 28.
67 Elmaleh, "Une Grande Figure de Judaisme Orientale", p. 11.
68 Schechtman, *On Wings of Eagles*, p. 167.
69 Patai, *The Vanished Worlds of Jewry*, p. 141.
70 Memorandum to the directors of the Zionist Organization, Jerusalem, from Yosef Sneh, Beirut, 26 November 1941, S25/1964, CZA.
71 Interview with Toufic Yedid Levy, Beirut, 28 June 1995.
72 Cohen, *The Jews of the Middle East*, p. 136.
73 Emile Saadia, "Le Grand Chef de la Jeunesse", in Elmaleh (ed.), *In Memoriam*, p. 33.
74 Stambouli, "Hommage à Joseph David Farhi", p. 57.
75 Ibid., 58.

76 Memorandum to the directors of the Zionist Organization, Jerusalem, from Yosef Sneh, Beirut, 26 November 1941, S25/1964, CZA.
77 Meeting of protest against the *numerus clausus*, January 1927, JSPP.
78 Y. D. Semach to the president of the *Alliance* in Paris, 14 January 1907, Liban I.G.2, AIUA.
79 R. Cohen (Beirut) to Dr I. Luria (Jaffa), 4 November 1918, S2/657, CZA.
80 Dr Joseph Rosenfeld to AIU (Paris), 10 July 1921, Syrie I.G.1, AIUA.
81 Profile of Moshe Kamhine, JSPP.
82 Ibid.
83 Kisch to Executive of the Jewish Agency (London), 19 October 1930, CZA L9/350b.
84 Ibid.
85 Eisenberg, *My Enemy's Enemy*, p. 82.
86 Letter from F. H. Kisch to Joseph Azar, 19 October 1930, L9/ 350b, CZA.
87 F. H. Kisch to Joseph Azar, 19 October 1930, L9/350b, CZA.
88 Ibid.
89 Eisenberg, *My Enemy's Enemy*, 82.
90 Ibid.
91 Kirsten E. Schulze, *Israel's Covert Diplomacy in Lebanon*.
92 To the management from the organizational department, Jerusalem, 16 December 1941, S25/1964, CZA.
93 To Delegation Committee, 1941, S25/1964, CZA.
94 Ibid.
95 Ibid.
96 Memorandum to the directors of the Zionist Organization, Jerusalem from Yosef Sneh, Beirut, 26 November 1941, S25/1964, CZA.
97 Conversation with the President of the Lebanese Republic, Mr Emil Eddé, Beirut, 22 September 1936, S25/22176, CZA.
98 Woolfson, *Prophets in Babylon*, p. 142.
99 Bracha Habas, *The Gate Breakers: A Dramatic Chronicle of Jewish Immigrants into Palestine* (New York: Herzl Press, 1963), pp. 237–8.
100 M. Marder, *Strictly Illegal* (London: Robert Hale, 1964), pp. 89–90.
101 Memorandum to the directors of the Zionist Organization, Jerusalem from Yosef Sneh, Beirut, 26 November 1941, S25/1964, CZA.
102 Ibid.
103 To the Management from the organization division, Jerusalem, 28 September 1941, S25/1964, CZA.
104 Ibid.
105 Eliahu Epstein to Prof. Sloshetz, 22 December 1937, S25/5580, CZA.
106 Kisch to Jewish Agency Executive (London), 19 October 1930, L9/350b, CZA.
107 Philip Mattar, *The Mufti of Jerusalem: Al-Hajj Amin al-Hussayni and the Palestinian National Movement* (New York: Columbia University Press, 1988), p. 33.
108 Joseph Azar to F. H. Kisch, undated, L9/350b, CZA.
109 Ibid.
110 Kisch to Executive of the Jewish Agency (London), 19 October 1930, L9/350b, CZA.

111 Azar to Kisch, undated report, L9/350b, CZA.
112 Ibid.
113 Kisch to Jewish Agency Executive (London), 19 October 1930, L9/350b, CZA.
114 For details see Eisenberg, *My Enemy's Enemy* and Schulze, *Israel's Covert Diplomacy in Lebanon*.
115 Eliahu Epstein (Beirut) to Moshe Shertok, 17 May 1933, CZA L9/350b.
116 "Le problème des minorites juives en Syrie et au Liban", 18 June 1936, Liban I.C.1, AIUA.
117 E. Penso to Alliance Headquarters (Paris), Beirut, 19 June 1936, Liban I.C.1, AIUA.
118 Stillman, *Jews in Arab Lands in Modern Times*, p. 274.
119 A. Rahmany, Director of the Alliance Israélite School, Liban I.C.4, AIUA.
120 Woolfson, *Prophets in Babylon*, p. 127.
121 Ben Zvi, 1 September 1937, S25/5580, CZA.
122 J. Farhi to Ben Zvi, 19 October 1937, S25/5580, CZA.
123 Schechtman, *On Wings of Eagles*, p. 168.
124 Ben Zvi to Yarblum (Paris), 1 September 1937, S25/5580, CZA.
125 Farhi to Ben Zvi, 19 October 1937, S25/5580, CZA.
126 Joseph David Farhi to Itzhak Ben Zvi, 28 October 1937, S25/5580, CZA.
127 Ibid.
128 Khayr al-Din al-Ahdab to Dr, Weizmann and M. Shertok, 23 August 1938, S25/5581, CZA.
129 *Le Jour*, 16 July 1938.
130 A. Rahmany, Director of the Alliance, Liban I.C.4, AIUA.
131 Khayr al-Din al-Ahdab to Dr Weizmann and M. Shertok, 23 August 1938, S25/5581, CZA.
132 E. Penso, Director of the Alliance Israélite Universelle (Beirut) to His Excellency Monsieur Puaux, High Commissioner of Lebanon and Syria, 27 July 1939, Liban I.C.1, AIUA.
133 Mattar, *The Mufti of Jerusalem*, pp. 88–9.
134 J. Farhi to Ben Zvi, 19 October 1937, S25/5580, CZA.
135 Eisenberg, *My Enemy's Enemy*, p. 81.
136 Eliahu Epstein (Beirut) to Moshe Shertok, 17 May 1933, L9/350b, CZA.
137 *L'Orient*, 13 June 1933.
138 Interview with Maronite Patriarch Antoine Arida, *Le Journal L'Aurore*, 17 June 1933.
139 Eliahu Epstein (Beirut) to Moshe Shertok, 17 May 1933, L9/350b, CZA.
140 Eliahu Epstein (Beirut) to Shertok, 17 May 1933, L9/350b, CZA.
141 Ibid.
142 Ibid.
143 Ibid.
144 Longrigg, *Syria and Lebanon under French Mandate*, p. 293.
145 Ibid., p. 298.
146 Stillman, *The Jews of Arab Lands in Modern Times*, pp. 114–15.
147 Interview with Nissim S. Dahan, New York, 18 March 1997.
148 Profile of Joseph Dichy Bey, JSPP.

149 Schechtman, *On Wings of Eagles*, p. 169.
150 Cohen, *The Jews of the Middle East*, p. 44.
151 Stambouli, "Hommage à Joseph David Farhi", p. 89.
152 Ziadeh, *Syria and Lebanon*, p. 65.
153 Schechtman, *On Wings of Eagles*, p. 169.
154 Joseph D. Farhi, Allocutions, Visite Officielle Alfred Naccache, December 1941, JSPP.
155 Stambouli, "Hommage à Joseph David Farhi", p. 91.

3 Lebanese and Israeli Independence: Questions of Identity

1 Picard, *Lebanon*, p. 68.
2 Longrigg, *Syria and Lebanon under French Mandate*, p. 320.
3 Ibid., p. 328.
4 Ziadeh, *Syria and Lebanon*, pp. 74–5.
5 Longrigg, *Syria and Lebanon under French Mandate*, pp. 331–2.
6 Letter from Beirut, 29 November 1943, FM2563/3, ISA.
7 El-Khazen, *The Communal Pact of National Identities*, p. 5.
8 Hanf, *Coexistence in Wartime Lebanon*, p. 72.
9 de Bar, *Communautés Confessionelles du Liban*, p. 157.
10 Picard, *Lebanon*, p. 71.
11 de Bar, *Communautés Confessionelles du Liban*, p. 157.
12 Patai, *Tents of Jacob*, p. 232.
13 Schechtman, *On Wings of Eagles*, p. 170.
14 Cohen, *The Jews of the Middle East*, p. 44.
15 Schechtman, *On Wings of Eagles*, p. 171 and Friedman, *Without Future*, p. 13.
16 Schechtman, *On Wings of Eagles*, p. 171.
17 Annual Report on the Lebanon for 1946, FO 371/61723, PRO.
18 Longrigg, *Syria and Lebanon under French Mandate*, p. 352.
19 Ibid.
20 To Bina, Re: The bombs in Beirut, 16 May 1946, FM 2563/3, ISA.
21 Interview with Alex and Nathan Sofer, Tel Aviv, 13 August 1995.
22 Mr Roberts to Mr Baxter, 30 May 1947, FO 371/61704, PRO. Also *Al-Amal*, 28 May 1947.
23 Ministère des Affaires Etrangères, Beirut, 4 June 1947, FO 371/61729, PRO.
24 Report Week ending 11 June 1947, FO 371/61710, PRO.
25 Interview with Vikki Angel, Jerusalem, 14 August 1995.
26 Interview with Stella Levy, Haifa, 16 August 1995.
27 Interview with Vikki Angel, Jerusalem, 14 August 1995.
28 Interview with Stella Levy, Haifa, 16 August 1995.
29 Woolfson, *Prophets in Babylon*, p. 142.
30 Interview with Vikki Angel, Jerusalem, 14 August 1995.
31 Ibid.
32 Eisenberg, *My Enemy's Enemy*, p. 83.
33 *Jewish Week* (New York), 25 February 1983.

34 Situation of the Jews in Syria and Lebanon, 31 August 1948, FM 2563/3, ISA.
35 Houston-Boswell to Foreign Office, 9 December 1947, FO 371/61743, PRO.
36 *Lebanon: A Country Study* (Washington, DC: Library of Congress, 1989), p. 70.
37 Ziadeh, *Syria and Lebanon*, p. 98.
38 Beirut Political Summary December 1947, British Legation, 6 February 1948, FO 371/68489.
39 Schechtman, *On Wings of Eagles*, 176.
40 Summary for January 1948, 2 March 1948, FO 371/68489, PRO.
41 S. Landshut, *Jewish Communities in the Muslim Countries of the Middle East* (London: Jewish Chronicle, 1950), p. 55.
42 Houston-Boswell to Foreign Office, Anti-Jewish activities in Lebanon, 15 January 1948, FO 371/68493, PRO.
43 Summary for April 1948, 28 May 1948, FO 371/68489, PRO.
44 Schechtman, *On Wings of Eagles*, p. 176.
45 Interview with Nissim S. Dahan, New York, 18 March 1997.
46 Summary for July, 19 August 1948, FO 371/68489, PRO.
47 Landshut, *Jewish Communities in the Muslim Countries of the Middle East*, p. 55.
48 Suleiman, *Political Parties in Lebanon*, 249. See also *Al-'Amal* editorials December 1947 and May 1948.
49 *Al-Ittihad al-Lubnani*, 22 December 1947.
50 *Al-Diyar*, 24 December 1947.
51 *Al-Hayat*, 27 December 1947.
52 *Al-Hayat*, 12 January 1948.
53 Landshut, *Jewish Communities in the Muslim Countries of the Middle East*, p. 56.
54 Conversation with Tarif Khalidi, Beirut, 27 June 1995.
55 *Encyclopedia Judaica*, p. 1545.
56 *The Jerusalem Post Magazine*, 20 August 1982.
57 British Legation to Ernest Bevin, 30 May 1948, FO 371/68495, PRO.
58 Mr Houston-Boswell to Foreign Office, 26 June 1948, FO 371/68495, PRO.
59 Beirut to Foreign Office, 21 July 1949, FO 371/75320, PRO.
60 Interview with Toufic Yedid Levy, Beirut, 28 June 1995.
61 Interview with Nathan and Alexander Sofer, Tel Aviv, 13 August 1995.
62 *Encyclopedia Judaica*, p. 1545.
63 The Jews detained in Lebanon, Foreign Ministry, Middle East Department, 25 July 1948, FM 2563/3, ISA.
64 Ibid.
65 Foreign Ministry, Middle East Department, 3 September 1948, FM 2563/3, ISA.
66 Interview with Nathan Sofer, Tel Aviv, 13 August 1995.
67 *Encyclopedia Judaica*, p. 1545.
68 Interview with Fuad Abu Nader, Beirut, 28 June 1995.
69 Interview with Nissim S. Dahan, New York, 18 March 1997.
70 *Encyclopedia Judaica*, p. 1543.

71 *The Jewish Times* (Baltimore), 17 September 1982.
72 Position of Jews in Lebanon, 28 May 1952, C-WDC/RG-59/Box 5448, National Archives and Records Administration (NARA).
73 Schechtman, *On Wings of Eagles*, p. 174.
74 Interview with Nissim S. Dahan, New York, 18 March 1997.
75 Ibid.
76 Ibid.
77 Ibid.
78 Interview with Joseph Lichtman, Jerusalem, 18 July 1995.
79 *La Voix Sepharde*, Septembre/Octobre 1982.
80 Ibid.
81 Interview with Nissim S. Dahan, New York, 18 March 1995.
82 Letter from Maurice Fisher (Paris) to Gershon Hirsch (Israel), 4 September 1949, FM 2565/3, ISA.
83 *The New York Times*, 21 February 1950.
84 *HaDor*, 17 March 1950.
85 Landshut, *Jewish Communities in the Muslim Countries of the Middle East*, p. 56.
86 Report from Ezra for the month of December 1945.
87 *Telegraph* (Beirut), 21 February 1946.
88 Abu Yusef to the Hazan, 15 May 1946, FM 2563/3, ISA.
89 Situation of the Jews of Syria and Lebanon, 31 August 1948, FM 2563/3, ISA.
90 News from Arab Countries, Situation of the Jews in Syria and Lebanon, 31 August 1948, FM 2563/3, ISA
91 *La Bourse Egyptienne*, 29 July 1948.
92 Friedman, *Without Future*, p. 28.
93 *Al-Diyar*, 13 December 1947.
94 Patai, *Vanished Worlds of Jewry*, p. 141.
95 Patai, *Tents of Jacob*, p. 232.
96 *An-Nahar*, 27 June 1995.
97 *La Revue du Liban*, 6 September 1980.
98 Schechtman, *On Wings of Eagles*, p. 172.
99 *Le Soir*, 30 October 1948.
100 Schechtman, *On Wings of Eagles*, p. 178.
101 Political Summary December 1949, FO 371/82266, PRO.
102 *Encyclopedia Judaica*, p. 1545.
103 Schechtman, *On Wings of Eagles*, p. 178.
104 Schechtman, *On Wings of Eagles*, p. 179.
105 Immigration of Jewish family to Israel from Lebanon, 21 March 1952, R-49–52, R-SM/RG 319, ID File, Military Intelligence Declassified, NARA.
106 M. Sasson, Re: Immigration of Jews from Lebanon to Israel, 14 November 1950, FM 2563/3, ISA.
107 Economic Summary February 1949, FO 371/75325, PRO.
108 "Smuggling in Lebanon", 29 April 1953, US/NARA/C-WDC, RG59, Box 2180, NARA.
109 *The Jewish Telegraph* (Manchester), 3 November 1982.

110 Interview with Ezra Tamir, Jerusalem, 2 August 1995.
111 Ibid.

4   The First Civil War: Conflict of Identities

1   *Le Soir*, 12 July 1951.
2   Undated report (probably 1950), FM 2563/3, ISA.
3   Position of the Jews in Lebanon, AMLEGATION, Beirut 634, RG 59, Box 5448, 28 May 1952, NARA.
4   Ibid.
5   Position of Jews in Lebanon, 28 May 1952, C-WDC/RG 59/Box 5448, NARA.
6   Report 61–52, "Jewish Officers in the Lebanese Army", 18 April 1952, R-SM, RG 319, ID File, Military Intelligence Declassified, NARA.
7   Ibid.
8   de Bar, *Communautés Confessionelles du Liban*, p. 157.
9   Longrigg, *Syria and Lebanon under French Mandate*, p. 339.
10 Ziadeh, *Syria and Lebanon*, p. 108.
11 Gates, *The Role of the Political Economy in Lebanon*, p. 15.
12 *Le Commerce du Levant*, 9 February 1952.
13 Michael Johnson, *Class and Client in Beirut: The Sunni Muslim community and the Lebanese state, 1840–1985* (London: Ithaca, 1986), p. 123.
14 Longrigg, *Syria and Lebanon under French Mandate*, p. 359.
15 Jewish Easter in Lebanon, AMLEGATION, Beirut 576, 2 May 1951, R 59, Box 5448, NARA.
16 Ibid.
17 Interview with Fuad Abu Nader, Beirut, 28 June 1995.
18 Picard, *Lebanon*, p. 56.
19 Entelis, *Pluralism and Party Transformation in Lebanon*, p. 103.
20 *Jewish Week* (New York), 25 February 1983.
21 Ziadeh, *Syria and Lebanon*, p. 116.
22 Interview with Toufic Yedid Levy, Beirut, 3 July 1995.
23 Ziadeh, *Syria and Lebanon*, p. 157.
24 *An-Nahar*, 26 April 1956.
25 Ministère des Anciens Combatants et Victimes de Guerre, 22 September 1964, JSPP.
26 Stambouli, "Hommage à Joseph David Farhi", p. 93.
27 Ibid., p. 98.
28 Y. Tchernovitz to Political Department, Jewish Agency for Palestine, 26 May 1943, FM 2563/3, ISA.
29 Ibid.
30 Nini, *Yehudei Agan HaYam HaTikhon nokhah Hitbolelut ve Imut im Tarbut HaMaarav (Assimilation and Westernization among the Jews of the Mediterranean Basin)*.
31 Berger, *The Arab World*, p. 251.
32 *Lebanon: A Country Study* (Washington, DC: Library of Congress, 1989), p. 70.

33 Undated report (probably 1950), FM 2563/3, ISA.
34 Woolfson, *Prophets in Babylon*, pp. 15–17.
35 S. Kahane to Dr A. Rosenfeld, Re: Hebrew Teachers and Textbooks for the Jewish Schools in Beirut, 2 June 1950,FM 2563/3, ISA.
36 S. Kahane (Middle East Research Department) to A. Rosenfeld (World Hebrew Union), "Hebrew teachers and books for Jewish schools in Beirut", 13 June 1950, FM 2563/3, ISA.
37 Eliahu Elmaleh to World Hebrew Covenant, 30 June 1950, FM 2563/3, ISA.
38 Undated report (probably 1950), FM 2563/3, ISA.
39 G. Avner, Israeli Legation Paris, Re: Hebrew teachers for the Jewish community in Lebanon, 21 February 1951, FM 2563/3, ISA.
40 S. Kahane, Middle East Department, to the Department for the Middle Eastern Jewry, Jewish Agency, 2 March 1951, FM 2563/3, ISA.
41 Schechtman, *On Wings of Eagles*, p.173.
42 Hommage à President Joseph Dichy Bey, Beirut, 25 April 1950, JSPP.
43 Joseph Dichy Bey, JSPP.
44 Loi Libanaise sur la competence des jurisdiction religieuses – commentaires sur Grand Rabbin Ouziel, JSPP.
45 Ibid.
46 Interview with Itzhak Levanon, Jerusalem, 2 August 1995.
47 Position of Jews in Lebanon, 28 May 1952, C-WDC/RG59/Box 5448, NARA.
48 Visit of a reliable man (Yosef Sedaka) to Beirut, 8 February 1954, FM 3751/23, ISA.
49 Ibid.
50 Interview with Itzhak Levanon, Jerusalem, 2 August 1995.
51 Visit of a reliable man (Yosef Sedaka) to Beirut, 8 February 1954, FM 3751/23, ISA.
52 Ibid.
53 Interview with Itzhak Levanon, Jerusalem, 2 August 1995.
54 *An-Nahar*, 26 April 1956.
55 L. Bernstein to Dr N. Goldmann, Tel Aviv, 30 December 1957, CZA.
56 Hanf, *Coexistence in Wartime Lebanon*, p. 116.
57 Picard, *Lebanon*, p. 73.
58 Entelis, *Pluralism and Party Transformation in Lebanon*, p. 174.
59 Hanf, *Coexistence in Wartime Lebanon*, p. 117.
60 Patai, *Vanished Worlds of Jewry*, p. 141.
61 Haddad, *Jews of Arab and Islamic Countries*, p. 59.
62 Schechtman, *On Wings of Eagles*, p. 180.
63 de Bar, *Communautés Confessionelles du Liban*, p. 157.
64 Suleiman, *Political Parties in Lebanon*, p. 34.
65 Haddad, *Jews of Arab and Islamic Countries*, p. 60.
66 de Bar, *Communautés Confessionelles du Liban*, p. 158.
67 Cohen, *The Jews of the Middle East*, p. 44.
68 Suleiman, *Political Parties in Lebanon*, p. 244.
69 de Bar, *Communautés Confessionelles du Liban*, p. 157.
70 Interview with Itzhak Levanon, Jerusalem, 2 August 1995.

71 Interview with Nissim S. Dahan, New York, 18 March 1997.
72 Interview with Toufic Yedid Levy, Beirut, 3 July 1995.
73 Ibid.
74 Fuad Khuri, *From Village to Suburb: Order and Change in Greater Beirut* (Chicago: Chicago University Press, 1975).
75 Hanf, *Coexistence in Wartime Lebanon*, p. 80.
76 Zenner and Deschen, "The Historical Ethnology of Middle Eastern Jewry", p. 25.
77 Ibid.

5 The Beginning of the Exodus

1 Telegram 401, State Department, 15 July 1958, RG 319, ACSI File, Unclassified, 1957–1958, NARA.
2 Department of the Army Intelligence Report R-229–55, Possibility of Resumption of Arab-Israeli Hostilities, 21 June 1955, R-SM, RG 319, ID File, ACSI, G-2 Military Intelligence, NARA.
3 Picard, *Lebanon*, p. 75.
4 Hanf, *Coexistence in Wartime Lebanon*, p. 120.
5 Ibid., p. 121.
6 Picard, *Lebanon*, p. 91.
7 Ibid., p. 79.
8 *Jewish Week* (New York), 25 February 1983.
9 Schechtman, *On Wings of Eagles*, p. 183.
10 Ibid.
11 Joe Golan (Geneva) to Nahum Goldman (New York), 30 September 1959, FM 3752/8, ISA.
12 *Filastin*, 25 September 1959.
13 Joe Golan (Rome) to Nahum Goldman (Goldman), 30 March 1959, FM 3752/8, ISA.
14 Cohen, *The Jews of the Middle East*, p. 135.
15 Schechtman, *On Wings of Eagles*, p. 182.
16 Cohen, *The Jews of the Middle East*, p. 135.
17 Ibid., p. 136.
18 Ibid., 137.
19 Reuven Shiloah to Foreign Ministry, 5 April 1959, FM 3752/8, ISA.
20 Schechtman, *On Wings of Eagles*, p. 182.
21 *Al-Hayat*, 22 July 1959.
22 Ibid.
23 Interview with Joseph Lichtman, Jerusalem, 18 July 1995.
24 Ibid.
25 Ibid.
26 Ibid.
27 *Jewish Week* (New York), 25 February 1983.
28 Joe Golan (Geneva) to Dr A. Steinberg (London), 30 September 1959, FM 3752/8, ISA.
29 Profile of Chief Rabbi Chaoud Chreim, JSPP.

30   Interview with Shlomo Leviatan, Shilo, 14 August 1995.
31   Inauguration of the Michkan Moche synagogue, 4 October 1966, JSPP.
32   Interview with Shlomo Leviatan, Shilo, 14 August 1995.
33   Interview with Shula Kishek Cohen, Jerusalem, 8 August 1995.
34   Interview with Shula Kishek Cohen, Jerusalem, 8 August 1995.
35   Ibid.
36   Ibid.
37   Interview with Nathan Sofer, Tel Aviv, 13 August 1995.
38   Cobban, *The Making of Modern Lebanon*, p. 101.
39   Interview with Shlomo Levitan, Shilo, 14 August 1995.
40   Kamal Salibi, *Crossroads to Civil War, 1958–76* (London: Ithaca Press, 1976), p. 30.
41   Ilan Peleg, *Begin's Foreign Policy, 1977–1983* (New York: Greenwood Press, 1987), p. 144.
42   Picard, *Lebanon*, pp. 80–1.
43   Yitzhak Rabin, *The Rabin Memoirs* (London: Weidenfeld & Nicolson, 1978), p. 48.
44   David Kimche, *The Last Option* (London: Weidenfeld & Nicolson, 1991), p. 126.
45   Cohen, *The Jews of the Middle East*, p. 79.
46   Patai, *Tents of Jacob*, p. 232.
47   Interview with Toufic Yedid Levy, Beirut, 28 June 1995.
48   *Encyclopedia Judaica*, p. 1545.
49   *The Jerusalem Report*, 24 October 1991.
50   *Encyclopedia Judaica*, p. 1545.
51   Richard Falk, "The Beirut Raid and the Law of Retaliation", in John Norton Moore, *The Arab-Israeli Conflict*, Vol. II: Readings (New Jersey: Princeton University Press, 1974), pp. 221–2.
52   Ibid., p. 223.
53   *New York Times*, 5 January 1969; see also Lebanese delegate Tekoah's statement before the UNSC, S/PV 1461, United Nations Archives (UNA).
54   Entelis, *Pluralism and Party Transformation in Lebanon*, pp. 197–8.
55   Salibi, *Crossroads to Civil War*, p. 41.
56   Ibid., pp. 42–3.
57   Hanf, *Coexistence in Wartime Lebanon*, p. 123.
58   Kimche, *The Last Option*, p. 26.
59   For the text of the Cairo Agreement see Yehuda Lucacs (ed.), *The Israeli–Palestinian Conflict: A Documentary Record* (Cambridge: Cambridge University Press, 1992), p. 456.
60   Peleg, *Begin's Foreign Policy*, p. 146.
61   Ian Black and Benny Morris, *Israel's Secret Wars: The Untold Story of Israeli Intelligence* (London: Hamish Hamilton, 1991), p. 265.
62   Salibi, *Crossroads to Civil War*, p. 51.
63   *Erev Shabbat*, 26 September 1986.
64   *The Telegram* (Toronto), 23 December 1969.
65   *Jewish Times* (Baltimore), 17 September 1982.
66   *Encyclopedia Judaica*, p. 1545.

67 Salibi, *A House of Many Mansions*, p. 196.
68 Ibid., p. 189.
69 Hanf, *Coexistence in Wartime Lebanon*, p. 77–9.
70 Action XXII (December 1964), 14 as quoted in Entelis, *Pluralism and Party Transformation in Lebanon*, p. 60.
71 *L'Orient*, 22 March 1968.
72 Entelis, *Pluralism and Party Transformation in Lebanon*, p. 110.
73 Picard, *Lebanon*, p. 103.
74 *An-Nahar*, 27 June 1995.
75 *La Diaspora*, 1986.
76 Friedman, *Without Future*, p. 17.
77 *Jewish Chronicle* (London), 2 July 1982.
78 Itamar Rabinovich, *The War for Lebanon, 1970–1985* (Ithaca: Cornell University Press, 1985) , pp. 37–41.
79 Hanf, *Coexistence in Wartime Lebanon*, pp. 125–8.
90 Ibid., 37.
81 Salim Nasr, "The Political Economy of the Lebanese Conflict", in Nadim Shehadi and Bridget Harney, *Politics and the Economy in Lebanon* (Oxford: Centre for Lebanese Studies, 1989), p. 44
82 Bard O'Neill, *Armed Struggle in Palestine: A Political–Military Analysis* (Boulder, CO: Westview Press, 1978), p. 15.
83 Rabinovich, *The War for Lebanon*, p. 41.
84 Lester Sobel (ed.), *Israel and the Arabs: The 1973 October War* (New York: Facts on File, 1974), p. 14.
85 *International Herald Tribune*, 25 September 1972.
86 Sobel, *Israel and the Arabs*, p. 17.
87 Ibid.
88 Sidney Bailey, *Four Arab-Israeli Wars and the Peace Process* (Basingstoke: Macmillan, 1990), p. 298. See also Salibi, *Crossroads to Civil War*, p. 66.
89 Salibi, *Crossroads to Civil War*, p. 66.
90 Ibid., 68.
91 Cobban, *The Making of Modern Lebanon*, p. 112.
92 Rabinovich, *The War for Lebanon*, p. 43. See also Salibi, *Crossroads to Civil War*, p. 68.
93 Lucacs (ed.), *The Israeli–Palestinian Conflict*, p. 457.
94 Hanf, *Coexistence in Wartime Lebanon*, p. 368.
95 Peleg, *Begin's Foreign Policy*, p. 146.
96 Cobban, *The Making of Modern Lebanon*, p. 113.
97 Ibid., p. 79.
98 Picard, *Lebanon*, p. 83.
99 Hanf, *Coexistence in Wartime Lebanon*, p. 173.
100 Schechtman, *On Wings of Eagles*, p. 182.
101 Courbage and Fargues, *Chrétiens et Juifs dans l'Islam arabe et turc*, p. 326.
102 El-Khazen, *The Communal Pact of National Identities*, p. 52.
103 Henry Kissinger, *Years of Upheaval* (Boston: Little, Brown & Company, 1982), p. 789.
104 Picard, *Lebanon*, p. 89.

105 Ibid., p. 105.
106 Roger Owen (ed.), *Essays on the Crisis in Lebanon* (London: Ithaca Press, 1979), p. 60.
107 Hanf, *Coexistence in Wartime Lebanon*, pp.177–8.
108 Hudson, *The Precarious Republic*, p. 60.
109 Ghassan Salame, "The Lebanese Crisis: Interpretations and Solutions", in Shehadi and Harney (eds.), *Politics and the Economy in Lebanon*, p. 55
110 Picard, *Lebanon*, p. 102–3.
111 UNRWA estimate as cited in Itamar Rabinovich and Yehuda Reinharz (eds.), *Israel in the Middle East* (Oxford: Oxford University Press, 1984), p. 352.
112 Zeev Schiff, *A History of the Israeli Army* (London: Sidgwick and Jackson, 1987), p. 241.
113 Interview with Joseph Abu Khalil, Beirut, 4 July 1995.
114 Interview with Yossi Alpher, Tel Aviv, 19 October 1993.
115 Rabinovich and Reinharz (eds.), *Israel in the Middle East*, p. 348.
116 Salibi, *Crossroads to Civil War*, pp. 107–8.
117 Rabinovich, *The War for Lebanon*, p. 49.
118 Ibid., p. 48.
119 Valerie Yorke, *Domestic Politics and Regional Security* (London: Gower for the International Institute for Strategic Studies, 1988), pp. 130–1; see also Richard Gabriel, *Operation Peace for Galilee* (New York: Hill and Wang, 1984), p. 41.
120 Gideon Rafael, *Destination Peace: Three Decades of Israeli Foreign Policy* (London: Weidenfeld & Nicolson, 1978), p. 362.
121 Picard, *Lebanon*, p. 117.
122 Hanf, *Coexistence in Wartime Lebanon*, p. 241.
123 *The Sentinel*, 24 July 1980.
124 Woolfson, *Prophets in Babylon*, p. 226.
125 *Erev Shabbat*, 26 September 1986.
126 *Israel Nachrichten*, 25 July 1978.
127 *The Jewish Chronicle* (London), 2 July 1982.
128 *La Voix Sepharade*, May/June 1983.
129 Ibid.
130 *Erev Shabat*, 26 September 1986.
131 *La Voix Sepharade*, May/June 1983.
132 *Erev Shabat*, 26 September 1986.
133 *The Sentinel*, 24 July 1980.
134 *Ohio Jewish Chronicle*, 2 September 1982.
135 *The Sentinel*, 24 July 1980.
136 *The Times*, 16 August 1982.
137 Interview with Shlomo Leviatan, Shilo, 14 August 1995.
138 Ibid.
139 *The Sentinel*, 24 July 1980.
140 Interview with Toufic Yedid Levy, Beirut, 28 June 1995.
141 *Ohio Jewish Chronicle*, 2 September 1982.
142 *Jewish Chronicle* (London), 2 July 1982.
143 *Israel Nachrichten* (Tel Aviv), 25 July 1978.

144 *Al Hamishmar*, 23 July 1978.
145 *The Sentinel*, 24 July 1980.
146 *Canadian Jewish News* (Toronto), 26 December 1980.
147 *The Jerusalem Post*, 29 October 1980.
148 *La Revue du Liban*, 6 September 1980.
149 Interview with Vikki Angel, Jerusalem, 14 August 1995.

6   The Israeli Invasion and Beyond: Renaissance or Decline?

  1 Peleg, *Begin's Foreign Policy*, p. 151. See also Abba Eban, *Personal Witness: Israel through my Eyes* (London: Jonathan Cape, 1992), p. 604. See also Rabinovich, *The War for Lebanon*, p. 122.
  2 Yair Evron, *War and Intervention in Lebanon* (London: Croom Helm, 1987), p. 117.
  3 Avner Yaniv, *Dilemmas of Security: Politics, Strategy and the Israeli experience in Lebanon* (Oxford: Oxford University Press, 1987), p. 115.
  4 Ibid., p. 101.
  5 Gabriel, *Operation Peace for Galilee*, p. 67.
  6 Ibid.
  7 Hanf, *Coexistence in Wartime Lebanon*, p. 259.
  8 Uzi Benziman, *Sharon: An Israeli Caesar* (London: Robson Books, 1987), p. 266.
  9 *Ma'ariv*, 27 June 1982.
 10 *Sha'ar Lematchil*, 15 June 1982.
 11 Interview with Zaki Levy, Metullah, 31 July 1995.
 12 Ibid.
 13 Ibid.
 14 *The Jerusalem Post Magazine*, 20 August 1982.
 15 Interview with Zaki Levy, Metullah, 31 July 1995.
 16 *The Jerusalem Post Magazine*, 20 August 1982.
 17 Ibid.
 18 Ibid.
 19 *Ma'ariv*, 27 June 1982.
 20 *Jewish Telegraph* (Manchester), 3 November 1982.
 21 *The Jerusalem Post Magazine*, 20 August 1982.
 22 *Jewish Times* (Baltimore), 17 September 1982.
 23 Ibid.
 24 *The Jewish Chronicle* (London), 2 July 1982.
 25 *The Times*, 16 August 1982.
 26 Ibid.
 27 *Ohio Jewish Chronicle*, 2 September 1982.
 28 *Jewish Times* (Baltimore), 17 September 1982.
 29 Interview with Toufic Yedid Levy, Beirut, 29 June 1995.
 30 Interview with Joseph Lichtman, Jerusalem, 18 July 1995.
 31 *Erev Shabbat*, 26 September 1986.
 32 *The Jerusalem Report*, 24 October 1991.
 33 Rabinovich, *The War for Lebanon*, p. 144.

34 Interview with Fuad Abu Nader, Beirut, 28 June 1995.

35 Kimche, *The Last Option*, p. 162.

36 Rabinovich, *The War for Lebanon*, p. 168.

37 Ibid.

38 Ibid.

39 Yaniv, *Dilemmas of Security*, p. 178.

40 Ibid.

41 Hanf, *Coexistence in Wartime Lebanon*, p. 307.

42 *The 1985 Tripartite Militia Agreement*, Middle East Reporter, 49/439 (1985), p. 21.

43 Hanf, *Coexistence in Wartime Lebanon*, p. 310.

44 Ibid.

45 *Actualité Juive*, 9 January 1987.

46 *Phoenix Jewish News*, 29 January 1986.

47 Ibid.

48 Friedman, *Without Future*, p. 17.

49 Interview with Toufic Yedid Levy, Beirut, 28 June 1995.

50 *L'Orient Le Jour*, 19 February 1986.

51 *Phoenix Jewish News*, 29 October 1986.

52 *La Diaspora*, 1986.

53 *Phoenix Jewish News*, 29 January 1986.

54 *Le Monde*, 14 January 1987.

55 *Globus*, 26 January 1993.

56 *L'Orient Le Jour*, 4 January 1987.

57 Ibid.

58 *Yeteed Neeman*, 19 August 1991.

59 *Hamodia*, 8 December 1991. *Al-Hamishmar*, 8 December 1991.

60 *Davar*, 30 December 1993.

61 "The Tai'f Agreement", *The Beirut Review* 1 (1991), 119–72.

62 *An-Nahar*, 27 June 1995.

63 *Hamodia*, 2 September 1992.

64 *Al Hamishmar*, 24 August 1993. *HaMachane HaHaredi*, 10 September 1993.

65 *Yateed Neeman*, 2 August 1993. *Al-Hamishmar*, 26 July 1993. *Hatzofe*, 13 July 1993. *Yediot Aharonot*, 23 July 1997.

66 Interview with Toufic Yedid Levy, Beirut, 28 June 1995.

67 Interview with Toufic Yedid Levy, Beirut, 28 June 1995.

68 *The Jerusalem Report*, 24 October 1991.

7 Conjectures, Considerations, and Conclusions: A Sentimental Journey

1 See for example, Joel Beinin, "Egyptian Jewish Identities: Communitarianism, Nationalisms, Nostalgias", *Stanford Humanitarian Review*, Vol. 5, No. 1 (1995).

2 Beinin, "Egyptian Jewish Identities: Communitarianism, Nationalisms, Nostalgias".

3 Salibi, *A House of Many Mansions*, pp. 233–4.

4   *Erev Shabbat*, 26 September 1986.
5   Interview with Camille Cohen Kishek, Bat Yam, 17 July 1995.
6   Interview with Moni Sfinzi, Bat Yam, 17 July 1995.

Bibliography

Archives

National Archives and Records Administration (NARA)
Central Zionist Archives (CZA)
Israel State Archives (ISA)
Jacques Stambouli Private Papers (JSPP)
Alliance Israelite Universelle Archives (AIUA)
Public Record Office (PRO)
Haganah Archives (HA)
Ben Zvi Archives (BZA)
United Nations Archives (UNA)

Newspapers and Magazines

Actualité Juive
Al-'Amal
The Beirut Review
La Bourse Egyptienne
Canadian Jewish News
Le Commerce du Levant
Davar
Al-Diyar
HaDor
Erev Shabbat
Filastin
Globus
Al-Ittihad al-Lubnaniya
Jerusalem Post
Jerusalem Report
Jewish Chronicle (London)
Jewish News (Detroit)
Jewish Telegraph (Manchester)
Jewish Times (Baltimore)
Jewish Week (New York)
Le Jour
Le Journal L'Aurore

Hamaggid
Al-Hamishmar
Hamodia
Hatzofe
International Herald Tribune
Israel Nachrichten
League of Nations Journal
Middle East Reporter
Le Monde
An-Nahar
New York Times
Ohio Jewish Chronicle
L'Orient
L'Orient-Le Jour
Phoenix Jewish News
La Revue du Liban
The Sentinel
Sha'ar LeMatchil
Le Soir
The Telegram (Toronto)
Telegraph (Beirut)
The Times ·
La Voix Sepharade
Yediot Aharonot
Yeted Neeman

Interviews

Joseph Abu Khalil, Beirut, 4 July 1995.
Fuad Abu Nader, Beirut, 28 June 1995.
Yossi Alpher, Tel Aviv, 19 October 1993.
Vikki Angel, Jerusalem, 14 August 1995.
Shula Kishek Cohen, Jerusalem, 8 August 1995.
Nissim S. Dahan, New York, 18 March 1997.
Camille Cohen Kichek, Bat Yam, 17 July 1995.
David Kimche, Jerusalem, 7 November 1993.
Itzhak Levanon, Jerusalem, 2 August 1995.
Shlomo Leviatan, Shilo, 14 August 1995.
Stella Levy, Haifa, 16 August, 1995.
Zaki Levy, Metullah, 31 July 1995.
Josef Lichtman, Jerusalem, 18 July 1995.
Reuven Merhav, Jerusalem, 4 November 1993.
Marcel Nahon, Holon, 9 August 1995.
Odette Ozon, Holon, 9 August 1995.
Moni Sfinzi, Bat Yam, 17 July 1995.
Alex Sofer, Givatayyim (Tel Aviv), 13 August 1995.
Nathan Sofer, Givatayyim (Tel Aviv), 13 August 1995.

Ezra Tamir, Jerusalem, 2 August 1995.
Toufic Yedid Levy, Beirut, 28 June 1995, 29 June 1995, 30 June 1995, and 3 July 1995.

Official Publications and Reference Works

Connaissance de Kataeb: Leur doctrine et leur politique nationales. Dans les declarations, messages, articles et lettres officielles, depuis 1936 de Pierre Gemayel, chef supérieur des Kataeb. Beirut: Imprimerie Jeanne d'Arc, 1948.
Cohn-Sherbock, *Atlas of Jewish History.* London: Routledge, 1994.
Encyclopaedia Judaica. Jerusalem: Keter, 1972.
Lebanon: A Country Study. Washington, DC: Library of Congress, 1989.

Books and Articles

Abitbol, Michel. "The Encounter between French Jewry and the Jews of North Africa: Analysis of a Discourse (1830–1914)", in Frances Malino and Bernard Wasserstein (eds.), *The Jews of Modern France.* Hanover, N.H.: University Press of New England, 1985.
Attie, Tofic. "Joseph David Farhi", in Abraham Elmaleh (ed.), *In Memoriam: Hommage à Joseph David Farhi.* Jerusalem: La Famille Farhi, 1948.
Bailey, Sidney. *Four Arab-Israeli Wars and the Peace Process.* Basingstoke: Macmillan, 1990.
de Bar, Luc Henri. *Les Communautés Confessionelles du Liban.* Paris: Edition Recherche sur les Civilisation, 1983.
Beinin, Joel. "Egyptian Jewish Identities: Communitarianisms, nationalism, nostalgias", *Stanford Humanities Review*, Vol. 5, No. 1 (1995).
Benjamin, J. J. *Acht Jahre in Asien und Afrika von 1846 bis 1855.* Hannover: Selbstverlag des Verfassers, 1859.
Berger, Morroe. *The Arab World.* London: Weidenfeld & Nicolson, 1962.
Benziman, Uzi. *Sharon: An Israeli Caesar.* London: Robson Books, 1987.
Black, Ian and Morris, Benny. *Israel's Secret Wars: The Untold Story of Israeli Intelligence.* London: Hamish Hamilton, 1991.
Chouraqi, André N. *Cent Ans d'Histoire: L'Alliance Israélite Universelle et la Renaissance Juive Contemporain (1860–1960).* Paris: Libraire Arthème Fayard, 1965.
Cobban, Helena. *The Making of Modern Lebanon.* London: Hutchinson, 1985.
Cohen, Hayyim J. *The Jews of the Middle East, 1860–1972.* Jerusalem: Israel University Press, 1973.
Courbage, Youssef and Fargues, Philippe. *Chrétiens et Juifs dans l'Islam arabe et turc.* Paris: Fayard, 1992.
Eisenberg, Laura Zittrain. *My Enemy's Enemy: Lebanon in Early Zionist Imagination, 1900–1948.* Detroit: Wayne State University Press, 1994.
Eban, Abba. *Personal Witness: Israel through my Eyes.* London: Jonathan Cape, 1992.
Elmaleh, Abraham. "Une Grande Figure de Judaisme Oriental", in Abraham Elmaleh (ed.), *In Memoriam: Hommage à Joseph David Farhi.* Jerusalem: La Famille Farhi, 1948.

Entelis, John P. *Pluralism and Party Transformation in Lebanon: Al-Kataib 1936–1970*. Leiden: E.J. Brill, 1974.

Evron, Yair. *War and Intervention in Lebanon*. London: Croom Helm, 1987.

Falk, Richard. "The Beirut Raid and the Law of Retaliation", in John Norton Moore, *The Arab-Israeli Conflict*, Vol. II: Readings. New Jersey: Princeton University Press, 1974.

Fawaz, Laila Tarazi. *An Occasion for War: Civil Conflict in Lebanon and Damascus in 1860*. London: Centre for Lebanese Studies and I.B.Tauris, 1994.

——. *Merchants and Migrants in Nineteenth-Century Beirut*. Cambridge, Mass: Harvard University Press, 1983.

Fayyad, Niqula. "Dhikrayat Adabiyya", *Muhadarat al-Nadwa al-Lubnaniyya*, No. 3–4, 25 June 1954.

Fischel, Walter (ed.). *Unknown Jews in Unknown Lands: The Travels of Rabbi d'Beth Hillel, 1824–1832*. New York: Ktav Publishing House, 1973.

Friedman, Saul. *Without Future: The Plight of Syrian Jewry*. New York: Praeger, 1989.

Gabriel, Richard. *Operation Peace for Galilee*. New York: Hill and Wang, 1984.

Gates, Carolyn. *The Historical Role of Political Economy in the Development of Modern Lebanon*. Oxford: Centre for Lebanese Studies, 1989.

Goitein, Shlomo. *Jews and Arabs: Their contacts through ages*. New York: Schocken, 1955.

——. *A Mediterranean Society: The Jewish Communities of the Arab World as Portrayed in the Documents of the Cairo Geniza*. Vol. I, Economic Foundations. Los Angeles: University of California Press, 1967.

Habas, Bracha. *The Gate Breakers: A Dramatic Chronicle of Jewish Immigrants into Palestine*. New York: Herzl Press, 1963.

Haddad, Heskel. *Jews of Arab and Islamic Countries: History, Problems, Solutions*. New York: Shengold Publishers, 1984.

Hanf, Theodor. *Coexistence in Wartime Lebanon: Decline of a State and Rise of a Nation*. London: The Centre for Lebanese Studies in association with I.B. Tauris, 1993.

Harris, William. *Faces of Lebanon: Sects, Wars and Global Extensions*. Princeton: Marcus Wiener Publishers, 1997.

Hourani, Albert. *Syria and Lebanon: A political essay*. London: Oxford University Press, 1946.

Hudson, Michael. *The Precarious Republic: Political Modernization of Lebanon*. Boulder, Co: Westview Press, 1985.

Johnson, Michael. *Class and Client in Beirut: The Sunni Muslim community and the Lebanese state, 1840–1985*. London: Ithaca, 1986.

el-Khazen, Farid. *The Communal Pact of National Identities: The Making and Politics of the 1943 National Pact*. Papers on Lebanon, No. 12. Oxford: Centre for Lebanese Studies, 1991.

Khuri, Fuad I. *From Village to Suburb: Order and Change in Greater Beirut*. Chicago: Chicago University Press, 1975.

Kimche, David. *The Last Option*. London: Weidenfeld & Nicolson, 1991.

Kissinger, Henry. *Years of Upheaval*. Boston: Little, Brown & Company, 1982.

Klein, S. "Das tannaitische Grenzverzeichnis Palästinas", *Palästina Studien* II, 1.

Kraemer, Gudrun. "Political Participation of the Jews in Egypt Between World War One and the 1952 Revolution", in Shimon Shamir, *The Jews of Egypt: A Mediterranean Society in Modern Times*. Boulder, CO: Westview Press, 1987.

Landshut, S. *Jewish Communities in the Muslim Countries of the Middle East*. London: Jewish Chronicle, 1950.

Laqueur, Walter. *Communism and Nationalism in the Middle East*. London, 1956.

Longrigg, Stephen Hemsley. *Syria and Lebanon under French Mandate*. Beirut: Libraire du Liban, 1958.

Lucacs, Yehuda (ed.). *The Israeli–Palestinian Conflict: A Documentary Record*. Cambridge: Cambridge University Press, 1992.

Marder, M. *Strictly Illegal*. London: Robert Hale, 1964.

Mattar, Philip. *The Mufti of Jerusalem: Al-Hajj Amin al-Hussayni and the Palestinian National Movement*. New York: Columbia University Press, 1988.

Nasr, Salim. "The Political Economy of the Lebanese Conflict", in Nadim Shehadi and Bridget Harney, *Politics and the Economy in Lebanon*. Oxford: Centre for Lebanese Studies, 1989.

Nini, Yehuda. *Yehudei Agan HaYam HaTikhon nokhah Hitbolelut ve Imut im Tarbut HaMaarav (Assimilation and Westernization among the Jews of the Mediterranean Basin)*. Jerusalem: Institute of Contemporary Jewry, Hebrew University, 1979.

O'Neill, Bard. *Armed Struggle in Palestine: A Political-Military Analysis*. Boulder, Co: Westview Press, 1978.

Owen, Roger (ed.). *Essays on the Crisis in Lebanon*. London: Ithaca Press, 1979.

Parfitt, Tudor. "Jewish Minority Experience in Twentieth-Century Yemen", in Kirsten E. Schulze, Martin Stokes and Colm Campbell (eds.), *Nationalism, Minorities and Diasporas: Identities and Rights in the Middle East*. London: I.B. Tauris, 1996.

Patai, Raphael. *The Vanished Worlds of Jewry*. London: Weidenfeld & Nicolson, 1981.

———. *Tents of Jacob: The Diaspora Yesterday and Today*. Englewood, N.J.: Prentice Hall, 1971.

Peleg, Ilan. *Begin's Foreign Policy, 1977–1983*. New York: Greenwood Press, 1987.

Picard, Elizabeth. *Lebanon: A Shattered Country*. New York: Holmes & Meier Publishers, 1996.

Rabinovich, Itamar. *The War for Lebanon, 1970–1985*. Ithaca: Cornell University Press, 1985.

Rabinovich, Itamar and Reinharz, Yehuda (eds.). *Israel in the Middle East*. Oxford: Oxford University Press, 1984.

Rabin, Yitzhak. *The Rabin Memoirs*. London: Weidenfeld & Nicolson, 1978.

Rafael, Gideon. *Destination Peace: Three Decades of Israeli Foreign Policy*. London: Weidenfeld & Nicolson, 1981.

Rodrigue, Aaron. *Images of Sephardi and Eastern Jewries in Transition: The Teachers of the Alliance Israélite Universelle, 1860–1939*. Seattle: University of Washington Press, 1993.

———. *French Jews, Turkish Jews: The Alliance Israélite Universelle and the Politics of Jewish Schooling in Turkey, 1860–1925*. Bloomington: Indiana University Press, 1990.

Roumani, Maurice. *The Case of the Jews from Arab Countries: A Neglected Issue*. Tel Aviv: World Organization of Jews from Arab Countries, 1978.

Rondot, Pierre. *Les Institutions Politiques du Liban*. Paris: Institut d'Etudes de l'Orient Contemporain, 1947.

Saadia, Emile. "Le Grand Chef de la Jeunesse", in Abraham Elmaleh (ed.), *In Memoriam: Hommage à Joseph David Farhi*. Jerusalem: La Famille Farhi, 1948.

Saadia, Joseph, "L'Amé de la Communauté de Beyrouth", in Abraham Elmaleh (ed.), *In Memoriam: Hommage à Joseph David Farhi*. Jerusalem: La Famille Farhi, 1948.

Sadgrove, P. C. "The Beirut Jewish Arab Theatre: A Question of Identity", in *Democracy in the Middle East*, BRISMES Conference Proceedings, July 1992.

Salame, Ghassan. "The Lebanese Crisis: Interpretations and Solutions", in Nadim Shehadi and Bridget Harney, *Politics and the Economy in Lebanon*. Oxford: Centre for Lebanese Studies, 1989.

Salibi, Kamal. *A House of Many Mansions: The History of Lebanon Reconsidered*. Los Angeles: University of California Press, 1988.

——. *Crossroads to Civil War, 1958–76*. London: Ithaca Press, 1976.

Schechtman, Joseph. *On Wings of Eagles: The Plight, Exodus, and Homecoming of Oriental Jewry*. New York: Thomas Joseloff, 1961.

Schiff, Zeev and Ya'ari, Ehud. *Israel's Lebanon War*. London: George Allen & Unwin, 1984.

Schiff, Zeev. *A History of the Israeli Army*. London: Sidgwick and Jackson, 1987.

Sobel, Lester (ed.). *Israel and the Arabs: The October 1973 War*. New York: Facts on File, 1974.

Schulze, Kirsten E. *Israel's Covert Diplomacy in Lebanon*. Basingstoke: St Antony's/Macmillan, 1998.

Stambouli, Jacques. "Hommage à Joseph David Farhi", in Abraham Elmaleh (ed.). *In Memoriam: Hommage à Joseph David Farhi*. Jerusalem: La Famille Farhi, 1948.

Stillman, Norman. *The Jews in Arab Lands in Modern Times*. New York: The Jewish Publication Society, 1991.

——. *The Jews of Arab Lands: A History and Source Book*. Philadelphia: Publication Society of America, 1979.

Suleiman, Michael W. *Political Parties in Lebanon: The Challenge of a Fragmented Political Culture*. New York: Cornell University Press, 1965.

Tsimhoni, Daphne. "Jewish–Muslim Relations in Modern Iraq", in Kirsten E. Schulze, Martin Stokes and Colm Campbell (eds.), *Nationalism, Minorities and Diasporas: Identities and Rights in the Middle East*. London: I.B. Tauris, 1996.

Woolfson, Marion. *Prophets in Babylon: Jews in the Arab World*. London: Faber and Faber, 1980.

Yaniv, Avner. *Dilemmas of Security: Politics, Strategy and the Israeli experience in Lebanon*. Oxford: Oxford University Press, 1987.

Yorke, Valerie. *Domestic Politics and Regional Security*. London: Gower for the International Institute for Strategic Studies, 1988.

Zenner, Walter P. "Jews in Late Ottoman Syria: External Relations", in Shlomo Deshen and Walter P. Zenner (eds.), *Jewish Societies in the Middle East: Community, Culture and Authority*. Washington, DC: University of America Press, 1982.

Zenner, W. P. and Deshen, S. "The Historical Ethnology of Middle Eastern Jewry", in Shlomo Deshen and Walter P. Zenner (eds.), *Jewish Societies in the Middle East: Community, Culture and Authority*. Washington: University Press of America, 1982.

Ziadeh, Nicola A. *Syria and Lebanon*. Beirut: Libraire du Liban, 1968.

Index